# Transgender Cops

Building on comparative research in the U.K. and the U.S.A., this is the first book focused specifically on transgender experiences within policing. It examines the issues faced by the transgender community within policing and explores how gender, and the non-conformity of it, is perceived within police cultures. Moreover, it provides an on-going critique of the queer criminology movement and why it is crucial to policing studies, emphasising the specific importance of transgender issues therein.

This empirical book provides qualitative data from American officers and English and Welsh constables on transgender police. The following research questions are addressed: What are the perceptions of cisgender officers towards transgender officers, and what are the consequences of these perceptions? What are the occupational experiences and perceptions of officers who identify as transgender within policing? Finally, what are the reported positive and negative administrative issues that transgender individuals face within policing? The author concludes by discussing the empirical, theoretical and policy contributions of this research and offers some final thoughts on policy recommendations and directions for future research.

A strong contribution to the literature in critical criminology and queer criminology, this book will also be of interest to those in the fields of gender studies, sociology, public administration, management studies and policing studies.

**Dr Heather Panter** is a retired police detective with over 2,000 hours of police-specific training and a combined 13 years of American law enforcement experience with local and federal police agencies. Currently, she is a senior lecturer at Liverpool's John Moore University where she is a programme leader in the BSc in Policing and Forensics and the programme leader in the MSc in Policing and Criminal Investigations.

# Routledge Critical Studies in Crime, Diversity and Criminal Justice

Edited by Sharon Hayes
*University of Newcastle, Australia*
and Patricia Faraldo Cabana
*University of A Coruña, Spain*

The works in this series strive to generate new conceptual and theoretical frameworks to address the legal, organisational and normative responses to the challenges that diversity and intersectionality present to criminal justice systems. This series aims to present cutting edge empirically informed theoretical works from both new and established scholars around the world.

Drawing upon a range of disciplines including sociology, law, history, economics and social work, the series encourages different approaches to questions of mobility and exclusion with a cross-section of theorists, empiricists and critical policy researchers. It will be key reading for scholars who are working in criminal justice, criminology, criminal law and human rights, as well as those in the fields of gender and LGBTI studies, migration studies, anthropology, refugee studies and post-colonial studies.

www.routledge.com/criminology/series/CDCJ

# Transgender Cops

## The Intersection of Gender and Sexuality Expectations in Police Cultures

Heather Panter

Routledge
Taylor & Francis Group

LONDON AND NEW YORK

First published 2018
by Routledge
2 Park Square, Milton Park, Abingdon, Oxon OX14 4RN

and by Routledge
711 Third Avenue, New York, NY 10017

*Routledge is an imprint of the Taylor & Francis Group, an informa business*

*British Library Cataloguing in Publication Data*
A catalogue record for this book is available from the British
Library

*Library of Congress Cataloging in Publication Data*
A catalog record for this book has been requested

ISBN: 978-1-138-22387-5 (hbk)
ISBN: 978-1-315-40370-0 (ebk)

Typeset in Times New Roman
by Wearset Ltd, Boldon, Tyne and Wear

This book is dedicated to those who unselfishly gave it all in policing, and those who still continue to make sacrifices. This book is also dedicated to the brave individuals in policing who challenge occupational biases and stay true to themselves.

# Contents

# Illustrations

## Figures

## Tables

# Series editor foreword

I am extremely pleased to be able to write the Foreword to this wonderful book. Not only is it timely, but it delivers a virtual treasure chest of empirical evidence and theoretical analysis on transgender police and the attitudes and contexts within which they work. As a retired police detective with a combined 13 years of American law enforcement experience with local and federal police agencies, and as a committed and vocal activist for LGBT+ in policing, academia and beyond, Heather Panter has the credibility as well as the skill to attack this task. Her research compares police culture between the United States and the United Kingdom with respect to officers' cognitive and social perceptions of LGBT+ identities, in a way that is both rigorous and compelling.

The timeliness of the work cannot be underestimated. Not only have LGBT+ issues come to the fore over the past decade, but transgender rights in particular have finally made it onto the political and social agendas. This is not to say that there is still not much to be done – indeed, simply being on the agenda does not by itself guarantee that the issues will be solved and the rights respected. A couple of recent examples serve to illustrate this.

In Brisbane, Australia, on 4 October, 2014, transgender woman, Mayang Prasetyo, was brutally murdered by her spouse in a bizarre case, the horrific circumstances of which were reported around the world. Mayang was a beautiful young woman who had met her husband aboard a cruise ship and migrated with him to Australia, where he worked as a chef, and she as a high-class escort. The day after the murder, local newspaper the *Courier Mail* ran a full page photograph of her posing in a bikini with the headlines: 'Monster Chef and the Shemale' and inside, 'Ladyboy and the Butcher'. Subsequent media coverage was more sympathetic, and the *Courier Mail* was shamed for its headline. Nevertheless, the media continued to lead with photographs of the victim in skimpy clothing (one exception being the *Guardian*), while emphasising her career choice and the way in which she was murdered, all with prurient interest. These disrespectful and discriminating reports are typical of the ways in which transgender individuals are framed in popular culture and politics in contemporary Western democracies.

In our society, transgender individuals are treated as second-class citizens, almost on a par with Muslim immigrants and asylum seekers, both of which are considered dangerous and threatening by many in Australia. Transgender people suffer the kind of discrimination and hate crime previously reserved for Aboriginal and LGB individuals, before laws and attitudes here changed in the 1960s and 1970s–1980s, respectively. Transgender persons are many more times likely to be victims of crime, particularly of domestic violence and other crimes of violence. And as we have seen recently in the United States, they are considered by the current leader of that nation as unfit to serve in the military. Not only must they suffer these egregious penalties, but they must also undergo the indignity of having themselves officially declared as 'gender dysphoric' in order to obtain sex reassignment surgery. This assumption of ill mental health is akin to the labelling of homosexuality as a mental illness in pre-millennial versions of the American Psychological Association's *Diagnostic and Statistical Manual*.

As I write this, my own government is conducting a nationwide, non-compulsory plebiscite on marriage equality for LGBT+ citizens. This $122 million postal vote asks people whether members of the federal parliament should conduct a 'conscience vote' about changing the Commonwealth Marriage Act to do away with the reference to marriage as being only between a man and a woman. As an out lesbian in my 60th year, I experienced much discrimination and homophobia in my early adult life – but over the past 15–20 years, I had grown confident that social attitudes were rapidly changing for the better. Certainly, being a respected academic helped shelter me from much of the crass homophobia still being experienced in working class and certain marginalised neighbourhoods. Nevertheless, I believed there was cause for hope, as around the world, other nations began first doing away with outdated sodomy laws and legalising civil partnerships and then marriage for LGBT+. Until recently, my queerness was just one small aspect of my overall identity. However, as the debate around same-sex marriage resounds throughout Australia, I am forced once again to confront – or be confronted by – my sexuality. While most of my colleagues, family and friends are decidedly and vocally on the YES side, from the start the NO campaign began to niggle its nasty little pincers into the conscience of the undecided. Thus, where before homophobes, transphobes and the generally ignorant would usually keep their own counsel out of politeness or fear of 'political correctness', they were now called upon to open up and give their ill-informed and demeaning opinions. Indeed, one of the main cases for NO is that marriage equality will encourage our children to become transgender! The sense of my sexuality as outside the norm that I now feel gives me some small sense of exactly what transgender individuals have been experiencing on a grander scale over the past decades, even as we LGBs were gaining ground. Their battle is no small matter, especially in the face of these latest onslaughts, and this book makes strides in raising awareness of and contributing to the amelioration of transgender rights and acceptance.

Methodologically, this book examines the narratives of transgender as well as straight individuals and their relative attitudes towards being transgender and how this relates to their experiences in the workplace. Policing is a particularly thought-provoking context for these narratives, not merely because of the often hypermasculine subculture characterising it, but also because police officers have both an inter- and intra-relationship with those who are transgender. Transgender people work within policing and as police officers, but outside policing, they are also subject to policing policies and practices in a way that is quite unique compared with other marginalised groups in society. Panter expertly unpacks these relationships and the impact they have on transgender cops.

*Transgender Cops* will appeal to many different audiences, including of course police officers and administrators, but also legislators, policy-makers, and those working within non-governmental organisations catering to and supporting LGB and transgender people. Panter's exceptionally coherent explanation of key terms and concepts in the opening chapter is a goldmine of information for police administrators in particular, as is her 'own reflective practice in police culture' in Chapter 4. Practitioners will also find the data analyses enlightening in terms of providing evidence of need for services and resources, while administrators will benefit from policy recommendations in Chapter 9. In terms of its contribution to queer criminology, the book stands out for its original empirical research and review of literature to date. Its appeal will be felt by junior and more experienced researchers alike, not to mention graduate students. The use of auto-ethnographic material in Chapter 4, followed by the analyses of trans narratives in later chapters, provides a unique contribution that I envisage will have considerable impact on the future of research into transgender issues. This is not a theoretical book, as Panter is careful to point out, but it does skilfully employ theoretical concepts in its analysis of the data, providing a well-rounded research tool. I look forward to witnessing its impact.

Sharon Hayes

*Co-editor, Routledge Critical Studies in Crime, Diversity and Criminal Justice. Conjoint Fellow, School of Humanities and Social Sciences, University of Newcastle, Australia*

# Abbreviations

ACPO    Association of Chief Police Officers
BME     Black and minority ethnic
GD      Gender dysphoria
GID     Gender identity disorder
HRT     Hormone replacement therapy
IPCC    Independent Police Complaints Commission
LGB     Lesbian, gay and bisexual
LGBT+   Lesbian, gay, bisexual, transgender and other sexuality/gender
        variants
NTPA    National Transgender Police Officer Association
TCOPS   Transgender Community of Police and Sheriffs
Trans   Transgender

# Introduction

MALE DETECTIVE: I mean; what I am trying to ask is why does he have to act like a sissy? Shit, I don't know ... I just don't get it; I think it is sick with two men being together. But lesbians, now that is sexy.

ME (AS A DETECTIVE): Geez ... I cannot imagine what you would think about someone who went through a sex change, like Officer Smith.[1]

MALE DETECTIVE: I think that is weird as shit. She was ugly as a man and even uglier as a woman. I heard she is dating men now but was dating women in the past. It's so weird. I don't think she should have been allowed back on the street. People look at her and don't know what to think. I am just glad she finally retired so I don't have to see her at our in-service[2] ... I am just glad I am retiring soon so it doesn't become a circus around here.

(Personal field notes, 2012)

I began the introduction of this book with the above dialogue because it sums up controversial police intersectional perceptions of sexuality, gender and performance within policing, which are explored throughout this book. Notably, this book fulfils several empirical and practitioner-based purposes. First, this book aids criminologists, and practitioners alike, in understanding how officers' perceptions might impact their interactions with LGBT+ individuals. It should be noted that police biases based on the foundation of sexuality and gender expectations clearly operate in the attitudes as they are expressed on the street, in the home, at the workplace and/or at social venues (Scraton and Chadwick, 1996). As such, LGBT+ bias displayed by officers should be extensively examined to determine if elements of 'institutional homophobia and transphobia' (LGBT Advisory Group, 2007: 8) exist within policing. There may have been progressive societal transformations, and public perceptions towards members of the LGBT+ community may have changed, but it is unclear if current policing is plagued with transgender bias. Further, it should be noted that once bias is institutionalised in any work setting, LGBT+ bias can become systematic and structured (Scraton and Chadwick, 1996).

Second, this book examines how a subcultural group of society (i.e. the police) who exist in a hypermasculine environment perceive gender expectations and trans identities. Notably, gender expectations are constructed and reinforced within society (i.e. socialised heteronormativity). Further, current legal classifications of gender often exclude the possibility of the existence of transgender identities through adherence to rigid gender binaries of 'male' and 'female' (Spade, 2008). Often social institutions exclude transgender identities and create substantial barriers to changing gender. Moreover, research has identified high levels of violent crime and discrimination against transgender people, which indicate an overall hostile climate (see Grant *et al.*, 2011; Spade, 2008; Worthen, 2016) for non-binary identities.

Third, researchers have shown in different occupations that trans employees experience substantial stigmas in workplace environments, which leads to increased reports of overt discrimination (see Barclay and Scott, 2006; Dietert and Dentice, 2009; Gagné *et al.*, 1997; Irwin, 2002). In addition to social obstacles and blatant discrimination, transgender individuals also experience higher levels of poverty, employment discrimination and homelessness than cisgender people (Grant *et al.*, 2011). Researchers have also shown that many transgender individuals are apprehensive of seeking help from the police due to potential victimisation or re-victimisation committed by the police (Grant *et al.*, 2011; Mogul *et al.*, 2011; Xavier *et al.*, 2007). Further, transgender women who engage in illegal work for their economic survival report a higher incidence of verbal, sexual and physical abuse by police officers than cisgender (i.e. non-transgender) sex workers (see Nemoto *et al.*, 2004; Valera *et al.*, 2000). As described above, transgender individuals, whether breaking or adhering to social norms and laws, face heightened risks of police abuse. Therefore, it is imperative that trans bias within policing should be subject to empirical scrutiny.

## Current failures in 'queer' criminology: why transgender identities should be included in LGBT+ police research

Groombridge's (1999) 'Perverse criminologies: the closet of Doctor Lombroso' points out that there is an empirical neglect of relationships between (homo)sexuality and policing. Despite the introduction of the 'queer criminology' movement that Groombridge (1999) calls for, there still appears to be an empirical neglect of relationships between (trans)sexuality and policing. Previous criminology researchers have notably explored LGB identities within policing (see Buhrke, 1996; Burke, 1993, 1994a, 1994b; Colvin, 2009, 2012; Jones and Williams, 2013), yet transgender identities have been neglected in criminology. By homogenising LGBT+ people's experiences, it marginalises the concerns of those who are perceived as the least privileged (see Cohen, 1997; Ward, 2008). Additionally, sociologists (see Hines, 2007; Namaste, 1996; Prosser, 1995, 1998; Rubin, 1996; Wilson, 2002) have argued that queer studies have fundamentally neglected transgender identities within the social sciences. Much like sociological 'queer' research, within the realm of 'queer criminology' there are perceived research divisions between LGB identities and transgender identities. Yet this book advocates for the inclusion of transgender identities within criminological and sociological research, placing both LGB and transgender identities within this modern 'queer criminology' movement.

Notably, there is a difference between one's sexual orientation (to whom one is sexually/emotionally/romantically attracted) and one's gender identity (how one identifies to one's own gender and how one identifies as man, woman, transgender, etc.), yet there is an intricate link between LGBT+ individuals collectively (Wilchins, 2004). Previous research has indicated that most transgender individuals also identify as LGB or previously identified as LGB. For example, the Transgender American Veterans Association and the University of California's Palm Center explored the experiences of transgender veterans while in and out of the U.S. military. Of those surveyed, 64 per cent identified as MTF, with 38 per cent identifying their sexual orientation as heterosexual, while the remaining 62 per cent identified as lesbian, gay, bisexual or another sexual identity (Bryant and Schilt, 2008).

Additionally, during the early stages of this research, I discovered that transgender members could not be so easily isolated from the LGB population due to the similarity of the respective biases they battle. There also exist theoretical similarities between LGB identities and transgender police identities, which make them difficult to separate at times. Several members of the transgender police community interviewed during my fieldwork stated that members of the LGB police community, at times, face a similar plight to their experiences of 'coming out', and hence should also be included under 'queer criminology'.[3] Therefore, LGB theoretical contributions will be examined contextually in the following chapters, which illustrate why transgender identities should be included within police research and queer criminology.

To explore the concept of transgender identities and biases further, cisgender biases within policing, how biases exist and how biases are expressed towards fellow transgender colleagues will also be examined.[4] This answers Groombridge's (1999) call for new empirical contributions to the field of 'queer criminology'. Additionally, personal transgender experiences mixed with police communal socialisation experiences will be explored.[5] I will not be extensively arguing for the feminist philosophical stance on transsexuality in terms of identity which gender construction is; instead I will be documenting the experiences and opinions of officers who identify as transgender in a hypermasculine environment and how they theoretically perceive they perform femininity/masculinity.

Further, conceptualising transgender police experiences in respect to the subjective and embodied experiences of gender differences is more explanatory in understanding the differences between gay bias and trans bias within policing. This process will involve a critique of the deconstruction of gender only in respect to analysing gender diversity in relationship to 'coming out', 'hiding in the closet', articulating gender diversity within policing, and accounting for significant moments of transgender experiences within policing. The multifaceted complex historical arguments surrounding gender, sex and identity are unfortunately beyond the scope of this book. Instead, previous theoretical concepts of sexuality and masculinity viewed through criminological, sociological and social psychological lenses will be used to better explore how socialised intersectional perceptions of gender and sexuality impact transgender police experiences.

## Intersectionality within policing studies

Coined by Crenshaw (1991), intersectionality posits how to interrogate how axes of race, class, gender and sexuality, that exist as interlocking systems and shape social identities, social problems and power relations. Relationality, social context, power, inequality and social justice interact with one another in society and contribute to intersectionality's complexity (Collins and Bilge, 2016). Collins and Bilge (2016) state 'Intersectionality is a way of understanding and analysing the complexity in the world, in people, and in human experience' (p. 25). Previously, Collins (2000) referred to intersectionality as:

> … particular forms of intersecting oppressions, for example, intersections of race and gender, or of sexuality and nation. Intersectional paradigms remind us that oppression cannot be reduced to one fundamental type and that all oppressions work together in producing injustice.
>
> (p. 18)

Arguably, identity existence is not confined to one social perception of institutional power structures surrounding gender and sexuality solely (excluding race, class, education levels, religion, disability, etc.).

Most transgender identities challenge androcentric, heterocentric, and normative micro-cultural expectations within policing. Negative reactions directed towards transgender identities are not solely the result of heteronormative sexuality expectations, but also how gender and sexuality are intertwined with perceptions of how 'gender is done' appropriately (see Perry, 2001; West and Zimmerman, 1987). As such, heterosocial pressures impact impressions of gender expression, gender identity, masculinity, femininity and non-heteronormative sexuality expectations. Transgender identities not only challenge gender expectations, they also are perceived as challenging heterosexual/non-heterosexual expectations of how gender is socially intertwined with sexuality and gender performances.

Heteronormative sexuality expectations often equate sexuality as being binary and opposite. For example, males (socially perceived as the opposite) of females in binary identity management are expected to be specifically attracted to each another. When there is a perceived change or variance in this heteronormative equation, per se, then the lines between gender expectations and sexuality become perceived as blurred. Therefore, transgender identities in a heteronormative equation may experience bias that is intersectional due to a combo of both heterosocial/homosocial expectations of gender and heterosocial/homosocial expectations of sexuality. In other words, it is questionable which identity faces the more oppression (i.e. gender expression or non-heteronormative sexuality expectations) excluding intersectional arguments surrounding race, class, education levels, religion, disability, etc. when examining bias. Referring to King (1988) and Zinn and Dill (1996), theoretical approaches that only take into account one system of oppression often provide 'homogenized and distorted views of marginalized groups, advancing the interests of more privileged individuals' (Meyer, 2012: 850).

## Book research objectives

As this is the first book based on empirical research to specifically examine non-transgender perceptions of transgender identities within policing alongside the occupational experiences of transgender police, this book addresses the following research questions:

1    What are the perceptions of cisgender officers towards transgender officers, and what are the consequences of these perceptions?
2    What are the occupational experiences and perceptions of officers who identify as transgender within policing?
3    What are the reported positive and negative administrative issues that transgender individuals face within policing?

## Book outline

The first portion of this book consists of several contextual chapters which explores key terms and theories.[6] During this process, literature is examined which conceptualise the subject of LGBT+ bias within policing. Chapter 1 explores how transgender identities are defined within the context of this research. In the remainder of Chapter 1, differences between heteronormativity, homophobia, heterosexism, heterosexist expressions and genderism are explored. Chapter 2 examines previous research to conceptualise the relationship between the police and trans communities. During this examination, American and British police interactions with the LGBT+ community are examined to better understand the social (un)acceptance of those who challenge heteronormative gender and sexuality expectations. As such, the distinction of gender identity and perceptions of sexuality are often blurred because I contend that transgender individuals and LGB individuals both experience somewhat similar types of discrimination based on gender ideologies. Yet, there are important differences between those who identify as transgender (one's gender identity) and those who identify as LGB (one's sexuality) (see Buhrke, 1996; Burke, 1993, 1994a, 1994b; Colvin, 2009, 2012; Grant *et al.*, 2011; Jones and Williams, 2013) and occupational experiences. Therefore, Chapter 2 will include literature of previous research conducted on those within policing and those outside policing, namely transgender perspectives and experiences with police.

Following up on Chapter 2, Chapter 3 focuses on theories of police culture and gender role ideology within police environments to better understand how bias can thrive through understanding occupational socialisation. This chapter is divided into two sections: one that examines theoretical concepts of gender identity and gender expression in respect to the role symbolic interactionism has upon perceptions of gendered bodies; and another which examines the social constraints of masculinity within policing.

Chapter 4 is my reflective exploration within policing through three distinct career phases: police academy, rookie and veteran. This chapter aims to provide examples demonstrating how and why LGBT+ identities encounter bias and conflict within policing. Chapter 5 focuses on the analytical and pragmatic issues surrounding comparative research on transgender and cisgender police within America, England and Wales. During this examination, who I am as a researcher and the influence it had upon this research will be examined. The remainder of this book involves the qualitative examination of trans identities within policing comparatively between the U.S., England and Wales. This examination consisted of a thematic analysis of findings from 39 interviews with officers and constables embedded within police culture.

Chapter 6 qualitatively compares and contrasts empirical research of American officers' opinions with those of British constables, in order to explore monolithic and/non-monolithic perceptions of those who do not reside within binary or heteronormative norms. This chapter, unlike Chapters 7 and 8, specifically focuses upon perceptions held of cisgender police (i.e. non-transgender) towards transgender identities within policing. This chapter focuses on categorisations of heteronormativity and gender ideologies alongside the consequences of their (mainly negative) perceptions of their transgender colleagues and the occupational environment of policing more broadly.

Chapter 7 dissects my empirical research on transgender participants' experiences to clarify social resistance within police cultures. A large portion of this chapter will explore how trans officers construct their gendered (or non-gendered) identities within policing while negotiating a hyper masculine environment where gender expectations are heightened. Further, this chapter will also explore the specific administrative challenges that transgender identities face when transitioning at work. More specifically, this chapter will theoretically consider why trans feminine identities differ from trans masculine identities within policing.

Chapter 8 specifically explores the administrative issues that members of the transgender policing community face. Following up on Chapter 7, this chapter will collectively examine what creates an inclusive transgender work environment versus an exclusionary work environment. During this examination, specific attention will be placed upon the role leadership and work policies play upon the diminishing (display of) transgender bias within police cultures.

Chapter 9 contains a summary of empirical findings and theoretical arguments which solidify future research implications within the realm of 'queer criminology'. This chapter reiterates the administrative policy implementations for those who are police practitioners that should be considered for future changes within policing, leading to a more inclusive and unbiased occupational realm for transgender police officers/constables.

## Notes

1   Pseudonym created to protect the identity of the officer in question.
2   *In-service* is annual police officer training required by agencies and mandated by American states to keep arrest powers (i.e. certification).
3   This is explored in Chapter 7.
4   This is explored in Chapter 6.
5   See Chapters 7 and 8.
6   Notably, throughout this piece, relevant theories are interwoven to aid in the construction of a theoretical backbone, which is explored in detail in Chapters 5, 6 and 7.

## References

Barclay, J. and Scott, L. 2006. Transsexuals and workplace diversity: a case of change management. *Personal Review* 4, pp. 1–30.

Bryant, K. and Schilt, K. 2008. *Transgender people in the U.S. military: summary and analysis of the 2008 Transgender American Veterans Association Survey*. Santa Barbara, CA: Palm Center.

Buhrke, R. 1996. *A matter of justice*. New York: Routledge.

Burke, M. 1993. *Coming out of the blue*. London: Continuum.

Burke, M. 1994a. Cop culture and homosexuality. *Police Journal* 65, pp. 30–39.

Burke, M. 1994b. Homosexuality as deviance: the case of the gay police officer. *British Journal of Criminology* 34, pp. 192–203.

Cohen, C. 1997. Punks, bulldaggers, and welfare queens: The radical potential of queer politics? *GLQ: A Journal of Lesbian and Gay Studies* 3(4), pp. 437–465.

Collins, P. 2000. Gender, black feminism, and black political economy. *Annals of the American Academy of Political and Social Science* 568(1), pp. 41–53.

Collins, P. and Bilge, S. 2016. *Intersectionality*. New York: John Wiley & Sons.

Colvin, R. 2009. Shared perceptions among lesbian and gay police officers: barriers and opportunities in the law enforcement work environment. *Police Quarterly* 12(1), pp. 86–101.

Colvin, R. 2012. *Gay and lesbian cops: diversity and effective policing*. London: Lynne Rienner Publishers.

Crenshaw, K. 1991. Mapping the margins: Intersectionality, identity politics, and violence against women of color. *Stanford Law Review* 43(6), pp. 1241–1299.

Dietert, M. and Dentice, D. 2009. Gender identity issues and workplace discrimination: The transgender experience. *Journal of Workplace Rights* 14, pp. 121–140.

Gagné, P., Tewksbury, R. and McGaughey, D. 1997. Coming out and crossing over: identity formation and proclamation in a transgender community. *Gender & Society* 11(4), pp. 478–508.

Grant, J., Mottet, L., Tanis, J., Harrison, J., Herman, J. and Keisling, M. 2011. *Injustice at every turn: a report of the National Transgender Discrimination Survey*. National Center for Transgender Equality and National Gay and Lesbian Task Force. [Online]. Available at: www.thetaskforce.org/downloads/reports/reports/ntds_full.pdf [accessed: 15 March 2014].

Groombridge, N. 1999. Perverse criminologies: the closet of Doctor Lombroso. *Social & Legal Studies* 8(4), pp. 531–548.

Hines, S. 2007. *Transforming gender: transgender practices of identity, intimacy and care*. Bristol: Policy Press.

Irwin, J. 2002. Discrimination against gay men, lesbians, and transgender people working in education. *Journal of Gay & Lesbian Social Services* 14(2), pp. 65–77.

Jones, M. and Williams, M. 2013. Twenty years on: Lesbian, gay and bisexual police officers' experiences of workplace discrimination in England and Wales. *Policing and Society: an International Journal of Research and Policy* 25(2), pp. 1–24.

King, D. 1988. Multiple jeopardy, multiple consciousness: The context of a black feminist ideology. *Signs*, 14, pp. 42–72.

LGBT Advisory Group. 2007. *Thematic review of lesbian gay bisexual transgender related murders*. [Online]. Available at: http://lgbtag.org.uk/documents/Murder Review_online_color.pdf [accessed: 20 March 2014].

Meyer, D. 2012. An intersectional analysis of lesbian, gay, bisexual, and transgender (LGBT) people's evaluations of anti-queer violence. *Gender & Society* 26(6), pp. 849–873.

Mogul, J., Ritchie, A. and Whitlock, K. 2011. *Queer (in)justice: the criminalization of LGBT people in the United States*. Boston, MA: Beacon Press.

Namaste, V. 1996. Tragic misreadings: queer theory's erasure of transgender subjectivity. In: Beemyn, B. and Eliason, M., eds. *Queer studies: a lesbian, gay, bisexual and transgender anthology*. New York: NYU Press.

Nemoto, T., Operario, D., Keatley, J. and Villegas, D. 2004. Social context of HIV risk behaviors among male-to-female transgenders of colour. *AIDS Care* 16(6), pp. 724–735.

Perry, B. 2001. *In the name of hate: understanding hate crimes*. New York: Psychology Press.

Prosser, J. 1995. No place like home: The transgendered narrative of Leslie Feinberg's Stone Butch Blues. *MFS Modern Fiction Studies* 41(3), pp. 483–514.

Prosser, J. 1998. *Second skins: the body narratives of transsexuality*. New York: Columbia University Press.

Rubin, H. 1996. Do you believe in gender? *Sojourner* 21(6), pp. 7–8.

Scraton, P. and Chadwick, K. 1996. The theoretical and political priorities of critical criminology. In: McLaughlin, E., Muncie, J. and Hughes, G., eds. *Criminological perspectives: essential readings*, 2nd edn. London: Sage, pp. 294–309.

Spade, D. 2008. Documenting gender. *Hastings Law Journal* 59, pp. 731–842.

Valera, R., Sawyer, R. and Schiraldi, G. 2000. Violence and post-traumatic stress disorder in a sample of inner city street prostitutes. *American Journal of Health Studies* 16(3), pp. 149–155.

Ward, J. 2008. *Respectably queer: diversity culture in LGBT activist organizations*. Nashville, TN: Vanderbilt University Press.

West, C. and Zimmerman, D. 1987. Doing gender. *Gender & Society* 1(2), pp. 125–151.

Wilchins, R. 2004. *Queer theory, gender theory: an instant primer*. Los Angeles, CA: Alyson Book.

Wilson, M. 2002. I am the prince of pain, for I am a princess in the brain: liminal transgender identities, narratives and the elimination of ambiguities. *Sexualities* 5(4), pp. 425–455.

Worthen, M. 2016. Hetero-cis-normativity and the gendering of transphobia. *International Journal of Transgenderism*, 17, pp. 31–57.

Xavier, J., Honnold, J. and Bradford, J. 2007. *The health, health-related needs, and life-course experiences of transgender Virginians*. Richmond, VA: Division of Disease Prevention through the Centers of Disease Control and Prevention, Virgina Department of Health.

Zinn, M. and Dill, B. 1996. Theorizing difference from multiracial feminism. *Feminist Studies* 22(2), pp. 321–331.

## Chapter 1

# The silent 'T' in LGBT+ police studies

## Transgender identification in America, England and Wales

No concrete numbers exist concerning the prevalence of transgender identification, but some research estimates that there are over 700,000 transgender individuals in the U.S.A. (Gates, 2011). Previous research based on gender reassignment surgeries performed each year in America indicates that between one out of every 500 and one out of every 2,500 people identify as transsexual (Conway, 2001). Notably, not all transgender individuals identify as transsexual, and some transsexuals may opt out of having gender reassignment surgery.

In the U.K., as in America, there exists no concrete estimate on the number of individuals who identify as transgender, but some research estimations are around 300,000–500,000 (Reed *et al.*, 2009). The prevalence of transsexual identities, based on reported NHS gender reassignment surgeries each year, indicate 20 per 100,000 patients have sought medical care for gender variance, with 6,000 undergoing surgical transition (Gender Identity Research and Education Society, GIRES, 2011). Research trends in the U.K. indicate an upward trend of 11 per cent undergoing gender reassignment surgeries every year, with an anticipated doubling of patients seeking out gender reassignment treatment every 5–6 years (Reed *et al.*, 2009). Arguably, trans identities are becoming more visible and are increasing in frequency within society (see Miles-Johnson, 2015; Panter, 2017).

It should be noted that empirical estimations of gender identities, with respect to transgender research, are difficult. First, some trans individuals may try to keep their trans status private, making them difficult to account for. Second, trans identities represent a broad spectrum of various gender identities and expressions. Historically, when we examine the prevalence of trans identities, previous research has only indicated a small proportion of those who actually identify as transgender. Western studies yield a range of $1:11,900$ to $1:45,000$ for trans feminine identities, and $1:30,400$ to $1:200,000$ for trans masculine identities (see Gates, 2011; Olyslager and Conway, 2007; Reed *et al.*, 2009). Notably, the statistics covering the prevalence of transsexuality and other forms of gender variance are difficult to measure and should be used with prudence.

## Conceptualising transgender identities

Wilchins (2002), as other gender researchers, contemplated what *transgender* actually means, stating that the term is 'used commonly in two ways: as both an identity and a descriptive adjective' (p. 60). Wilchins (2002) points out that as an identity, the question of gender itself can be raised. As a descriptive adjective, Wilchins (2002) further questions if transitioning genders is something we *are* or something we *do* (p. 60). Conflicting arguments between gender theorist who understand gender as 'doing' and transgender activists claiming trans identity as 'being' (Wilchins, 2002) have led to further questions.[1] Notably, within academic discourses and within the transgender community, language surrounding any challenge to 'conventions of legitimate gender' (Stryker, 1994: 84) will always be contentious. As such, I must openly confess to readers that as a criminologist interested in policing studies, the complex multifaceted arguments of gender existentialism will be minimally covered within this book. Therefore, readers must be aware that linguistic terms which are associated with transgender subjectives are not encompassing terms within gender existentialism arguments. Further, I do not contend that my research participants' voices represent the various transgender communities as a whole. Therefore, the main focus of this book is not on how transgender subjectives are defined in the social sciences, instead the focus primarily is on how gender and sexuality ideologies within policing influence (trans)gender identities within policing.

Notably, gender researchers have frequently defined the transgender community as a social grouping that consists of various subgroup identities. These identities include transsexuals, intersex individuals, gender variant identities and cross-dressers. Sociologists contend that there is terminological confusion within this transgender assemblage (see Rizzo, 2006). Johnson (2012) states:

> Transitioning is something that always necessitates some form of movement across or between the socially established binary genders, but it must be acknowledged that when theorists or individuals refer to the collective *trans*, they mean different things in terms of both identities and practices.
>
> (p. 608)

Whittle (2000), a major contributor to transgender studies, provided a useful explanation of why *trans* is an encompassing term for those who challenge binary genders:

> … transgender is an umbrella term used to define a political and social community which is inclusive of transsexual people, transgender people, cross-dressers (transvestites), and other groups of 'gender variant' people such as drag queens and kings, butch lesbians, and 'mannish' or 'passing' women. 'Transgender' has also been used to refer to all persons who express gender in ways not traditionally associated with their sex. Similarly, it has also been

used to refer to all persons who express gender in non-traditional ways, but continue to identify as the sex of their birth.

(p. 65)

As Whittle (2000) illustrates, a sociological framework of the word transgender is beneficial to better understand gender diversity.

Theoretically, Prosser (1995, 1998) differentiated transsexuals as individuals who search for a gendered 'home' versus gender variant individuals who live on the 'borderlands' between genders under a transgender assemblage. Prosser (1995, 1998) and Rubin (1996) argued that a distinction should be made between subjective experiences of gender variant identities under the assemblage of 'transgender' and transsexuals in order to avoid the 'universalizing of trans' (Prosser, 1998: 201). Therefore, this book explores some essentialist categories separately, not in an effort to imply that all transgender narratives are alike, but instead to highlight that different members of the transgender community experience similar reported incidents of transgender bias within policing itself. Notably, much like Halberstam's (1998) research, this subgrouping of essentialist categories is not used to argue as to what constitutes a 'real' transgender identity; instead this book will be examining the politics of transgender mobility within policing.

Therefore, in accordance with other researchers (see Erich *et al.*, 2010; Gagné *et al.*, 1997; Miles-Johnson, 2013, 2015), this research defines *transgender* as including the following individuals: those who have had gender reassignment surgery to change from one biological sex to the other; those taking hormones and other medications to help transition their physical body from one to another; those who dress as the gender opposite of their biological sex because they feel they belong to the wrong sex; those who privately dress as the gender opposite of their biological sex for personal or erotic reasons;[2] those who desire to be the opposite gender of their biological sex; and those individuals who do not identify or associate with stereotypical binary gender categories.

### Transsexuals

A transsexual individual can be defined as a 'male' or 'female' that, through biological or psychological factors, expresses a particular binary gender role and potentially wants biological congruity with their gender preference (Kane-DeMaios, 2006). For an individual to be medically diagnosed as transsexual, three criteria must be met: (1) they must possess the desire to live and be accepted as a member of their adopted gender; (2) this must typically be accompanied by the desire to make their body as congruent as possible with the preferred sex through surgery and hormone treatment; (3) they must have the trans identity present for years; and (4) the identity is not a system of a mental disorder or a chromosomal abnormality (Whittle, 2000). Transsexual identities are typically classified as FTM or MTF. Female-to-male (i.e. FTM, transman) is an individual who has transitioned or is in the process of transitioning to male, identifies as male and was previously assigned female at birth. Male-to-female (i.e. MTF, transwoman) is an individual who has transitioned or is in the process of transitioning to female, identifies as female and was previously assigned male at birth.[3]

In accordance with other researchers (see Erich *et al.*, 2010; Gagné *et al.*, 1997; Law *et al.*, 2011), transsexuals within the context of this book will be identified as: those who have had gender reassignment surgery to change their biological sex to another, and/or those taking hormones and other medications to help transition their physical body from one sex to another. Notably, not all transsexuals will want to take hormones, and some may be unable to take hormones for medical reasons. Yet, transsexual identities are often connected to some form of surgical intervention (e.g. clitotoplasty, mastectomy, metoidioplasty, oophorectomy, orchidectomy, penectomy, phalloplasty, vaginoplasty, etc.).[4] These medical and surgical interventions occur in the transsexual community because their assigned birth gender does not match their gender, and thus medical treatment is needed to make their bodies conform to the gender with which they identify. Arguably, because of stereotypical binary gender role ideology within society, transsexuals often feel the need to take every possible means to medically and socially conform to the gender role to which they feel they belong. Tragically, some transsexual identities are both societal victims and societal perpetrators of socialised reinforced binary constructs of 'male' and 'female' gender, unlike other members of the transgender community.[5]

### Intersex identities

Besides transsexual identities, one transgender identity that is typically underresearched under the transgender assemblage are those who identify as intersex. Like transsexual identities, intersex individuals are also victims of socialised reinforced binary constructs. Yet, unlike transsexual identities, some intersex identities are medically forced without consent from birth to physically conform to a gender binary. This typically occurs when the parents of an intersexed child force them to undergo medical procedures after birth or during childhood because they possess genitalia assigned to both sexes. In this type of scenario, although rare, parents choose which gender they believe their child will physically present better than the later or their preferred sex of their child. Yet some intersex identities do not possess both biological genitalia, leaving some intersex individuals to make surgical and/or medical gender realignment decisions later on in life.

Typically, a chromosomal disorder is associated with individuals who are intersexed. It should be noted that intersex individuals, a phenomenon also known as sexual dimorphism, could be considered trans, but some view themselves as separate from transsexuals. Intersex individuals possess immediate or atypical combinations of physical features that usually distinguish male from female. This can include individuals who have non-XX or non-XY, Turner syndrome, Klinefelter syndrome, Kallmann syndrome, androgen insensitivity syndrome, partial androgen insensitivity syndrome, congenital adrenal hyperplasia, late onset congenital adrenal hyperplasia, vaginal agenesis, or idiopathic hypogonadotropic hypogonadism (Blackless *et al.*, 2000). It should be noted that the actual occurrence of an individual being born as intersex is roughly between 0.1 per cent and 2 per cent (Blackless *et al.*, 2000) and they comprise a very small portion of the transgender population, hence why they are typically under-researched. Notably during the course of this research, I only secured one interview with an intersex officer. As such, this research will instead mainly focus on transsexual officers, transgender officers, gender variant individuals and cross-dresser officers, since the one intersexed officer I interviewed considered himself a transman, despite his medical diagnosis of being intersexed.

### Gender variants

Gender variance is very different to transsexual identities, intersex identities and cross-dresser identities. Someone who identifies as gender variant is an individual who does not conform to the stereotypical 'male' or 'female' category assigned to them at birth. They identify as non-binary because their sex differentiation is inconsistent with the binary sex characteristics associated with the structure and working of their brain (Office for National Statistics, 2009), and thus they reject any social conformity to binary gender systems. Gender variant identities can be distinguished typically into five unique categories (from Stringer, 2009). These are:

1    both man and woman (i.e. androgyne);
2    neither man nor woman (i.e. agender, neutrois, non-gendered);
3    moving between two or more genders (i.e. gender fluid);
4    third gendered or other-gendered (includes those who prefer 'genderqueer' or 'non-binary' to describe their gender without labelling it otherwise);
5    having an overlap or blur of gender and orientation and/or sex (i.e. girlfags and guydykes).[6]

Notably, gender variant participants in this research either were biologically assigned female, had their breasts removed and had an androgynous type of haircut; or were biologically assigned male, took HRT to grow their breasts and had an androgynous type of haircut. Participants who identified as 'genderqueer' chose not to take higher levels of HRT[7] to lose muscle mass or have noticeable changes in their voice depth. Instead they took HRT to present themselves in an androgynous way. Notably, some gender variant individuals may choose not to undergo any medical treatment at all, but both English and Welsh genderqueer research participants disclosed that they underwent medical procedures (i.e. surgery, HRT, hormone blockers, etc.).

## Cross-dressers

Cross-dressers, known as transvestites[8] in the U.K., dress for personal or sexual arousal in the clothing associated with the opposite gender than they were assigned at birth, and they typically have no desire to change or alter their biological sex (McBride and Hansson, 2010). The act of cross-dressing involves wearing clothing that is stereotypically associated with 'males' or 'females' (e.g. male cross-dressers wearing make-up, wigs, dresses and high heels). Often the act of cross-dressing is done in secret to avoid social rejection or social alienation.

One notable controversial cross-dresser researcher (Blanchard, 1989) examined why males engage in acts of transvestitism. Blanchard (1989) introduced his theory of autogynephilia to refer to 'a male's propensity to be sexually aroused by the thought of himself as a female' (p. 616). Blanchard theorised that cross-dressers develop an error in erotic target localisation; in other words, they locate their erotic target (towards women) on themselves rather than on other people (Veale et al., 2010). Therefore, in the case of cross-dressers, individuals become attracted to parts of the female body that the garment is worn over (e.g. female underwear and bras). Further, Blanchard stated that sexual arousal in cross-dressers may diminish or even disappear due to age, hormone treatment and genital surgery, yet for some, the desire to live as a woman does not diminish and may grow stronger. Notably, a significant number of transgender individuals have voiced disagreement with Blanchard's model because it is too narrow, and a majority of cross-dressers often do not want to change sex (see Dreger, 2008; Lawrence, 2007; Veale et al., 2010).

Unlike Blanchard (1989), Garber (1992) described cross-dressers as a representative example of a 'category crisis', as they are 'disrupting and calling attention to cultural, social, or aesthetic "dissonances"' (p. 16). Therefore, Garber (1992) contended that cross-dressers challenge the notion of a fixed or coherent identity of perceptions of binary genders. The practice of cross-dressing therefore could be perceived as being a transgender practice that embraces gender as a deconstructive tool. Countering Garber's arguments, Namaste (1996) stated that this theoretical critique of cross-dressers 'reduced the transvestite to a mere tropological figure, a textual and rhetorical device' (p. 189). By doing so, Namaste (1996) argues that this critique 'undermined the possibility of "transvestite as a viable identity in and of itself"' (p. 189).

Research from the U.S.A. estimates that 2–5 per cent of males engage in frequent (e.g. clubs/private) cross-dressing (Reed et al., 2009). The American Psychological Association (2013) has reported that 2–3 per cent of the cisgender male population occasionally engage in cross-dressing privately. In the U.K., estimates are that one in ten men have cross-dressed or will do so, which conflicts with any foregoing figures (Reed et al., 2009). Reed and colleagues estimated that 1 per cent of the British cisgender male population (i.e. around 235,000 men) cross-dress. Notably, there are no studies on the prevalence of females who engage in cross-dressing.

Cross-dressers, unlike other transgender identities, have the desire to dress as the opposite binary sex because the clothing is associated with the opposite sex. For cross-dressers, wearing opposite-sex clothing is about the gender role that is assigned to particular garments. Some cross-dressers also have the desire to act out the mannerisms associated with the opposite sex. While cross-dressers could arguably possess degrees of gender dysphoria, it is not strong enough or consistent enough that they feel compelled to live full-time as the opposite sex. Therefore, cross-dressing is often seen as fetishist in nature and is often viewed as a part-time transgender activity (see Blanchard *et al.*, 1989; Langstrom and Zucker, 2011) that can be controlled at will, unlike other trans identities. Some theorists even go as far as saying that cross-dressers are not trans at all and cross-dressing is not an identification, yet this research has indicated that some cross-dressers do identify as transgender and that the trans police community views them as transgender.[9]

As with the cisgender population, there exist variations in the performance of masculinity and femininity within the cross-dressing world. Those who participate in 'high drag' make more apparent attempts at dressing in opposite-sex attire than those who participate in 'low drag'. I observed this during my fieldwork, when cross-dressing officers would wear high heels, an elaborate hairdo (in the form of a wig), make-up and deemed feminine jewellery. As one participant told me:

> We don't play around. When we dress in drag it is serious business; some of us can even 'pass' if we go out.

Comparatively, those who participate in 'low drag' may don make-up and accessories because they have learned rudimentary aspects of female impersonation as it is understood to a cisgender male.

Yet some types of cross-dressing activities which are not fetishist in nature can be undertaken out of other personal desires, such as for performance reasons (e.g. drag queens, drag kings, female impersonator, male impersonator, etc.). Often those in cross-dressing performance roles are stigmatised into fundamental and inseparable parts, show business and gay sexuality (Newton, 1998). Newton argued that female impersonators are a choice status in 'the deviant career of the homosexual in the homosexual community, or the status is one of those offered by the community' (1998: 44).

## Heteronormativity

In American and British societies, heterosexual norms are constructed and reproduced spatially throughout policing. The term 'heteronormativity' encompasses the notion that certain cultural beliefs regarding sexuality and social expectations of heterosexual love, sex and reproduction are exclusive in society (Hubbard, 2008). As Herek (1992) states:

Heterosexuality is equated ideologically with 'normal' masculinity and 'normal' femininity, whereas homosexuality is equated with violating the norms of gender.

(p. 97)

The links between traditional gender role ideology and anti-homosexual sentiment have been frequently suggested in sociology and criminology, yet there exists empirical criminological neglect on how traditional gender role ideology can impact anti-transgender sentiments. This gender role ideology relies upon a binary sex system in which 'normal' attraction occurs between two gendered types of bodies defined as opposites (Schilt and Westbrook, 2009). Therefore, heterosexuality and gender identity could arguably rely upon social perceptions of genitalia which is influenced by heteronormativity, even though during most social interactions, genitals may not be visible (Schilt and Westbrook, 2009). Socially, there exists a perception that a person's gender matches their 'biological' credentials (Schilt and Westbrook, 2009). In other words, due to heteronormativity there is an assumption that gendered appearances reflect biologically sexed realities (West and Zimmerman, 1987).[10]

## Homophobia

In recent decades, there has been a psychosocial movement that has described homophobia as a general dislike of LGBT+ individuals and/or an opposition to their political claims directed towards attaining equal rights in modern democratic systems. The term 'homophobia' has become common vernacular in society, which denotes negativity towards gay sexualities in general (Mason, 2002). George Weinberg (1972) first proposed a new type of phobia, which was 'the dread of being in close quarters with homosexuals' (p. 4). Weinberg (1972) proposed an unorthodox view to describe a mental illness resulting in hatred, fear or avoidance of homosexuals founded upon a complex interaction between socialised notions of heteronormativity and internalised conflicts. By proposing that homophobia was a result of a social pathology instead of a personal pathology, Weinberg (1972) contended that homophobia was constructed by society to be viewed as an illness. In other words, it implicated that society was to blame for the consequences for homophobia, and not those who are non-heteronormative. This rejected the prevailing cultural assumption of the time, that non-heteronormative identities were an individualised pathology. Similarly, this new social phenomenon in the form of a phobia suggested that homophobia specifically afflicted certain sexually repressed individuals. Weinberg's (1972) theory – that placing prejudiced individual homophobes into a clinical pathologised category conflicted with the essentialist model of identity – was challenged by other psychotherapists at the time (Tomsen, 2009).

Academically, psychologists Hudson and Ricketts (1980) stated that the term 'homophobia' has been diluted because literature includes any negative attitude, belief or action towards gay sexualities. Further, Hudson and Ricketts (1980) criticised previous social science studies for not making a distinction between intellectual attitudes towards non-heterosexual sexualities (homonegativism/ transnegativism) and affective responses towards gay and some transgender individuals (homophobia/transphobia). Hudson and Ricketts (1980) defined homophobia as an emotional or affective response – including fear, anxiety, anger, discomfort and aversion – that some individual experiences in interacting with those who do not identify as heterosexual, which may or may not include a cognitive component. Hudson and Ricketts were not alone in their criticisms of how the social sciences have ignored any operational definition of what the term 'homophobia' means.

Since Hudson and Ricketts' study, several social scientists have made attempts to properly define what homophobia is and how it should be used in the social sciences (Fyfe, 1983; Bernstein, 1994; Rowan, 1994; O'Donahue and Caselles, 1993). Further, historically, the term 'homophobia' itself has theoretically ignored structural, institutional, political and normative assumptions (Peel, 2001). Therefore, it is vital to establish what homophobia is in the context of this research to better understand its potential impact on trans identities before theoretical components of transgender-specific biases are examined in the chapters to come.

For the purposes of this criminological research, homophobia is used to describe individuals who have an irrational fear of being in close proximity to members of the LGBT+ community, based upon socialised constructs of heteronormativity. Homophobia is thus limited in its representation of discrimination as the product of individual fear. Therefore, homophobia does not, as a construct, encapsulate the precarious societal pathology that is directly implicated in anti-LGBT+ victimisation (Smith *et al.*, 2012). Much like Hudson and Ricketts (1980), I contend that homophobia is an affective response based upon socialised heteronormativity that makes it difficult for an officer to be around, detain, arrest, talk to and casually interact with, an individual who is LGBT+. In other words, homophobia is a complex mixture of individual attitudes towards non-heteronormative identities and the social constructs of heteronormativity (i.e. heterosexism).

## Heterosexism

LGBT+ activists and researchers often prefer the term 'heterosexism' because it offers a structural dimension and suggests parallels with other forms of disadvantage linked to prejudice (Tomsen, 2009; Burn *et al.*, 2005). In lesbian and gay psychology, and even in some feminist theoretical works, the term 'heterosexism' is preferred due to the perception that heterosexism is a pervasive cultural and ecological phenomenon rather than simply incidents experienced by some individuals. In other words, homophobia concerns the individual and heterosexism refers to cultural arena. Table 1.1 displays how the term 'heterosexism' has evolved and its discrepancies within gender studies, occupational studies, sociology and psychology.[11]

*Table 1.1* How the term 'heterosexism' has been historically defined in social science literature

| Academic | Date | Definition |
|---|---|---|
| Neisen | 1990 | The continued promotion of a heterosexual lifestyle and the subordination of gay and lesbian lifestyles. |
| Sears | 1997 | A belief in the superiority of heterosexuals or heterosexuality evidenced in the exclusion, by omission or design, of non-heterosexual persons in policies, procedures, events, or activities. |
| Herek | 2004 | The cultural ideology that maintains social prejudice against sexual minorities. |
| Alden and Parker | 2005 | The belief system that posits superiority of heterosexuality over gay sexualities. |

Herek (1990) defined heterosexism as an ideological system that denies, denigrates and stigmatises non-heterosexual behaviour. Herek (1990) further broke down heterosexism into: (1) cultural heterosexism (encompassing the stigmatisation, denial or denigration of non-heterosexuality in cultural institutions within public institutions) and (2) psychological heterosexism (a person's internalisation of cultural heterosexism, which erupts into homophobia). Herek (1992) additionally proposed that cultural heterosexism is based in society, customs, religion and legal institutions; and, comparatively, psychological heterosexism is based on the attitude and behaviour of individuals. Cultural heterosexism, therefore, will be critically examined in this research along with components of psychological heterosexism. Notably, within police culture, much like other social groups, there is an assumption that the world must be heterosexual, and it assumes that sexuality and gender are intertwined, yet never separated. This reinforces societal expectations of how gender should be performed and reinforces cultural underpinnings of binary gender ideology.

Further, psychologists Herek (1990) and Kinsman (2004) advocated for the usage of the term 'heterosexism' due to the social stigma of an anti-gay sentiment and the argument that a phobia implies that a person's attitude towards LGBT+ individuals is the product of fear (Mason, 2002). Herek (2000) further advocated for the term 'heterosexism' in additional research in which he identifies heterosexism as an 'ideological system that denies, denigrates, and stigmatizes any non-heterosexual form of behaviour, identity, relationship, or community' (p. 316). Therefore, the usage of the term 'heterosexism' shifts the emphasis from unique individuals' attitudes to include social customs and institutions as part of the problem without excluding it (Peel, 2001). Hence, I am specifically using the term 'heterosexism' when exploring components of police culture, which encompasses police social customs and the institution itself.

## Heterosexist expressions

Notably, heterosexism centres upon normalising and privileging heterosexuality. Heterosexism highlights social beliefs, and a more dynamic way of thinking about prejudiced behaviours. The expression of heterosexism is linked to factors such as gender role traditionalism, which includes adherence to traditional and rigid social constructions about what constitutes appropriate male and female behaviour (see Goodman and Moradi, 2008; Hoover and Fishbein, 1999; Theodore and Basow, 2000); religiosity (see Herek and Capitanio, 1996; Laythe *et al.*, 2001); intolerance and prejudice of out-groups (i.e. those who are not part of a dominant group in society; see Hegarty and Pratto, 2001; Wickberg, 2000); and social power imbalances (e.g. dominant groups in society that retain power by minimising the influence of marginalised groups; see Bernstein *et al.*, 2003; Wickberg, 2000). Similarly, Herek (1984) theorised that heterosexist behaviour is a result of less personal contact with LGB identities; not engaging in LGB behaviour or identifying as LGB; perceptions that peers hold the same anti-gay attitudes; living in geographical regions where more negative attitudes towards LGB identities exist; being older and less educated; believing in more conservative religious ideology; holding traditional sex role ideologies; having more negative views about sexuality and expressing more guilt about sexuality; and possessing an authoritative type of personality.

Besides these characteristics that can implicate the expression of heterosexism, demographic factors of gender (see Hegarty and Pratto, 2001; Herek, 2002); ethnicity (see Herek and Capitanio, 1996); age and educational level (see Herek, 1994) can also influence the expression of heterosexism. Notably, the collective expression within police culture of both gender role ideology and heterosexism can impact the amount of displays of anti-LGBT+ bias in occupational realms. Further, previous research has shown that intensity of heterosexism at the individual level can vary and be impacted by gender (Connell, 1995; Kimmel, 1994); age (Kite and Whitley, 1998; Morrison *et al.*, 1997); religious ideology (Birken, 1997; Herek, 1984; Peplau *et al.*, 1993); and adherence to gender role ideology (Cotton-Huston and Waite, 2000). Arguably, in an arena (e.g. policing) where gender roles are heightened, it makes sense to conclude that collective expression of heterosexism as a cultural phenomenon can manifest.

Therefore, heterosexist attitudes can manifest in certain attitudes and behaviours, including verbal and physical abuse as extreme outliers. Attitudes and behaviours can range from avoidance through fear to avoidance through aggression. This can include negative talk, social exclusion of those that are LGBT+, verbal insults and threats, changing bathroom behaviour, spreading rumours, requesting transfers from police units occupied with LGBT+ members, occupational discrimination and telling anti-gay jokes.

Herek (1984) suggested that expressions of heterosexist attitudes and behaviours can serve as personal functions for certain people. These functions include: those who categorise reality based on previous interactions (experiential); those who use their behaviour to cope with conflicts and anxieties by projecting themselves onto others (defensive); and those who use abstract ideological concepts to express closely linked notions of self (symbolic). Notably, heterosexist behavioural correlates and their expressions can vary in usage and occurrence towards LGBT+ identities.

## Genderism

Genderism, not to be confused with transphobia, is the incorporating of binary beliefs that there are, or should be, only two biological genders that comprise males and females. This binary bias concept can consist of perceptions based on visual representation, psychological representation and emotional representation that stereotypically rest within the binary constraints of what an individual identifies as a 'male' and/or a 'female'. Much like heterosexism, how cultural belief systems perceive what being a 'man' or a 'woman' means can perpetuate and encourage biases that uphold transitional gender role ideologies. Notably, these perceptions, which constitute as 'male' and/or 'female', are products of gender socialisation and social gender conformism.

In contrast, transphobia is an emotional phobia – meaning, essentially, fear and avoidance – of those who identify as transgender (Hill and Willoughby, 2005). Comparatively, genderism is the broad ideology that encompasses and reinforces the negative evaluation of gender non-conformity (Hill, 2002; Hill and Willoughby, 2005). For the purposes of this research, 'genderism' will also be used to describe the bias that individuals have towards those individuals who identify as transgender, transsexual, gender variant and cross-dressers. Genderism is a cultural belief that perpetuates negative feelings, judgements and biases about people who do not conform to sociocultural and stereotypical assumptions of 'male' identities and 'female' identities. Therefore, genderism, like heterosexism, is a series of internalised beliefs or externalised beliefs formed through socialisation within group cultures. As such, genderism is a source of social oppression and psychological shame that is dissimilar but slightly analogous to heterosexist experiences of individuals who identify as LGB. Further, it is possible, if not highly probable, for a trans-identified individual to experience both heterosexism and genderism at the same time, due to both biases having a reliance upon concepts of gender ideology.

It could be argued that negative workplace experiences for transgender police officers occur due to an extreme manifestation of the dominant cultural values of genderism. Therefore, collective expression of both gender role ideology and cultural genderism within policing can impact the amount of displayed trans biases. It should be noted that stereotypical perceived binary gender norms, embraced by the term 'genderism' within this research, are the foundation of all anti-trans discrimination (Serano, 2007).

## Intersectional genderism

Some researchers have suggested that non-binary gender non-conformity in outward traits, such as voice, movement and appearance, occurs frequently within the LGB population and could in theory be perceived as transgender in nature (Ambady *et al.*, 1999; Bailey, 2003) due to social reliance upon traditional gender role ideologies. Previous studies have documented that the LGB community are more likely to experience childhood gender non-conformity than their heterosexual-identified counterparts (Bailey and Zucker, 1995). Further, previous research has theorised that some gay men defeminise as they reach adulthood in reaction to persistent social pressure (see Bell *et al.*, 1981; Harry, 1983a, 1983b; Landolt *et al.*, 2004; Taywaditep, 2001). Notably, it could be argued that lesbians who identify or are perceived as 'masculine' or 'butch' add to extraneous confusion on non-binary gender conformity by being perceived as rejecting stereotypical assumptions of femininity. As such, some 'butch' or 'masculine' lesbians are often socially adopted into the transgender community by those who identify as trans. This gender non-conformity can blur the line between what a perceived member of the LGB community is and what can be constituted as transgender. This potential blurring of gender non-conformity makes the connection between sexual orientation and gender non-conformity extraneous for some outside observers, specifically those who are not LGBT+ identified.

In addition, research has suggested that a negative heterosexual attitude towards gender non-conformity impacts the expectation that lesbians are masculine and gay men are feminine (see Haddock *et al.*, 1993; Kite and Deaux, 1987; Madon, 1997; Martin, 1990). Arguably, this can influence and conflict with the highly masculinised gender perceptions within policing in relationship to masculinity. It should be noted that gender non-conformity in men may be interpreted as a sign of weakness within society (Haddock and Zanna, 1998; Theodore and Basow, 2000; Tomsen, 2002) and potentially within police culture itself (Buhrke, 1996; Burke, 1993, 1994a, 1994b; Colvin, 2009, 2012). As such, the ultimate visually perceived sign of binary gender non-conformity arguably resides with those individuals who are transitioning from male to female or, to a lesser extent, female to male.

Besides the negative attitudes some heterosexuals possess towards binary gender non-conformity, some research has suggested that LGB individuals themselves have negative attitudes towards transgender individuals (see Skidmore *et al.*, 2006; Bailey *et al.*, 1997; Bell and Weinberg, 1978; Laner, 1978; Laner and Kamel, 1977; Laner and Laner, 1979, 1980). Further, Bailey *et al.* (1997) and Taywaditep (2001) found that negative opinions and attitudes within lesbian and gay communities may contribute to additional problems for non-binary gender conforming individuals. Therefore, for research purposes, I collectively analysed LGB cisgender participants with heterosexual cisgender participants to explore if LGB police officers and constables express any negative attitudes towards transgender individuals as previous research has indicated.[12]

## Chapter summary

This chapter has highlighted the terminological differences between gender as a performance, gender as an identity and the intersectionality of different forms of bias towards those who identify as transgender. As previously discussed, the intersectional perceptions of binary gender and sexuality are often difficult to separate when specifically examining transgender communities. As Herek (1992) stated:

> Heterosexuality is equated ideologically with 'normal' masculinity and 'normal' femininity, whereas homosexuality is equated with violating the norms of gender.
>
> (p. 97)

Notably, gender role ideology relies upon a binary sex system in which 'normal' attraction occurs between two gendered types of bodies defined as opposites (Schilt and Westbrook, 2009). As such, any identity, whether a sexual one or a gendered one, will face different forms of bias if they are viewed as violating heteronormative gender and sexual ideologies. Arguably, non-trans identities can face both heterosexism and genderism if they identify as LGB; this is inimitable but somewhat similar to the heterosexism and genderism that transgender identities often confront. Further, this chapter has examined how heterosexism can be linked to adherence to traditional and rigid social constructions of gender, regardless of gender identity or the performance of a gender. Chapter 1 has built the partial foundation of the theoretical and ontological issues, which Chapter 2 and Chapter 3 will follow-up upon.

## Notes

1  This will be explored in Chapter 3.
2  Notably, there is a difference between gender as an identity and gender as a performance. Yet, during this research, I found that the division between the two was at times very blurred, with transgender identities claiming they were a cross-dresser in the past.
3  Please refer to Appendix B for other common useful terms.
4  Please refer to Appendix B.
5  This is explored in detail in Chapter 8, where I introduce my *trans feminine subcultural hierarchy concept*.
6  This is explored in Chapter 8.
7  HRT, hormone replacement therapy.
8  A 'transvestite' is typically a culturally offensive word in America and is not socially accepted as a way to describe a cross-dresser, yet British participants use and embrace the term.
9  This is explored in Chapter 8.
10  This will be explored further in Chapter 3.
11  Selected definitions were obtained from a literature search, which yielded 52 different articles in 17 different peer-reviewed journals, with the key words 'homophobia' and 'heterosexism'.
12  See Chapter 6.

## References

Ambady, M., Hallahan, B. and Conner, B. 1999. Accuracy of judgments of sexual orientation from thin slices of behaviour. *Journal of Personality and Social Psychology* 77(3), pp. 538–547.

Bailey, J., Kim, P., Hills, A. and Linsenmeier, J. 1997. Butch, femme, or straight acting? Partner preferences of gay men and lesbians. *Journal of Personality and Social Psychology* 73, pp. 960–973.

Bailey, J. and Zucker, K. 1995. Childhood sex-typed behavior and sexual orientation: A conceptual analysis and quantitative review. *Developmental Psychology* 31, pp. 43–55.

Bailey, M. 2003. *The man who would be queen*. Washington, DC: The Joseph Henry Press.

Bell, A. and Weinberg, M. 1978. *Homosexualities: a study of diversity among gay men and women*. New York: Simon & Schuster.

Bell, A., Weinberg, M. and Hammersmith, S. 1981. *Sexual preference: its development in men and women*. Bloomington, IN: Indiana University Press.

Bernstein, G. 1994. A Reply to Rowan. *Behavior Therapist* 17, pp. 185–186.

Bernstein, M., Kostelac, C. and Gaardner, E. 2003. Understanding heterosexism: Applying theories of racial prejudice to homophobia using data from a southwestern police department. *Race, Gender & Class* 10, pp. 54–74.

Birken, L. 1997. Homosexuality and totalitarianism. *Journal of Homosexuality* 3, pp. 1–16.

Blackless, M., Charuvastra, A., Derryck, A., Fausto-Sterling, A., Lauzanne, K. and Lee, E. 2000. How sexually dimorphic are we? Review and synthesis. *American Journal of Human Biology* 12(2), pp. 151–166.

Blanchard, R. 1989. The concept of autogynephilia and the typology of male gender dysphoria. *Journal of Nervous and Mental Disease* 177(10), pp. 616–623.

Buhrke, R. 1996. *A matter of justice*. New York: Routledge.

Burke, M. 1993. *Coming out of the blue*. London: Continuum.

Burke, M. 1994a. Cop culture and homosexuality. *Police Journal* 65, pp. 30–39.

Burke, M. 1994b. Homosexuality as deviance: the case of the gay police officer. *British Journal of Criminology* 34, pp. 192–203.

Burn, S., Kadlec, K. and Rexer, R. 2005. Effects of subtle heterosexism on gays, lesbians, and bisexuals. *Journal of Homosexuality* 49(2), pp. 23–38.

Colvin, R. 2009. Shared perceptions among lesbian and gay police officers: barriers and opportunities in the law enforcement work environment. *Police Quarterly* 12(1), pp. 86–101.

Colvin, R. 2012. *Gay and lesbian cops: diversity and effective policing*. London: Lynne Rienner Publishers.

Connell, R. 1995. *Masculinities*. Berkeley, CA: Stanford University Press.

Conway, L. 2001. *How frequently does transsexualism occur?* [Online]. Available at: http://ai.eecs.umich.edu/people/conway/TS/TSprevalence.html [accessed: 6 November 2017].

Cotton-Huston, A. and Waite, B. 2000. Anti-homosexual attitudes in college students: predictors and classroom interventions. *Journal of Homosexuality* 38, pp. 117–133.

Dreger, A. 2008. The controversy surrounding The Man Who Would Be Queen: a case history of the politics of science, identity, and sex in the internet age. *Archives of Sexual Behavior* 37(3), pp. 366–421.

Erich, S., Tittsworth, J. and Kersten, A. 2010. An examination and comparison of trans-sexuals of color and their white counterparts regarding personal well-being and support networks. *Journal of GLBT Family Studies* 6(1), pp. 25–39.

Fyfe, B. 1983. 'Homophobia' or homosexual bias reconsidered. *Archives of Sexual Behavior* 12, pp. 549–554.

Gagné, P., Tewksbury, R. and McGaughey, D. 1997. Coming out and crossing over: identity formation and proclamation in a transgender community. *Gender & Society* 11(4), pp. 478–508.

Garber, M. 1992. *Vested interests: cross-dressing and cultural anxiety*, New York: Routledge.

Gates, G. 2011. *How many people are lesbian, gay, bisexual and transgender?* The Williams Institute [Online]. Available at: http://escholarship.org/uc/item/09h684x2 [accessed: 6 November 2017].

Gender Identity Research and Education Society (GIRES) 2011. *The number of gender variant people in the UK – update 2011*. [Online]. Available at: https://uktrans.info/attachments/article/197/Prevalence2011.pdf [accessed 6 November 2017].

Goodman, M. and Moradi, B. 2008. Attitudes and behaviors toward lesbian and gay persons: Critical correlates and mediated relations. *Journal of Counseling Psychology* 55, pp. 371–384.

Haddock, G. and Zanna, M. 1998. Authoritarianism, values, and the favorability and structure of anti-gay attitudes. In: Herek, G., ed. *Stigma and sexual orientation: understanding prejudice against lesbians, gay men, and bisexuals*. Newbury Park, CA: Sage, pp. 82–107.

Haddock, G., Zanna, M. and Esses, V. 1993. Assessing the structure of prejudicial attitudes: The case of attitudes toward homosexuals. *Journal of Personality and Social Psychology* 65, pp. 1105–1118.

Halberstam, J. 1998. Transgender butch: Butch/FTM border wars and the masculine continuum. *GLQ: A Journal of Lesbian and Gay Studies* 4(2), pp. 287–310.

Harry, J. 1983a. Defeminization and adult psychological well-being among male homosexuals. *Archives of Sexual Behavior* 12, pp. 1–19.

Harry, J. 1983b. Parasuicide, gender, and gender deviance. *Journal of Health and Social Behavior* 24, pp. 350–361.

Hegarty, P. and Pratto, F. 2001. Sexual orientation beliefs: their relationship to anti-gay attitudes and biological determinist arguments. *Journal of Homosexuality* 41(1), pp. 121–135.

Herek, G. 1984. Beyond homophobia: a social psychological perspective on attitudes towards lesbians and gay men. *Journal of Homosexuality* 10, pp. 1–21.

Herek, G. 1990. The context of anti-gay violence: notes on cultural and psychological heterosexism. *Journal of Interpersonal Violence* 5(3), pp. 316–33.

Herek, G. 1992. The social context of the crimes: notes on cultural heterosexism. In: Herek, G and Berrill, K., eds. *Hate crimes: confronting violence against lesbians and gay men*. Newbury Park, CA: Sage, pp. 89–104.

Herek, G. 1994. Assessing attitudes towards lesbian and gay men: A review of empirical research with the ATLG scale. In: Greene, B. and Herek, G., eds. *Lesbian and gay psychology: theory, research, and clinical applications*. Thousand Oaks, CA: Sage, pp. 206–228.

Herek, G. 2000. The psychology of sexual prejudice. *Current Directions in Psychological Research* 9(1), pp. 19–22.

Herek, G. 2002. Heterosexuals' attitudes towards bisexual men and women in the United States. *Journal of Sex Research* 39, pp. 264–274.

Herek, G. and Capitanio, J. 1996. 'Some of my best friends': intergroup contact, concealable stigma, and heterosexuals' attitudes toward gay men and lesbians. *Personality and Social Psychology Bulletin* 22, pp. 412–424.

Hill, D. 2002. Genderism, transphobia and gender bashing: A framework for interpreting anti-transgender violence. In: Wallace, B. and Carter, R., eds. *Understanding and dealing with violence: a multicultural approach.* Thousand Oaks, CA: Sage, pp. 113–136.

Hill, D. and Willoughby, B. 2005. The development and validation of the genderism and transphobia scale. *Sex Roles* 53(7/8), pp. 531–544.

Hoover, R. and Fishbein, H. 1999. The development of prejudice and sex role stereotyping in white adolescents and white young adults. *Journal of Applied Developmental Psychology* 20, pp. 431–448.

Hubbard, P. 2008. Here, there, everywhere: the ubiquitous geographies of heteronormativity. *Geography Compass* 2/3, pp. 640–658.

Hudson, W. and Ricketts, W. 1980. A strategy for the measurement of homophobia. *Journal of Homosexuality* 5, pp. 356–371.

Johnson, K. 2012. Transgender, transsexualism, and the queering of gender identities: Debates for feminist research. *Handbook of Feminist Research*, pp. 606–626.

Kane-DeMaios, J. 2006. *Crossing sexual boundaries: transgender journeys, uncharted paths.* New York: Prometheus Books.

Kimmel, M. 1994. Masculinity as homophobia: fear, shame, and silence in the construction of gender identity. In: Brod, H. and Kaufman, M., eds. *Theorizing masculinities.* Thousand Oaks, CA: Sage, pp. 119–141.

Kinsman, G. 2004. Men loving men: the challenge of gay liberation. In: Murphy, P.F., ed. *Feminism and masculinities.* Oxford: Oxford University Press, pp. 165–181.

Kite, M. and Deaux, K. 1987. Gender belief systems: Homosexuality and the implicit inversion theory. *Psychology of Women Quarterly* 11, pp. 83–96.

Kite, M. and Whitley, B. 1998. Do heterosexual women and men differ in their attitudes toward homosexuality? A conceptual and methodological analysis. In: Herek, G., ed. *Stigma & sexual orientation: understanding prejudice against lesbians, gay men and bisexuals.* Thousand Oaks, CA: Sage, pp. 39–61.

Landolt, M., Bartholomew, K., Saffrey, C., Oram, D. and Perlman, D. 2004. Gender nonconformity, childhood rejection, and adult attachment: A study of gay men. *Archives of Sexual Behavior* 33, pp. 117–128.

Laner, M. 1978. Media mating II: 'Personals' advertisements of lesbian women. *Journal of Homosexuality* 4, pp. 41–61.

Laner, M. and Kamel, G. 1977. Media mating I: Newspaper 'personals' ads of homosexual men. *Journal of Homosexuality* 3, pp. 149–162.

Laner, M. and Laner, R. 1979. Personal style or sexual preference: Why gay men are disliked. *International Review of Modern Sociology* 9, pp. 212–218.

Laner, M. and Laner, R. 1980. Sexual preference or personal style? Why lesbians are disliked. *Journal of Homosexuality* 5, pp. 339–356.

Langstrom, N. and Zucker, K. 2011. Transvestic fetishism in the general population. *Journal of Sex and Marital Therapy* 31(2), pp. 87–95.

Law, C., Martinez, L., Ruggs, E., Hebl, M. and Akers, E. 2011. Trans-parency in the workplace: How the experiences of transsexual employees can be improved. *Journal of Vocational Behavior* 79(3), pp. 710–723.

Lawrence, A. 2007. Becoming what we love: Autogynephilic transsexualism conceptualized as an expression of romantic love. *Perspectives in Biology and Medicine* 50(4), p. 506.

Laythe, B., Finkel, D. and Kirkpatrick, L. 2001. Predicting prejudice from religious fundamentalism and right-wing authoritarianism: A multiple-regression approach. *Journal of the Scientific Study of Religion* 40, pp. 1–10.

Madon, S. 1997. What do people believe about gay males? A study of stereotype content and strength. *Sex Roles* 37, pp. 663–685.

Martin, C. 1990. Attitudes and expectations about children with nontraditional and traditional gender roles. *Sex Roles* 22, pp. 151–165.

Mason, G. 2002. *The spectacle of violence: homophobia, gender and knowledge.* New York: Routledge.

McBride, R. and Hansson, U. 2010. *'The luck of the draw'. A report on the experiences of trans individuals reporting hate incidents in Northern Ireland.* Belfast: Institute for Conflict Research.

Miles-Johnson, T. 2013. LGBTI variations in crime reporting: how sexual identity influences decisions to call the cops. *Sage Open* April–June, pp. 1–15.

Miles-Johnson, T. 2015. Perceptions of group value: how Australian transgender people view policing. *Policing and Society: an International Journal of Research and Policy*, pp. 1–20.

Morrison, T., McLead, L., Morrison, M., Anderson, D. and O'Connor, W. 1997. Gender stereotyping, homonegativity and misconceptions about sexually coercive behavior among adolescents. *Youth and Society* 28, pp. 451–465.

Namaste, V. 1996. Tragic misreadings: queer theory's erasure of transgender subjectivity. In: Beemyn, B. and Eliason, M., eds. *Queer studies: a lesbian, gay, bisexual and transgender anthology.* New York: NYU Press.

Newton, E. 1998. The queens. In: Nardi, P. and Schneider, B. *Social perspectives in lesbian and gay studies.* London: Routledge, pp. 38–50.

O'Donahue, W. and Caselles, C. 1993. Homophobia: Conceptual, definitional, and value issues. *Journal of Psychopathology and Behavioral Assessment* 15, pp. 177–195.

Office for National Statistics 2009. *Trans data position paper.* Newport: ONS.

Olyslager, F. and Conway, L. 2007. On the calculation of the prevalence of transsexualism. *World Professional Association for Transgender Health 20th International Symposium.* September 2007. Chicago, IL: WPATH, p. 2010.

Panter, H. 2017. Pre-operative transgender motivations for entering policing occupations. *International Journal of Transgenderism*, pp. 1–13.

Peel, E. 2001. Mundane heterosexism: understanding incidents of the everyday. *Women's Studies Forum* 24(5), pp. 541–554.

Peplau, L., Hills, C. and Rubin, Z. 1993. Sex role attitudes in dating and marriage: a 15-year follow-up of the Boston Couples Study. *Journal of Social Issues* 40, pp. 31–52.

Prosser, J. 1995. No place like home: The transgendered narrative of Leslie Feinberg's Stone Butch Blues. *MFS Modern Fiction Studies* 41(3), pp. 483–514.

Prosser, J. 1998. *Second skins: the body narratives of transsexuality.* New York: Columbia University Press.

Reed, B., Rhodes, S., Schofield, P. and Wylie, K. 2009. *Gender variance in the UK: prevalence, incidence, growth and geographic distribution.* Available at: www.scribd.com/document/218815457/2009-Gender-Variance-in-the-UK-Prevalence-Incidence-Growth-an-Geographic-Distribution. [accessed 6 November 2017].

Rizzo, A. 2006. Italy in an uproar over transvestite in the ladies room; as Parliament debates issue, its creditability, already under fire, endures further ridicule. *The Houston Chronicle*, p. 21.

Rowan, A. 1994. Homophobia: A new diagnosis for DSM-W? *Behavior Therapist* 17, pp. 183–184.

Rubin, H. 1996. Do you believe in gender? *Sojourner* 21(6), pp. 7–8.

Schilt, K. and Westbrook, L. 2009. Doing gender, doing heteronormativity: 'gender normals', transgender people, and the social maintenance of heterosexuality. *Gender and Society* 23, pp. 440–464.

Serano, J. 2007. *Whipping girl: a transsexual woman on sexism and the scapegoating of femininity*. Berkeley, CA: Seal Press.

Skidmore, W., Linsenmeier, J. and Bailey, J. 2006. Gender non-conformity and psychological distress in lesbians and gay men. *Archives of Sexual Behavior* 35(6), pp. 685–697.

Smith, I., Oades, L. and McCarthy, G. 2012. Homophobia to heterosexism: Constructs in need of re-visitation. *Gay and Lesbian Issues and Psychology Review* 8(1), pp. 34–44.

Stringer, J. 2009. *GenderQueer and Queer Terms. Trans & Queer Wellness Initiative.* [Online]. Trans, Genderqueer, and Queer Terms Glossary available at: www.ebony.com/wp-content/uploads/2015/10/Trans_and_queer_glossary.pdf [accessed: 10 November 2017].

Stryker, S. 1994. My words to Victor Frankenstein above the village of chamounix: performing transgender rage. *GLQ: A Journal of Gay and Lesbian Studies* 1(3), pp. 237–254.

Taywaditep, K. 2001. Marginalization among the marginalized: Gay men's negative attitudes towards effeminacy. *Journal of Homosexuality* 42, pp. 1–28.

Theodore, P. and Basow, S. 2000. Heterosexual masculinity and homophobia: A reaction to the self? *Journal of Homosexuality* 40, pp. 31–48.

Tomsen, S. 2002. Victims, perpetrators and fatal scenarios: A research note on anti-homosexual male homicides. *International Review of Victimology* 9, pp. 1–28.

Tomsen, S. 2009. *Violence, prejudice and sexuality*. New York: Routledge.

Veale, J., Clarke, D. and Lomax, T. 2010. Biological and psychosocial correlates of adult gender-variant identities: A review. *Personality and Individual Differences* 48(4), pp. 357–366.

Whittle, S. 2000. *The transgender debate: the crisis surrounding gender identity*. Reading: South Street Press.

Wilchins, R. 2002. Deconstructing trans. In: Nestle, J., Howell, C. and Wilchins, R., eds. *Genderqueer: voices from beyond the sexual binary*. Los Angeles, CA: Alyson Publications, pp. 53–63.

Weinberg, G. 1972. Hate crime: a review essay. *Current Issues in Criminal Justice* 11(2), pp. 357–361.

West, C. and Zimmerman, D. 1987. Doing gender. *Gender and Society* 1, pp. 125–151.

Wickberg, D. 2000. Homophobia: on the cultural history of an idea. *Critical Inquiry* 27, pp. 42–57.

## Chapter 2

# Previous police research on LGBT+ identities

## Previous research on non-heteronormative bias within policing

Historically, police interactions and social relationships with members of LGBT+ communities have been strained and plagued with accusations of negative conduct and/or LGBT+ bias. Research (see Dworkin and Yi, 2003; Herek *et al.*, 1999, 2002) has previously suggested that sexual minorities are subject to enacted stigma in the form of prejudice and harassment, are stereotyped as deviants and are targets of victimisation and discrimination because of their perceived non-conformity with binary gender systems (Grossman and D'Augelli, 2006). Prior to the 1970s, LGBT+ people were often labelled as criminals, psychopaths, sinners and perverts (Sarbin, 1996). Further, gay sexualities and transsexuality are perceived as representing aspects of 'social disorder' or 'social deviance', and officers previously enforced laws centred on behaviour associated with gay sexuality and transsexuality (see Rumens and Broomfield, 2012). Historically, transgender individuals around the world have been aggressively targeted by law enforcement, arrested, charged and prosecuted specifically because of their non-heteronormative presentations of gender (see Dwyer, 2011; Eskridge, 1997; Gross, 2009). Further, LGBT+ individuals have expressed distrust in reporting crimes and feelings of being unprotected due to their perceived opinions of the police (Williams and Robinson, 2004; Grant *et al.*, 2011).

Early criminological research on LGB police officers focused on the idea that being gay and being a police officer represented dual and often conflicting identities (Burke, 1993; Leinen, 1993). Previous researchers attempted to understand how officers, as regulators of deviance, reconciled a 'deviant' behaviour within policing (see Burke, 1994a, 1994b; Leinen, 1993). These studies disclosed that police officers often reported that lines of division, distrust and resentment exist between gay and straight officers (Sklansky, 2006). It is well-documented that the relationship between the LGBT+ community and the police have been historically plagued with hostility, with accusations of misconduct (see Cook, 2007; Greenberg Traurig LLP, 2011; Steed, 2011; Pena, 2009); but questions remain around how heteronormative perceptions of sexuality specifically impact police perceptions of the transgender community.

Arnott (1994) concluded that straight police officers, who make up the bulk of police forces, are fearful of gays and lesbians and appear to be 'homophobic' in general. It has been contended that the occupational culture of policing creates negative attitudes about minority individuals (Leinen, 1993) and over-policing that has been over-zealous and arbitrary in its application of gross indecency laws with regard to sexual behaviour in public places (Derbyshire, 1990; Seabrook, 1992; Valverde and Cirak, 2003). As such, police regulations of behaviour have impacted on how the LGBT+ community perceives the police. Researchers have also found evidence that some homophobic/transphobic crimes are actually perpetrated by police officers themselves (Herek, 1989; Berrill, 1992; Grant *et al.*, 2011).

## Gay and blue: previous research on LGB police

Ground-breaking research in the study of lesbian and gay police officers initially began with Stephen Leinen's *Gay Cops* (1993) and Marc Burke's *Coming Out of the Blue* (1993). While Leinen's (1993) research focused on the narratives of 41 lesbian and gay officers in New York City and Burke's (1993) research focused specifically on constables in the U.K., both works examined the discrimination and harassment that gay and lesbian officers faced when managing their sexual identity as police officers. Notably, Burke's study (1993) of nine forces in England and Wales demonstrated that widespread prejudices and biases existed within policing towards police colleagues who identify as LGB.

Burke (1993) additionally disclosed three major findings in his research. First, gay sexualities represent an aspect of social deviance that the police have had to address in the past, which creates a volatile socialised environment between LGBT+ communities and the police (Burke, 1993). Second, normative characteristics of masculinity in police culture (i.e. emphasis on control, physical aggression and competition) place little emphasis on 'feminine' qualities that have been associated with gay male sexuality (Burke, 1993). Third, gay and lesbian officers reported that police work and organisations are understood to represent conservative elements within society, which are linked to anti-gay attitudes (Burke, 1993). Burke (1993) argued that the reported biases, prejudices and discrimination were based on heteronormative perceptions of gay sexuality's social stereotypes, which are connected with effeminacy and weakness. Further, the perceived sexual deviance of gay sexualities challenged the conservative, conformist and binary gender role assumptions that are connected with the masculine subcultural macho ethos, which is constructed within police culture and impacts police mentality.

Burke (1994a, 1994b), in additional studies, stated that the macho subculture of policing and the police's role as regulators of deviance makes it difficult for police to adopt or accept a non-conformist orientation, such as gay sexualities. Burke (1994a, 1994b) found that non-equal rights, machismo culture and the police as regulators of deviance, are all factors that make it difficult for police culture to accept non-heteronormative behaviour. This non-heteronormative behaviour can be described as non-conformity of stereotypical sexual norms.

It should be noted that since Leinen's (1993) and Burke's (1993, 1994a, 1994b) pivotal, yet dated, research, 27 states in the U.S.A. and over 200 local jurisdictions have prohibited employment discrimination on the basis of sexual orientation (Human Rights Campaign, 2010) and English and Welsh police agencies are now among some of the most gay-friendly employers (Stonewall, 2010).

Bernstein and Kostelac (2002) conducted a survey that examined the relationship between attitudes and behaviours towards lesbian and gay sworn officers,[1] illustrating gay bias within American law enforcement. Bernstein and Kostelac surveyed 222 officers belonging to a medium-sized police department in the south-west. They found that unmarried males discriminate more frequently against, and have more negative attitudes towards, non-heterosexuals than married males. Bernstein and Kostelac theorised that single, unattached officers view that they face more of a possibility of being labelled LGB than their married counterparts. This same study found that heterosexual women in law enforcement held a more positive view towards lesbians, due to the possibility of their direct experiences in workplace gender discrimination (Bernstein and Kostelac, 2002). The same survey showed that 30–40 per cent of heterosexual sworn officers indicated that gays and lesbians would not be treated the same or would not be taken as seriously in the criminal justice system. Additionally, 69 per cent of police respondents disclosed that LGB officers do not belong in law enforcement, and 85 per cent reported that gay men would not be able to perform their job as well as others (Bernstein and Kostelac, 2002).

Miller *et al.* (2003) conducted a study of how gay and lesbian officers construct their identities within a traditionally masculine, heterosexually dominated police organisational environment in the U.S.A. This study addressed gay and lesbian officers' perceptions of their work environment in a Midwestern city. Miller and colleagues found that gay and lesbian officers sensed patterns of social exclusion as well as overt sexist and anti-gay behaviour within the police organisation. Every officer in the sample of this study stated that they had heard or been the target of anti-gay or lesbian jokes or derogatory slang (Miller *et al.*, 2003). Additionally, Miller and colleagues contended that police heterosexism has created a hostile environment towards gay men and lesbians, with police ignoring and sometimes even contributing to violence perpetrated against LGB individuals. This coincides with Herek's (1989) and Berrill's (1992) previous findings with regard to police officers themselves perpetrating violence against LGB populations.

Colvin (2012), in his qualitative and quantitative examination of LGB police officers in Washington, DC (America), and within Hampshire and Wiltshire constabularies (England), found that LGB officers in America (71 per cent of 66 respondents) and England (72 per cent of 243 respondents) reported that they had good relationships with heterosexual co-workers, supervisors and subordinates. While this suggests an overall friendly and inclusive police cultural environment, Colvin found LGB discrimination in promotion, assignments and evaluations in both American and English police agencies. Colvin examined attitudinal barriers, with 67 per cent of American officers and 50 per cent of English constables reporting anti-gay attitudes as the most frequently faced attitudinal barrier (Figure 2.1).[2] Besides homophobic comments, being treated like an outsider, feeling social isolation, tokenism (being selected as the single minority to stave off claims of discrimination), repeated LGB harassment and retaliation were additional complaints LGB officers reported when attitudinal barriers were examined.

More recently, Jones and Williams (2013) surveyed 836 police officers in England and Wales across 43 forces and measured three areas of employment: training, deployment and promotion (Table 2.1). Jones and Williams' survey also asked respondents to identify personal characteristics, which included their sexual orientation, rank, ethnicity and membership of LGB employment groups. They found that gay men reported more incidents of discrimination in training, deployment and promotion than lesbian and bisexual officers (Jones and Williams, 2013).

Additionally, Jones and Williams found that officers from large and small departments who identify as LGB were more likely to experience discrimination

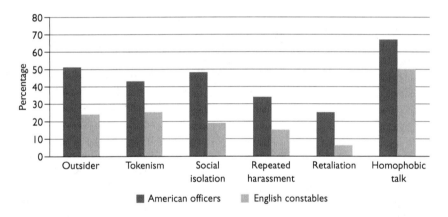

*Figure 2.1* Differential treatment of LGB police.

Source: adapted from Colvin 2012.

*Table 2.1* Prevalence of discrimination among LGB police (%)

|  | Discrimination in training | Discrimination in deployment | Discrimination in promotion |
|---|---|---|---|
| Gay male officers | 11 | 13.5 | 6.9 |
| Gay female officers | 8.2 | 10.6 | 3.2 |
| Bisexual male officers | 5.1 | 3.8 | 1.3 |
| Bisexual female officers | 1.7 | 0.0 | 1.7 |

Source: adapted from Jones and Williams, 2013.

in training and in deployment than LGB officers from medium-sized departments. Overall, one-fifth of self-identified LGB police officers in England and Wales reported some type of discrimination within policing. This study is beneficial, as social advances have been made since earlier research, with anti-discrimination laws, equal benefits ordinances and legalised same-sex marriages (see Weeks, 2007).

## Previous research on transgender perceptions of the police

Researchers have stated that transgender individuals are one of the most victimised groups within society and are likely to face more abuse by the police than other stigmatised groups (see Berman and Robinson, 2010; Edelman, 2014; Miles-Johnson, 2013a, 2013b; Redfern, 2014). Previous research from America and the U.K. have documented specific forms of discrimination, prejudice, bias and violence against trans individuals (see Clements-Nolle *et al.*, 2006; Gagné *et al.*, 1997; Grant *et al.*, 2011; Grossman and D'Augelli, 2006, 2007; Hill, 2002; McNeil *et al.*, 2012; Tee and Hegarty, 2006; Witten and Eyler, 1999). As stated by Mogul *et al.* (2011):

> The policing of queer sexualities has been arguably the most visible and recognised point of contact between LGBT people and the criminal justice system.
>
> (p. 47)

For transgender identities specifically, the likelihood of an increased chance of encounters with law enforcement can occur because of decreased opportunities for employment and housing. These decreased opportunities can often force a disproportionate number of trans individuals to engage in sex work and drug sales as a means for survival (see Bassichis, 2009; Weinberg *et al.*, 1999). Cochran *et al.* (2002) found that trans women sex workers are more likely to have a history of arrest and conviction than cisgender sex workers. Human Rights Watch (2012) found that in four U.S. cities, trans women who were stopped and in possession of condoms were frequently arrested for solicitation, no matter what activity they engaged in. Clearly, a small number of transgender individuals engage in sex work, but often policing loosely associates transgender (particularly feminine) identities with deviant sexualities and sex work (Stotzer, 2014). Stotzer states that this association occurs due to a policing assumption that transgender identities have no legitimate reason to be seen in public. This is apparent in the disproportionate amount of reporting unjustified arrests and stops of transgender identities by the police (see Grant *et al.*, 2011; Stotzer, 2009; Xavier *et al.*, 2007).

A study conducted for the National Center for Transgender Equality, by Grant *et al.* (2011) researched 6,450 individuals who identified as being transgender.

One of the key findings of this large body of research conducted in the U.S.A. was that one-fifth (22 per cent) of respondents who had interacted with the police reported harassment by police due to bias, with 6 per cent reporting physical assault and 2 per cent reporting sexual assault by police officers because they were transgender or gender non-conforming (Figure 2.2). It should be noted that FTM-identified individuals reported more police incidents of harassment than MTF-identified individuals, yet complaints of sexual assault perpetrated by the police against MTF were higher than those against FTM (Grant *et al.*, 2011). See Figures 2.2–2.4 for an analysis of Grant *et al.*'s (2011) key findings.

Another key finding of this research was that FTMs reported higher levels of perceived disrespect than their MTF counterparts, with gender non-conforming individuals reporting the highest amount of perceived police disrespect (Figure 2.3) (Grant *et al.*, 2011).

Further, it appeared that police harassment and assault had an apparent deterrent effect on respondents' willingness to ask for help from law enforcement, with 46 per cent reporting that they were uncomfortable seeking help from the police (Grant *et al.*, 2011). Nemoto *et al.* (2011) also found that out of 573 MTF participants, more than two-thirds reported that they have been ridiculed or embarrassed by American police because of their transgender identity or expression.

When examining research on the denial of police services, Grant *et al.* (2011) disclosed that 20 per cent of participants reported that they were denied equal service by police compared with their cisgender counterparts, with FTM and gender non-conforming individuals reporting higher rates of police harassment than their MTF and transgender counterparts. Notably, variations exist in the comfort levels in seeking police help within the trans sample of Grant *et al.*'s (2011) study (Figure 2.4).

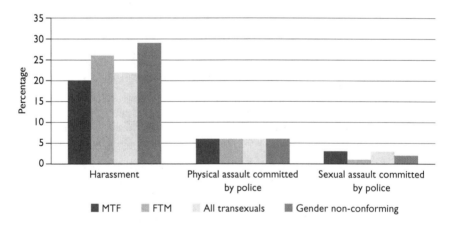

*Figure 2.2* Trans reported harassment and assault perpetrated by police officers.
Source: Grant *et al.* 2011.

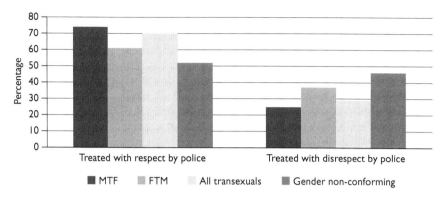

*Figure 2.3* Trans reported opinions on interactions with police officers.
Source: Grant *et al.* 2011.

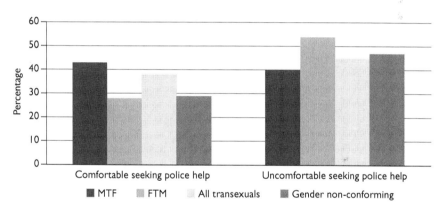

*Figure 2.4* Trans comfort levels in seeking police assistance when needed.
Source: Grant *et al.* 2011.

Empirically, transgender identities disclosed that they are wary of police interaction due to the potential for victimisation or re-victimisation by police (see Grant *et al.*, 2011; Stotzer, 2009; Xavier *et al.*, 2007). Stotzer (2013) found that trans women and trans men reported higher percentages of being arrested in Hawaii (39 per cent and 47 per cent, respectively) than cisgender lesbian/ bisexual women (14 per cent), and cisgender gay/bisexual men (19 per cent), and gender non-conforming gay/bisexual men (27 per cent) and gender non- conforming lesbian/bisexual women (17 per cent). Sousa (2002) found that higher percentages of trans women (45.5 per cent) than trans men (18.2 per cent) reported harassment or verbal abuse by the police. Green (2012) found that Alaskan transgender people have a higher percentage of being verbally harassed or abused by the police than 11 per cent of gay/bisexual cisgender men and 4.7

per cent of lesbian/bisexual cisgender women. Looking at American studies, data suggests that transgender people face more victimisation at the hands of the police (see Grant *et al.*, 2011), more arrests than LGB cisgender individuals (see Stotzer, 2013) and more reports of police harassment (see Grant *et al.*, 2011).

Additionally, the relationship between American law enforcement and trans individuals appears very precarious when examining crime reporting rates. As previously stated, Grant *et al.* (2011) found 46 per cent of trans individuals were uncomfortable seeking help from the police. Xavier *et al.* (2007) found that Virginians who participated in a transgender health study reported that 83 per cent had been victims of sexual assault but did not disclose the incidents to police, with 70 per cent of physical assault victims not reporting the incidents to the police. Lombardi *et al.* (2002) found that 41.3 per cent of transgender participants never reported violent criminal incidents to the police. Sousa (2002) found that among criminal victimisation, only 25 per cent of their sample disclosed that they reported the incidents to police.

Besides the fear of harassment, fear of physical assault, fear of sexual assault, and fear of arrest, transgender identities often disclose a general uncomfortableness when interacting with the police (see Carson, 2008; Grant *et al.*, 2011). Witten (2003) found that transgender identities avoided interacting with the police due to fear of abuse by the legal system, with over half of participants disclosing a fear of ridicule, that their report would not be taken seriously or had previous negative experiences that dissuaded them from reporting another criminal incident (Galvan and Bazargan, 2012). Further, Galvan and Bazargan (2012) found that 71 per cent of trans Latinos from Los Angeles reported negative police interactions overall.

When examining research of the genderqueer community specifically, data suggests that they face rates of discrimination and violence that are similar to, if not higher than, transsexuals within America. Harrison *et al.* (2012) found that genderqueer identities face more physical assaults (32 per cent compared with 25 per cent); more police harassment (31 per cent compared with 21 per cent); and more unemployment (76 per cent compared with 56 per cent) than transsexual identities.

In comparison, there is minimal research that examines police harassment and discrimination against transgender and gender non-conforming individuals in England and Wales. One notable body of European research that offers some evidence of the extent of officer interactions with transgender individuals was conducted by the Scottish Transgender Alliance. McNeil *et al.* (2012) surveyed 889 Scottish transgender-identified individuals for the Trans Mental Health Study (the largest trans survey in Europe) and discovered that out of 665 respondents, 14 per cent had reported some form of police harassment for being transgender, with 34 per cent worried about potential future police harassment (McNeil *et al.*, 2012).

From an international research perspective, Miles-Johnson (2013a, 2013b, 2015a, 2015b, 2015c, 2015d, 2016) examined transgender identities within

Australia. Miles-Johnson (2015a) found that the damaging effects of police hostility and discrimination towards the transgender community stemmed from the aggression directed towards transgender identities in general. As such, this hostility has led to a lack of trust and confidence that the transgender community has towards the police (see Miles-Johnson, 2013a; Moran and Sharpe, 2004). Miles-Johnson (2015a) found that the Australian transgender community commonly reported negative experiences with the police and during their interaction with the police. Further, participants perceived that Australian officers did not accept their gender identity (Miles-Johnson, 2015a). Miles-Johnson's (2015a) sample disclosed that police officers were disrespectful and displayed 'unprofessional and harassing behaviours' (p. 184) towards the transgender community. Notably, as previously stated in this chapter, this is similar to the perceptions held by international cisgender LGB communities.

### Trans and blue: previous research on transgender police

Currently, there exists very scant literature which specifically examines transgender identities within policing. Sears *et al.* (2013) examined transgender identities collectively in a report of LGBT+ identities in law enforcement. Notably, this study examined all types of personnel within law enforcement, which included correction officers, federal agents, local policing, federal policing and probation officers in America. Sears *et al.* (2013) found that out of 60 transgender law enforcement personnel, 90 per cent reported negative experiences within their departments. Of those who reported negative experiences, 15 per cent reported that they were terminated; 37 per cent reported being threatened with termination; 68 per cent reported homophobic verbal attacks; 18 per cent reported physical attacks from colleagues; and 53 per cent felt that their safety was jeopardised due to social isolation from their peers within policing (Sears *et al.*, 2013). Sears and colleagues theorised that because transgender identities are underrepresented within law enforcement, reports of discrimination are more frequent. Further, they contended that discrimination likely reduces the overall diversity among law enforcement personnel, which in turn can create additional barriers between the LGBT+ community and law enforcement agencies (Sears *et al.*, 2013).

Panter (2017) examined the motivations for American, English and Welsh transsexual identities for entering policing as an occupation. Panter argued that instead of avoiding a perceived volatile binary gendered environment, pre-transition transsexual identities are more likely to seek out a career in policing due to hyper masculine expectations of the job itself. Panter also found that both MTF and FTM pre-transition identities seek refuge within policing to ease internal conflicts as a result of gender dysphoria (i.e. pre-transition distress) prior to transition. Further, Panter found that pre-transition MTF identities chose to enter policing to combat their gender dysphoria by proving their 'masculinity' and FTM identities enter policing to foster and embrace their 'masculinity'.

## Chapter summary

This chapter has examined previous research on LGBT+ perspectives of the police and previous research on LGBT+ identities within policing. As illustrated by previous studies on heterosexism within police culture and how LGB communities perceive the police, there are indications that some police, or certain police cultures, possess heterosexist views towards LGB identities (see Buhrke, 1996; Burke, 1993, 1994a, 1994b; Colvin, 2009; Jones and Williams, 2013) and heterosexist/genderist attitudes towards transgender identities (see Grant *et al.*, 2011). Therefore, arguably there is a socialised connection between gender and sexuality when exploring heterosexism. I believe it would be naive to assume that only LGB identities face components of homophobia, heterosexism and heteronormativity. Transgender officers who are negotiating police culture may, like their LGB counterparts, be susceptible to anti-homosexual sentiments.[3] While some LGB experiences and perceptions are similarly aligned with trans experiences and perceptions, notable differences exist between the LGB and the trans communities. For example, members of the transgender community face more fears of harassment, more fears of physical assault, more fears of sexual assault and more fears of arrest from the police than LGB populations (see Carson, 2008; Grant *et al.*, 2011).

## Notes

1  Sworn officers are officers who are given the power to arrest and who have completed the mandatory training.
2  American respondents ($n=66$) and English respondents ($n=243$).
3  This will be explored in Chapters 7 and 8.

## References

Arnott, J. 1994. Gays and lesbians in the criminal justice system. In: Hendricks, J. and Byers, B., eds. *Multicultural perspectives in criminal justice and criminology*. Springfield, OH: Charles C. Thomas Publishing, pp. 211–213.

Bassichis, D. 2009. '*It's war in here': a report on the treatment of transgender and intersex people in New York state men's prisons*. Sylvia Rivera Law Project.

Berman, A. and Robinson, S. 2010. *Speaking out: stopping homophobic and transphobic abuse in Queensland*. Queensland: Australian Academic Press.

Bernstein, M. and Kostelac, C. 2002. Lavender and blue: attitudes about homosexuality and behavior towards lesbians and gay men among police officers. *Journal of Contemporary Criminal Justice* 18(3), pp. 302–328.

Berrill, K. 1992. Anti-gay violence and victimization in the United States: An overview. In: Herek, G. and Berrill, K., eds. *Hate crimes: confronting violence against lesbians and gay men*. Newbury Park, CA: Sage, pp. 19–35.

Buhrke, R. 1996. *A matter of justice*. New York: Routledge.

Burke, M. 1993. *Coming out of the blue*. London: Continuum.

Burke, M. 1994a. Cop culture and homosexuality. *Police Journal* 65, pp. 30–39.

Burke, M. 1994b. Homosexuality as deviance: The case of the gay police officer. *British Journal of Criminology* 34, pp. 192–203.

Carson, L. 2008. *Physical and emotional health needs of transgender individuals in Philadelphia: summary of key findings*. Philadelphia, PA: Public Health Management Corporation.

Clements-Nolle, K., Marx, R. and Katz, M. 2006. Attempted suicide among transgendered persons: the influence of gender-based discrimination and victimization. *Journal of Homosexuality* 51, pp. 53–69.

Cochran, B., Stewart, A., Ginzler, J. and Cauce, A. 2002. Challenges faced by homeless sexual minorities: Comparison of gay, lesbian, bisexual, and transgender homeless adolescents with their heterosexual counterparts. *American Journal of Public Health* 92(5), pp. 773–777.

Colvin, R. 2009. Shared perceptions among lesbian and gay police officers: barriers and opportunities in the law enforcement work environment. *Police Quarterly* 12(1), pp. 86–101.

Colvin, R. 2012. *Gay and lesbian cops: diversity and effective policing*. London: Lynne Rienner Publishers.

Cook, M. 2007. Queer conflicts: love, sex and war, 1914–1967. In: Cook, M., ed. *A gay history of Britain: love and sex between men since the middle ages*. Oxford: Greenwood World Publishing, pp. 145–177.

Derbyshire, P. 1990. Gays and the police. *Police Review* 8, pp. 1144–1145.

Dworkin, S. and Yi, H. 2003. LGBT identity, violence, and social justice: The psychological is political. *International Journal for the Advancement of Counseling* 25, pp. 269–279.

Dwyer, A. 2011. 'It's not like we're going to jump them': How transgressing heteronormativity shapes police interactions with LGBT young people. *Youth Justice* 11(3), pp. 203–220.

Edelman, E. 2014. Walking while transgender. Necropolitical regulations of trans feminine bodies of colour in the nation's capital. In: Haritaworn J., Kuntsman, A. and Posocco, S., eds. *Queer necropolitics*. New York: Routledge, pp. 172–190.

Eskridge, W.N. Jr. 1997. Challenging the apartheid of the closet: establishing conditions for lesbian and gay intimacy, nomos, and citizenship, 1961–1981. *Hofstra Law Review* 25, p. 817.

Galvan, F. and Bazargan, M. 2012. *Interactions of Latina transgender women with law enforcement*. Los Angeles, CA: Bienestar Human Services Incorporated.

Gagné, P., Tewksbury, R. and McGaughey, D. 1997. Coming out and crossing over: identity formation and proclamation in a transgender community. *Gender & Society* 11(4), pp. 478–508.

Grant, J., Mottet, L., Tanis, J., Harrison, J., Herman, J. and Keisling, M. 2011. Injustice at every turn: a report of the National Transgender Discrimination Survey. *National Center for Transgender Equality and National Gay and Lesbian Task Force* [Online]. Available at: www.thetaskforce.org/downloads/reports/reports/ntds_full.pdf [accessed: 5 November 2017].

Green, M. 2012. *Anchorage LGBT discrimination survey: final report*. Anchorage, AK: Identity Inc. [Online]. Available at: http://alaskacommunity.org/wp-content/uploads/2012/03/akq_final_report.pdf [accessed: 6 November 2017].

Greenberg Traurig LLP. 2011. APD.SOP 20.20§3.4.1 Final report regarding the planning, execution, and subsequent conduct related to the 'Eagle Raid' [Online]. Available at:

http://clatl.com/images/blogimages/2011/06/29/1309357414-eagle_report_city.pdf [accessed: 10 May 2011].

Gross, A. 2009. Gender outlaws before the law: the courts of the borderlands. *Harvard Journal of Law and Gender* 32(1), pp. 165–230.

Grossman, A. and D'Augelli, A. 2006. Transgender youth: Invisible and vulnerable. *Journal of Homosexuality* 51, pp. 111–128.

Grossman, A. and D'Augelli, A. 2007. Transgender youth and life-threatening behaviors. *Suicide and Life-Threatening Behavior* 37(5), pp. 527–537.

Harrison, J., Grant, J., Herman, J. 2012. A gender not listed here: genderqueers, gender rebels, and otherwise in the National Transgender Discrimination Survey. *LGBTQ Policy Journal at the Harvard Kennedy School* 2, pp. 13–24.

Herek, G. 1989. Hate crimes against lesbians and gay men: Issues for research and policy. *American Psychologist* 44, pp. 948–955.

Herek, G., Cogan, S. and Gilliss, J. 2002. Victim experiences of hate crimes based on sexual orientation. *Journal of Social Issues* 58, pp. 319–399.

Herek, G., Gillis, J. and Cogan, J. 1999. Psychological sequelae of hate-crime victimization among lesbian, gay, and bisexual adults. *Journal of Consulting and Clinical Psychology* 67, pp. 945–951.

Hill, D. 2002. Genderism, transphobia and gender bashing: A framework for interpreting anti-transgender violence. In: Wallace, B. and Carter, R., eds. *Understanding and dealing with violence: a multicultural approach.* Thousand Oaks, CA: Sage, pp. 113–136.

Human Rights Campaign. 2010. Issue: Workplace [Online]. Available at: www.hrc.org/issues/workplace/equal_opportunity/equal_opportunity_laws.asp [accessed: 6 November 2017].

Human Rights Watch. 2012. Sex workers at risk: condoms as evidence of prostitute in four U.S. cities. [Online]. Available at: www.hrw.org/report/2012/07/19/sex-workers-risk/condoms-evidence-prostitution-four-us-cities [accessed: 6 November 2017].

Jones, M. and Williams, M. 2013. Twenty years on: Lesbian, gay and bisexual police officers' experiences of workplace discrimination in England and Wales. *Policing and Society: An International Journal of Research and Policy* 25(2), pp. 1–24.

Leinen, S. 1993. *Gay cops.* New Brunswick, NJ: Rutgers University.

Lombardi, E., Wilchins, R., Priesing, D. and Malouf, D. 2002. Gender violence: Transgender experiences with violence and discrimination. *Journal of Homosexuality* 42, pp. 89–101.

McNeil, J., Bailey, L., Ellis, S., Morton, J. and Regan, M. 2012. Trans Mental Health Study 2012 [Online]. Available at: www.scottishtrans.org/Uploads/Resources/trans_mh_study.pdf [accessed: 6 November 2017].

Miles-Johnson, T. 2013a. Confidence and trust in police: How sexual identity difference shapes perceptions of police. *Current Issues in Criminal Justice* 25, p. 685.

Miles-Johnson, T. 2013b. LGBTI variations in crime reporting: how sexual identity influences decisions to call the cops. *SAGE Open* April–June, pp. 1–15.

Miles-Johnson, T. 2015a. Perceptions of group value: how Australian transgender people view policing. *Policing and Society: An International Journal of Research and Policy,* pp. 1–20.

Miles-Johnson, T. 2015b. 'They don't identify with us': perceptions of police by Australian transgender people. *International Journal of Transgenderism* 16(3), pp. 169–189.

Miles-Johnson, T. 2015c. Perceptions of group value: how Australian transgender people view policing. *Policing and Society: An International Journal of Research and Policy*, pp. 1–20.

Miles-Johnson, T. 2015d. Policing transgender people. *SAGE Open* 5(2).

Miles-Johnson, T. 2016. Policing diversity: examining police resistance to training reforms for transgender people in Australia. *Journal of Homosexuality* 63(1), pp. 103–136.

Miller, S., Forest, K. and Jurik, N. 2003. Diversity in blue: lesbian and gay police officers in a masculine occupation. *Men and Masculinities* 5(4), pp. 355–385.

Mogul, J., Ritchie, A. and Whitlock, K. 2011. *Queer (in)justice: the criminalization of LGBT people in the United States (Vol. 5)*. Boston, MA: Beacon Press.

Moran, L. and Sharpe, A. 2004. Violence, identity and policing: The case of violence against transgender people. *Criminal Justice* 4(4), pp. 395–417.

Nemoto, T., Bodeker, B., and Iwamoto, M. 2011. Social support, exposure to violence and transphobia, and correlates of depression among male-to-female transgender women with a history of sex work. *American Journal of Public Health* 101(10), pp. 1980–1988.

Panter, H. 2017. Pre-operative transgender motivations for entering policing occupations. *International Journal of Transgenderism*, pp. 1–13.

Pena, A. 2009. Inter-Office Communication C09–012 (Aller/Chapman) Investigation [Online]. Available at: www.motherjones.com/files/TABC_report.pdf [accessed: 7 November 2017].

Redfern, J. 2014. Best practices to improve police relations with transgender individuals. *Journal of Law Enforcement* 3(4).

Rumens, N. and Broomfield, J. 2012. Gay men in the police: identity disclosure and management issues. *Human Resource Management* 22(3), pp. 283–298.

Sarbin, T. 1996. The deconstruction of stereotypes: homosexuals and military policy. In: Herek, G., Jobe, J. and Carnery, R., eds. *Out in force: sexual orientation and the military*. Chicago, IL: University of Chicago Press, pp. 177–196.

Seabrook, M. 1992. Homosexuality and the police. *New Law Journal* 142, pp. 325–326.

Sears, B., Hasenbush, A. and Mallory, C. 2013. *Discrimination against law enforcement officers on the basis of sexual orientation and gender identity: 2000 to 2013*. The Williams Institute [Online]. Available at: http://escholarship.org/uc/item/3h220044 [accessed: 7 November 2017].

Sklansky, D. 2006. Not your father's police department: making sense of the new demographics of law enforcement. *Journal of Criminal Law & Criminology* 96(3), pp. 1209–1243.

Sousa, A. 2002. A victimization study of transgendered individuals in San Francisco, California. Master's thesis. San Jose University (paper 2245).

Steed, S. 2011. Investigation and disposition (addendum for court settlement) OPS File #09-c-0387-MISC. [Online]. Available at: www.atlantaga.gov/home/showdocument?id=36 [accessed: 6 November 2017].

Stonewall. 2010. Workplace Equality Index 2010 [Online]. Available at: www.stonewall.org.uk/workplace [accessed: 6 November 2017].

Stotzer, R. 2009. Violence against transgender people: A review of United States data. *Aggression and Violent Behavior* 14(3), 170–179.

Stotzer, R, 2013. LGBTQI Hawai'i: A needs assessment of the lesbian, gay, bisexual, transgender, queer, and intersex communities in the state of Hawai'i, Suppl. 2:

*Findings by gender identity/expression*. Honolulu, HI: Myron B. Thompson School of Social Work, University of Hawai'i, Manoa.

Stotzer, R. 2014. Law enforcement and criminal justice personnel interactions with transgender people in the United States: a literature review. *Aggression and Violent Behavior* 19(3), pp. 263–277.

Tee, N. and Hegarty, P. 2006. Predicting opposition to the civil rights of transpersons in the United Kingdom. *Journal of Community and Applied Social Psychology* 16, pp. 70–80.

Valverde, M. and Cirak, M. 2003. Governing bodies, creating gay spaces: Policing and security issues in 'gay' downtown Toronto. *British Journal of Criminology* 43, pp. 102–121.

Weeks, J. 2007. *The world we have won: the remaking of erotic and intimate life*. New York: Routledge.

Weinberg, M, Shaver, F. and Williams, C. 1999. Gendered sex work in the San Francisco Tenderloin. *Archives of Sexual Behavior* 28(6), pp. 503–521.

Williams, M. and Robinson, A. 2004. Problems and prospects with policing the lesbian, gay and bisexual community in Wales. *Policing and Society* 14(3), pp. 213–232.

Witten, T. 2003. Transgender aging: An emerging population and an emerging need. *Review Sexologies* 12(4), pp. 15–20.

Witten, T. and Eyler, E. 1999. Hate crimes and violence against the transgendered. *Peace Review* 11, 481–469.

Xavier, J., Honnold, J., Bradford, J. 2007. The health, health-related needs, and lifecourse experiences of transgender Virginians. Centers of Disease Control and Prevention, Virginia Department of Health. [Online] Available at: www.vdh.virginia.gov/epidemiology/DiseasePrevention/documents/pdf/THISFINALREPORTVol.1.pdf [accessed: 6 November, 2017].

## Chapter 3

# Gendered divisions and social spaces within policing

## Arguments surrounding binary notions of gender subjectivity

The material of this book cannot dismiss the broad nuanced arguments that underpin political movements and theoretical notions of gender identity. There has been a substantial amount of debate over binary notions of gender subjectivity. This has occurred for three major reasons. First, transgender studies are theoretically and empirically tied to observations and personal accounts by both trans and non-trans scholars (for example see Bornstein, 1994; Rubin, 1996, 2003). Second, when examining nuanced arguments of gender identity and ideology, some academics state that transgender identities are a threat to lesbian subjectivity (see Jeffreys, 2003) or are a threat to gay male subjectivity. As such, sexuality and gender identity, while much different from one another, are frequently viewed as interconnected. This has led to further theoretical complications within studies of gender identity politics.

Third, Bornstein (1994), Halberstam (1998), Hines (2007), along with many other trans scholars have argued for a specific academic focus on transgender subjectivities instead of the more traditional binary notions of gender subjectivity. Namaste (2005) and Prosser (1998) have further addressed Bornstein's, Halberstam's and Hines' arguments by stressing that there should be a clear division between transsexual and transgender subjectives. Johnson (2012) states:

> Transitioning is something that always necessitates some form of movement across or between the socially established binary genders, but it must be acknowledged that when theorists or individuals refer to collective *trans*, they may mean different things in terms of both identities and practices.
>
> (p. 608)

## Post-structuralism approaches to gender identity: symbolic interactionism

Goffman repeatedly scorned any affiliation with symbolic interaction, often claiming to be a Durkeimian structuralist instead (Scheff, 2005). Yet his work, *The Presentation of Self in Everyday Life* indirectly implied otherwise. Goffman (1959), through dramaturgical metaphor (stage, zoning, front and back regions, masquerade, etc.), argued that interaction is an engagement between individual(s) and audience(s), to whom individuals perform and who, in turn, interpret their actions. For Goffman (1959):

> ... the self [is] a performed character ... not an organic thing that has specific location ... [the performer and] his body merely provide the peg on which something of a collaborative manufacture will be hung for a time.
>
> (pp. 252–253)

Thus, behind Goffman's analyses of interaction lies an active, prior, conscious and performing self. Scheff (2005) highlights that Goffman moves away from a rigid structuralist stance to a more arguable symbolic interactionist stance when he examines the motives of the actors (namely Chapters Four–Six). In *Presentation of Self in Everyday Life* (1959), it is apparent that Goffman was quite conscious of the significance of the body to identity, social order and emotional order in respect experiences of embodiment. As Goffman (1959) stated:

> In our society, the character one performs and one's self are somewhat equated and this self-as-character is usually seen as something housed within the body of the possessor ... I suggest that this view is ... a bad analysis.... While this image is entertained *concerning* the individual ... this [body] itself does not derive from its possessor, but from the whole scene of his action, being generated by that attribute of local events which renders them interpretable by witnesses. A correctly staged and preformed scene leads the audience to impute a [body] to a performed character, but this imputation – this [body] – is a *product* of a scene that comes off, and is not a *cause* of it. The [body], then as a performed character, is not an organic thing that has a specific location, whose fundamental fate is to be born to mature, and to die; it is a dramatic effect arising diffusely from a scene that is presented, and the characteristic issue, the crucial concern, is whether it will be credited or discredited.
>
> (pp. 252–253)

Here, Goffman stresses that the body is essentially made, moulded and manipulated in ritualised social and cultural contracts. In simplest terms, Goffman is stating that the body is something that people do and there exists an active process by which the body is realised and made meaningful (embodiment). Therefore, the body is '... systematically produced, sustained, and presented in everyday life ... which is realized and actualized through a variety of social regulated activities or practices' (Turner, 1984: 24).

Notably, I am aware of the pragmatic tradition of symbolic interactionism: people who merely 'have' a body actively 'do' a body. For example, Butler (1990) with her arguably symbolic interactionist[1] reinvention of the concept of performativity and Goffman (1959) with his gender deconstruction consisting of moments of attribution and iteration in a social process of 'doing' masculinity and femininity in a performative interval may appear at odds. Yet, both describe social presentation as fundamentally dramaturgical. Notably, while gender may, or may not, be performative in nature during different intervals of social interactions, I would contend with both Butler and Goffman that there are valid arguments that a majority of individuals conform to socialised gender expectations.

While I do not subscribe to the notion that every aspect of gender performativity is a theoretical performance and being transgender is syllogistically subversive, I agree (much like Butler and Goffman) with some components of dramaturgistic thinking. First, embodied gender is sometimes articulated socially in ways which are similarly expressed by others during social interactions (Brissett and Edgley, 2005).[2] Therefore, gender is not simply constructed but radically influenced by contingent aspects of society itself. Second, dramaturgy entails a complex system of understanding founded upon how social order is sustained in dramatic body-rituals, which are socially bound and imposed by moral orders (Vannini and Waskul, 2013). In the context of this research, I believe gender can be presented and produced by social influences that are personal and communal at the same time. As such, social identities are not just privately held, they are also held by individuals who share, define and negotiate through interaction (Blumer, 1969). Notably, one cannot quickly dismiss gender as strictly due to performative discourse,[3] instead it makes more sense to conceptualise how specific social interactions influence aspects of embodiment how individuals expect other to conform to it.

## Social constraints: gender construction

From the moment we are born, we are socialised to conform or adapt to binary gender roles that exist within society. Often this binary socialisation begins during infancy, and at times during pregnancy. For example, we associate baby girls with the colour pink and boys with the colour blue,[4] and often nurseries are painted in the baby's respective colours. Or, girls are told to play with certain toys because they are girls' toys, while boys are told to play with others. As such, gender construction is the process of how we are taught to socially conform or socially behave in accordance with societal expectations of our assigned biological gender (i.e. genderism). Thus, almost all humans are socially institutionalised, per se, to conform to binary gendered systems.

Developmental psychologists Bussey and Bandura (1999), modelled a concept of gender identity development as a self-categorisation from birth to adolescence, based upon gender institutionalism. Notably, developmental psychologists disagree upon the exact constituents of and best explanations for the development of gender, with most research perspectives focused on one's sense of gender self-categorisation evolving from birth as opposed to being fixed in nature (see also; Kohlberg, 1966; Martin *et al.*, 2002). Yet, the social influence of a binary gender system allows for gender self-categorisation to occur within a child's perceived label within a gender group and eventually internalises into a self-categorised gender label (Tate *et al.*, 2014). Therefore, social developmental influences upon binary gender must be understood to conceptualise social meanings of 'male' and 'female'.

As such, arguments in this book rely upon intersectional theories of the social construction of gender both within personal and professional social environments. This is similar to works completed by Garfinkel (1967), Kessler and McKenna (1978), West and Zimmerman (1987) and Schilt (2010). As such, throughout this book it is contended that social experiences which rely upon cultural workings of gender difference are constantly reinforced by the social maintenance of gender construction and often gender inequality.

Obviously nuanced arguments of 'gender essentialism' (Greer, 1999) cannot be ignored when discussing theories of gender construction. 'Essentialist' arguments situate gender experiences by placing paramount importance on the idea that physiology contributes to identity. Notably, some radical feminists have previously argued that transwomen can never lay claim to 'womanhood' (see Greer, 1999; Grosz, 1994; Jeffreys, 2003; Raymond, 1980). When examining Greer's (1999) research, Johnson (2012) states: 'transwomen are constructed as the bastards of the feminist movement: infiltrating and penetrating female spaces, impersonating and annihilating their mothers, not just in a "weird" or "freakish" sense' (p. 612). As Johnson points out, Raymond (1980), Jeffreys (2003), and other 'gender essentialist' feminists fail to present anti-essentialist, post-structuralist arguments for gender when examining the tenuous claim that *all* women have a claim to the identity category of woman if they are 'feminist'. Notably, here lies the main issue when conducting transgender research: by claiming essentialist categories of gender, researchers continue to take part in another form of gender oppression, which is the antithesis of feminism. Thankfully, most arguments over 'essentialism' have primarily faded away in progressive feminist circles.

'Gender essentialism' aside, one cannot discuss post-structuralist accounts of gender without exploring the influence feminist philosopher Judith Butler (1990) had upon current transgender theories. Butler argued that a philosophical paradigm involving the binary categories of sex and gender are too socially restrictive for feminist understandings of transsexuality and conflict with sociological perceptions of 'heterogender' (Butler, 1997). Butler further stated that gender must be produced by the body and exist as an unchangeable identity to maintain the order of heterosexuality (i.e. 'heterogender'). Therefore, the interweaving concepts of heterosexuality, heteronormativity and the performance of gender are fundamental in Butler's (1990, 1993, 1997) theories.

Butler's ideas on the social performance of gender can be theoretically beneficial for conceptualising how some people enact gendered behaviours and how people perceive the gendered behaviours of others. Butler (1990) stated in her theory of performativity that the concept of sex relates to biological male or female body constructs, and gender refers to the social meaning of such bodies.

Further, Butler's *Gender Trouble* (1990) described how cross-dressing could emphatically elucidate the meaning of gender performativity and that all gender is performative. Butler (1990) ontologically examined cisgender males who performed acts of 'femininity' as an example of gender performativity which replicated traditional patriarchal norms, where gender rules were compulsively and frequently acted out to reinforce naturality (Hines, 2006; Prosser, 2006). Butler (1990) argued that 'being' is reducible to the form of 'appearing' (Johnson, 2012). Butler (1990), by using performances of drag, argued that there is no ontological 'truth' to 'being' male or female; rather, every aspect of gender is performed (Johnson, 2012). Butler (1990) further contends that 'there is no 'real' male or female body, only an unattainable ideal to aspire to become' (Johnson, 2012: 615). Butler, who adopted Foucault's 'genealogical analysis' (1977: 142) of binary concept of 'sex' and 'gender', theorised that transgender individuals, butch lesbians, drag kings and drag queens, do not become empirical examples of gender performativity illustrating the inessentiality of sex and the non-originality of heterosexuality (Prosser, 2006). These acts of 'gender trouble', as Butler (1990) described them, showed how the naturalisation of gender may be challenged both socially and politically.

Obviously, Butler's (1990, 1993, 1997) works have led to contention within transgender studies, as Namaste (2000) points out that her contribution has led to a notion that a hierarchical division exists 'between the newly celebrated "transgenderist" and the relegated "transsexual"' (Johnson, 2012: 615). Yet, key trans theorists (e.g. Stryker, 1994, 1998; Bornstein, 1994; Wilchins, 1995) embraced Butler's language surrounding 'performativity' to dispute previous notions of gender essentialism. As Stryker (1998) states:

> Transgender phenomena have achieved critical importance (and critical chic) to the extent that they provide a site for grappling with the problematic relation between the principles of performativity and a materiality that, which inescapable, defies stable representation, particularly as experienced by embodies subjects.
>
> (p. 147)

It was not until Butler's more recent work *Undoing Gender* (2004) that she specifically wrote at length about transsexuality while addressing how heteronormativity itself influences anti-trans violence. To sum up Butler's more recent work, she describes the human body as a container for an inner gendered self, which is culturally established, thus reinforcing the argument that gender is constructed socially regardless of sexed bodies (Butler, 2004). Butler's (2004) argument notably focuses on the 'subversion of identity' and has led to debates in respect to what extent gender variant individuals (who do not conform to binaries) should be included under sociological queer theory. While Butler has powerful theoretical and philosophical claims about human autonomy, it must be understood that there exists a greater range of masculinities and femininities which are unfixed to binary concepts of the sexed body. In other words, masculinity and femininity are not owned by any gendered body; instead, they are governed by socialised gender ideologies. This governance of socialised gender ideologies was founded upon ethnomethodological theories of gender (see Garfinkel, 1967; West and Zimmerman, 1987) which argue that social interactions create mechanisms that maintain a gender system, which is visible (Schilt and Westbrook, 2009).

Besides ontological arguments for gender performativity, some researchers have turned to phenomenological and psychoanalytic accounts to better theorise trans embodiment. Serano (2007) argued that despite the social constraints of binary gender expectations and social gender conformity, there exists a subconscious sex that occurs in all of us, regardless of our biological gender signifiers. Serano describes a subconscious sex that exists within transgender populations as a battle between a person's subconscious sex and a person's presentation of gender, thus leading to conflict when examining gender identification. As such, there exist problematic divisions between how gender is socially and politically viewed and what the actual definition of 'gender identity' is: there exists a gender that we choose to identify as, and a gender that we subconsciously feel ourselves to be (see Serano, 2007). Understanding and focusing on the concept of a subconscious sex that is separate from an individual's gender identity allows for the examination of how the subconscious sex can manifest into the acceptance and existence of transsexualism (Serano, 2007). For most individuals, particularly cisgender individuals, this subconscious sex corresponds to their gender presentation without having questions about their subconscious sex, but for others their subconscious sex conflicts with their biological sex or their sex presentation; this can lead to gender conflict or gender dysphoria.[5]

Worthy of mention due to its sociological significance is Feinberg's (1993) *Stone Butch Blues*, a novel which played an important, informative role in the examination of genderqueer identities and social constructivism. In this novel, Jess, the main character, moves from the category of 'butch' (in butch-femme lesbian subculture) to the category of 'transsexual', and then recognises that transition from female to male is likewise unfulfilling (Feinberg, 1993; Prosser, 1995). Jess then self-identifies as occupying a middle ground, identifying simply as a 'he-she'. Feinberg's (1993) work has notably drawn attention to the genderqueer movement, yet there is still a neglect of empirical examinations of genderqueer identities within the social sciences.

## 'Doing' male and female: the gender attrition process

Birdwhistell (1970) rejected notions that genitals are markers for 'male' or 'female' identities because genitals are typically hidden in social situations. As such, Birdwhistell argued that 'tertiary sexual characteristics' (i.e. facial expressions, movement, body posture, etc.) are instead the primary markers for social gender construction. I would tend to agree somewhat with Birdwhistell, that our understanding of gender differences is reliant upon how we understand gender displays and how we recognise gender instead of genital constructs.

Socially, we descriptively recognise how gender can be perceived as a typical 'male' or typical 'female' identity. For example, 'women' typically have longer hair, longer fingernails, walk differently, project different mannerisms and dress differently from a 'typical male'.[6] Notably, when a 'female' displays 'non-typical' characterisations, she is still a 'woman' whether she is being (non-verbally) masculine or feminine. Yet, this gender attribution process only highlights how binary gender can be socially constructed and reinforced, as Butler (1990) argued.

In order to better understand gender variants (i.e. genderqueer identities),[7] we must further understand how this gender attribution process occurs socially. Gender as a socialisation process involves the interpretations of interactions between a gender 'displayer' and gender 'attributors' (Kessler and McKenna, 2006). During this process, the 'attributor' visually and sometimes auditorily interprets what they define as being 'male' or 'female'. As such, gender markers are learned through previous interactions through socialisations reliant upon cultural influences. In the process of becoming a social actor in a binary environment, the 'attributor' not only constructs their perception of 'male' and 'female' gender, they also reinforce these perceptions in how they themselves 'display' their own gender. Conversely, the 'displayer' presents their socialised gender cues, so that other 'attributors' can interpret their gender as being 'male' or 'female'. Culturally, these gender cues accentuate social gender by selective perception (Kessler and McKenna, 2006). Therefore, this gender attribution process exists as a continuum within sociocultural groups and within certain particular social constructs based on social interactions (Garfinkel, 1967).

To put this into context, it is not uncommon for 'women' as 'attributor' to view someone who dresses as masculine in nature ,with short hair as being a male 'displayer' or discrediting the naturalness of understood social norms. This occurs because secondary gender cues (i.e. hair styles, clothing styles, etc.) are more visually apparent than primary and tertiary sexual characteristics (see Birdwhistell, 1970). Therefore, being perceived as violating and/or discrediting a social role as a 'displayer', the person in question is not a 'successful' gender performer and disrupts the social continuum of the gender attrition process. This is how and where social conflict and bias can manifest.

## Bathrooms and other gender segregated issues within policing

When examining open spaces, it is understood that power is equitable. Yet once socially open spaces become perceived as closed spaces, there is a social shift in how identities become perceived. Within these closed social spaces, categories of sex (man/woman) and gender (masculinity/femininity) become more apparent due to socialised constructs of sex and gender identity. Feminist scholars have contended that public space is not a neutral space, but instead it is gendered areas in which power in enacted (Gardner, 1989). One of the most observable areas where power is enacted within social spaces is within sex-segregated areas.

Foucault (1977) suggested that discipline is concerned with the regulation of bodies in three ways: (1) the division of space allocated for specific functions; (2) a panoptic design that facilitates and emboldens surveillance; (3) the production of docile, appropriately gendered bodies. Space in gendered bathrooms is divided through enclosure and partitioning in the construction of functional spaces (Bender-Baird, 2016). As such, sex-segregated spaces (i.e. gendered bathrooms) force a regulation of gender binaries: (1) through a person's forced selection between men's and women's rooms; and (2) further regulation through methods of gender policing.

Sex-segregated toilets highlight and magnify socialised understandings of gender and sexuality in respect of 'male' and 'female' constructs; it is understandable why these areas serve as an area of contention for non-binary identities. This heteronormalisation (i.e. the intersection of sex and gender constructs) of gender-segregated spaces further highlights visual differences that exist in a binary gendered world. As previously stated, gender, from birth until adulthood, relies upon physiology, which contributes to gender identity (see Hines, 2003, 2010). As such, in any publicly shared social arena where subtle differences may exist, they will become more apparent and perceived as relevant. This relevancy leads to tension between those who are socially perceived as subjectively conforming to socialised binary gendered expectations versus those who are perceived as not conforming. This non-conformity threatens those who believe they are compliant by visually disrupting core belief systems which are founded upon socialised perceptions of sex and gender since birth. This occurs because gender is one of the first socialised constructs in which we learn and recognise social and individual differences.

As such, gendered public toilets simultaneously uphold and regulate opposing binaries. Gender ideologies are therefore influenced by the assumption that gender presentation, identity and biological sex are interconnected. This in turn reinforces cisgender privileges by allowing those to interpret feminine gender presentation and attributes to female physical characteristics (e.g. long hair, visible breasts, feminine clothing, make-up, etc.). Often this taken-for-granted perceived gender norm exists in geographically binaried segregated spaces (see Cresswell, 1996, 1999; Browne, 2004). As gendered spaces are strictly 'panopotic' (Foucault, 1977), individuals who appear to others as being 'out of place' are more strictly gender policed in sex-segregated spaces. As such, those who do not adhere to these cisgender 'female' expectations are more susceptible to be challenged or confronted for being perceived as not being 'female' in a 'female' segregated area. Browne (2004), Doan (2010) and Halberstam (1998) refer to this as the 'bathroom problem'. This obviously causes a great deal of distress to anyone, regardless of transgender or cisgender status, being affected by this cisgender perception of binary existence. Yet, more often it impacts the transgender and butch lesbian communities more than others.

For the trans community specifically, binaried bathrooms require self-surveillance of how they are presenting gender and their reaction to the reception they may receive in gendered spaces. Further, this encourages a forced compliance to binary 'norms'. Therefore, as Bender-Baird (2016) refers to it, 'trans people are not simply reinforcing the power structure; rather, they are responding to it and making conscious decisions regarding how to operate in the situation they are forced into' (p. 986).

Further exploring how gender is differentiated in certain social contexts (i.e. gender segregated areas within police workplaces), theoretically it is again beneficial to examine Goffman (1977). Goffman argued that social interactions, spaces and institutions have been constructed in ways that highlight gender differences. He stated that gender performance is often framed as though they come from within (as a consequence of gender differences), but he believed that it was through this process that gender differences are produced. Goffman (1977) noted:

> The functioning of sex-differentiated organs is involved, but there is nothing in this functioning that biologically recommends segregation; that arrangement is totally a cultural matter.... [T]oilet segregation is presented as a natural consequence of the difference between the sex-classes, when in fact it is rather a means of honoring, if not producing, this difference.
>
> (p. 316)

While Goffman used the gendered segregation of toilets as an example of how 'normative' gendered differences are highlighted, his theoretical concept could also include other visual-gendered distinctions (e.g. clothing and hair styles).[8]

### Misgendering and violence in gender segregated areas

In reference to perceptions of genital constructs, Juang (2006) stated: 'In the transphobic imagination, the bathroom becomes the extension of a genital narcissism' (p. 247). Bender-Baird (2016) points out that people believe that 'there is always a correlation between genitals and gender presentation and that gender segregation of bathrooms is based on genital configuration' (p. 987). Besides gendered toilets serving as an area that highlights and reinforces gender ideologies, these spaces also serve as a hostile area where misgendering occurs. Gender misreadings entail visual double takes, verbal challenges to a person's right to be in the restroom, to calling security guards and even arrests (Cavanagh, 2010). Cavanagh states that hostile public responses are often justified by public safety narratives. Browne (2004) highlighted, gender-segregated toilets have become locations for attacks on women who are misrecognised as men.

Browne's (2004) research built upon Halberstam's (1998) argument that areas of gender segregation and the policing of gender in toilets are by-products of heteronormativity. Greed (2003) stated that this occurs because toilets are perceived as a 'male territory' (p. 198) that excludes women and children because of fears of sexual violence or indecent exposure. Often this perception of a 'male territory' occurs because of visual-gendered distinctions that exist as a result of sexed characteristics (Bornstein, 1994). First, the absence of a penis is viewed as a primary gender attribution. As Bornstein (1994) stated '… it has little or nothing to do with vaginas. It's all penises or no penises' (p. 22).[9] Second, the presence of breasts also tends to be a primary gender attribution (Hale, 1996). Kessler and McKenna (1978) noted the importance of breasts for those transitioning: the growing of breasts[10] for MTFs for achieving socially convincing feminine self-presentations; and the removal of breasts for FTMs for achieving socially convincing masculine self-presentations. Third, the presence or absence of reproductive organs (i.e. uterus, ovaries, etc.), which either allow pregnancy or possessing hormones within 'normal' ranges of one's age group is also attributed to gender attribution (Hale, 1996). Hale goes on to describe that gender attribution can further be allocated to having an occupation acceptable for a woman/or man, engaging in feminine or manly leisure pursuits (i.e. hobbies) and being heterosexual.

Often misgendering is the root cause of the violence that occurs in public restrooms. In *Queering Bathrooms: Gender, Sexuality, and Hygienic Imagination*, Cavanagh (2010) theoretically mapped the findings from 100 interviews of LGBT+ individuals regarding public bathrooms. Cavanagh (2010) highlighted that these areas reinforce gender and sexuality norms which results in personal harm to describe examples of harassment, humiliation, arrest and physical violence. This theoretical analysis is not surprising considering Vade (2002) found in a qualitative study of transgender people in San Francisco that:

> … out of 116 responses from those who did not identify as male or female, 48 people took the time to write out specific bathroom experiences, all negative. These experiences ranged from harassment to violence to getting fired.
>
> (p. 2)

Herman (2013) conducted a survey of 93 trans and gender non-conforming individuals who either work or live in Washington, DC and found that 70 per cent of respondents reported experiencing one or more issues within public bathrooms. These issues included denial of access to facilities, verbal harassment and physical assault. Herman reported that 9 per cent of the individuals reported experiencing actual physical assault. Those experiences included: having been physically removed from the bathroom, hit or kicked, physically intimidated and/or cornered and slapped. Additionally, one MTF participant reported that she had been sexually assaulted while using the men's bathroom. Further, Herman reported that 54 per cent of respondents reported different types of health problems due to 'holding it' (p. 75) in an effort to avoid using public bathroom confrontations. These included dehydration, urinary tract infections, kidney infections and other kidney issues (Herman, 2013). Unfortunately, no matter which bathroom one can use, if you are socially perceived by others as being gender non-conforming, you face physical and medical dangers when deciding which gendered bathroom to use.

On a more personal level, as a butch lesbian and often viewed as others as a non-conforming gender identity, unlike Lucal (1999: 787),[11] I do not view gendered segregated spaces as an 'adventure' because it is unknown what the public reaction will be when entering these spaces. Much like Seelman's (2014, 2016) research participants disclosed, I have personally experienced being questioned whether I belong in the women's restroom, stared at and denied access or told to leave. As such, I personally understand how female public restrooms create anxiety and fear and often I avoid them at all cost, to avoid embarrassing confrontations. If avoiding the bathroom is not an option, masculine identified lesbians much like the trans feminine community, may adjust clothing to make the visual appearance of breasts more noticeable or ask a more deemed 'feminine' friend to accompany them to the toilet to avoid gender policing (see Browne, 2006; Cavanagh, 2010; Devor, 1989; Lucal, 1999). I can attest that emotionally it is very damaging when someone states that you are not 'woman enough' to use a deemed 'female' area if you self-identify as a woman. By doing so, gender policing conveys that you are failing in the performance of womanhood and are not worthy of the same status of other women within normal social environments.

Munt (1998) stated that public bathrooms serve as sites where gender is tested and proved. This 'test' can easily be failed if one is not understood as being a 'woman' in 'women' public spaces or a 'male' in 'male' public spaces. Skeggs (2001) argued further that those 'who appear feminine are authorized and granted power (in a small space) to evaluate others' (p. 302). Arguably, 'women' or 'men' may feel they are depowered in other social situations and may be more likely to embrace this small amount of perceived power to 'evaluate others' or physically challenge others.[12] I would argue that those who feel more depowered in their social lives, are more likely to be confrontational in gendered areas.

## Structural constraints: nuances of 'police culture'

Policing has historically been synonymous with masculinity, hyper masculinity, and dichotomous gendered roles (see Brown and Heidensohn, 2000; Colvin, 2012; Loftus, 2008; Westmarland, 2001). Police organisations are 'gendered' (Acker, 1990) and many male officers do not accept women in policing (Chan *et al.*, 2010; Mallicoat and Ireland, 2013; Prokos and Padavic, 2002). Policing as a social environment not only recognises male (non)conformity, but also socially reinforces expectations of binary masculinity.

Acker (1990) stated:

... advantage and disadvantage, exploitation and control, action and emotion, meaning and identity, are patterned through and in terms of a distinction between male and female, masculine and feminine.

(p. 442)

As such, the structural constraints of binary genders are rigidly *encouraged* and *enforced* within police culture itself. Within police cultures, it is apparent masculinity is somewhat actively encouraged (see Brown and Heidensohn, 2000; Colvin, 2012; Loftus, 2010; Westmarland, 2001). During this *encouragement*, per se, social norms are enforced. Ely and Meyerson (2010) state that cis-males exert a significant effort to demonstrate their masculinity in order to prove they fit within occupational roles. Pasciak and Kelley (2013) further contend that the outcome of this cis-male social pressure to conform to idealised masculinity can lead to negative perceptions held by fellow colleagues. Nolan (2009) goes a step further and states that this failure of social gendered conformity can lead to perceptions of weakness, and therefore ridicule and shame from peers.

Through this *encouragement* of a masculine ethos within policing, the perceived antithesis of masculinity, i.e. femininity, is perceived as threatening. Women (who symbolically represent femininity) have been met with significant resistance from male rank-and-file officers who continue to believe that women are unfit for the physical and emotional demands of policing (Chan *et al.*, 2010), or that they pose a threat to the male-oriented occupational solidarity of policing (Balkin, 1988). This social dominance of masculinity within policing further *encourages* a gendered hierarchy of male dominance within policing. Further, with this *encouragement* comes further resistance in how gender ideologies manifest. For example, to further assert masculine dominance, resistance to femininity can manifest in the sharing of war stories, telling sexists jokes, sexual harassment and tales of sexual exploits to display toughness (Cockburn, 1988; Connell, 1987) frequently occur. Other forms of femininity resistance, or rejection, can occur in this social environment via this hierarchy by the devaluing of women through highlighting the difference between men and women in order to confirm the masculine nature of the job by emphasising that women are unfit for policing (Cockburn, 1988). Martin (1999) stated that feminine identities in policing are expected to either accept their biological inferiority or strive to overcome it by adopting masculine traits. This is how binary gender is arguably structurally enforced within policing.

Notably, I do not subscribe to nuanced arguments that collective police culture is a 'monolithic' concept. Often monolithic assumptions about police culture are seen as too universalistic or deterministic. Chan (1996) previously stated that 'police culture has become a convenient label for a range of negative values, attitudes and practice norms among police officers' (p. 110). Often this 'convenient' concept of monolithic grouping serves as an explanation for negative bias within criminology, yet police culture and the sociology of police culture is much more complex. While attempting to explain negative bias within policing, criminologists must not simply dismiss it a product of police culture, instead we should seek to understand why officers have certain views. Furthermore, individual personal variables are not accounted for when categorising police as one large subgroup. These affected variables can range from religious beliefs, racial beliefs, cultural beliefs, theories on gender and theories on sexuality. Additionally, officers bring to the field of policing their unique perspectives, histories, experiences and personal identities to the job. Intrinsically, these variables are what consist of a personal belief system that may or may not be affected by raptness into cop culture itself.

Yet, there exists two conflicting theoretical orientations when examining police culture: police officers (independent of geographical location) have similar perceptions about their work, how they perform it and how they perceive the police role to be fulfilled because they are exposed to similar situations and problems within policing environments (see Brown, 1992; Skolnick, 2011); or police culture is not a unitary construct, but consists of several individual, social and contextual factors (Manning, 2007). Nonetheless, it could be argued that police forces in modern democratic societies (i.e. England, Wales and America) do face similar basic pressures that create the framework for a 'characteristic culture' (Reiner, 2010: 116). These basic similar pressures may vary in intensity (Reiner, 2010). Hence, it makes more sense to compare how these perceptions influence group behaviour than to assume police culture is the same across all democratic societies. In other words, aspects of the 'working personality' (Skolnick, 1966) and 'characteristics of a proper police officer' (Heidensohn, 1992) described in the context of a socially generated culture should be explored monolithically instead of as generalisations formed within this socially generated culture. Within the context of this book, it is contended that masculinity is a characteristic of this 'working personality' and therefore cannot be separated from policing, as it is viewed as a characteristic for successful policing performance. As such, I fully acknowledge that there exist various subcultures that may impact perceptions and attitudes within policing when conducting international research. Yet, when examining how binary gender is socially *encouraged* and *enforced* within American and British policing, 'monolithic' arguments are more apparent than other arguments towards other 'monolithic' assumptions.

## Structural constraints: masculinity, gender identity and 'police culture'

Karen Horney (1932) theorised that masculinity is built on overreactions to femininity, and there exists a connection to the construct of masculinity through the subordination of women. There still exist questions in respect to how the overreactions to femininity interact with males who appear to be effeminate, a stereotypical gay male or a transsexual individual. Connell (1995) states that patriarchal culture interprets gay men as lacking masculinity; this interpretation is linked to the assumption, that American and British culture makes about the mystery of sexuality, that opposites attract. Connell further states that gay men present the dilemma about masculinity for men who are attracted to other men. It should be noted that hegemonic (i.e. exaggerated masculinity) masculine police ideology typically defines gay men as effeminate. As such, gay masculinity is a contradiction for a gender order structured by the way cultural systems exist, much like those who challenge gender roles within the transgender realm.

It could be argued that LGBT+ identities are the repository of whatever is symbolically expelled from hegemonic masculinity in patriarchal ideology within policing. Modern societies view heterosexual men as dominant and gay men as subordinate (Connell, 1995). Gay theorists and feminists share the perception that mainstream masculinity is fundamentally linked to power, organised for domination and resistant to change because of power relations (Connell, 1995). As such, the occupation of policing brandishes a tremendous amount of power over the citizens they are sworn to protect. With the increase in the feelings of empowerment, the groundwork for a negative macho culture magnifies, and those who display any signs of perceived femininity could face conflict when integrating into police culture.

Contemporary British and American societies view sexuality as dichotomised and perceive bisexuality as demonstrating that sexuality is unstable (Connell, 1995). This dilemma has grown to encompass and conflict with lesbianism and those who are transgender or refuse to be classified in stereotypical gender binaries. Further, bisexuality is viewed as an alternation between heterosexuals and gay connections (Connell, 1995). As with bisexuality, there exists psychological conflict with understanding and the classification of transsexuality. This conflict and polarity exists between the binary sexes, since society catalogues individuals as 'male' or 'female'; this can help to explain why some individuals have conflicting feelings about understanding and accepting transgender individuals, arguably within police ideology.

As discussed previously, heteronormative divisions within policing are closely connected with dominant forms of masculinity within policing. The boundary between straight and gay is blurred with the boundary between masculine and feminine in heteronormative ideology. Gay men are viewed as feminised men and lesbians as masculinised women (Connell, 1995). Consequently, the infusion of hegemonic masculinity within policing may provide a compelling explanation as to why lesbians are more likely to be accepted by their police colleagues. Furthermore, it also helps explain why FTM transgender individuals are much more likely to be accepted than gay officers or MTF transgender officers.[13] While gay sexuality itself was considered the repressed truth of conventional masculinity, those who are transgender can be viewed as further leading to conflict with the social ideology of dichotomous gender roles.

Due to social influences of heteronormativity, police work is still heavily influenced by hegemonic masculinity, with a distinction drawn between the men's work of crime-fighting and the women's work of social service activities

(Fielding, 1994). West and Zimmerman (1987) state policing entails 'socially gendered perceptual, interactional, and micro-political activities that cast particular pursuits as expressions of masculine and feminine "natures"' (p. 126). This dichotomous division perpetuates further reinforcement of gender-role ideologies and occupational assumptions of 'masculine' and 'feminine' job performance suitability (see Fielding, 1994; Garcia, 2003; McCarthy, 2013). Fielding and Fielding (1992) have theorised that the mere presence of women (i.e. femininity) can symbolically undermine the traditional masculine ethos of policing itself and could be perceived as a threat to masculinity. Doran and Chan (2003) argued that the crime-fighting and coercive nature of police work equates policing with masculinity. As such, researchers contend that this ethos, in turn, leads to stereotypical assumptions that policing is more fitted to a male existence (Appier, 1998; Crank, 1998; Heidensohn, 1992).

Westmarland (2001) stated that police work is reliant upon physical abilities, such as running, jumping over fences, climbing buildings, crawling through overturned cars and fighting; these activities serve as a legitimate outlet for masculine aggression at work. Fielding (1988), Heidensohn (1994) and Uildriks and Van Mastrigt (1991) suggest that individuals may assert their masculinity in perceived social environments, like policing, where the acceptable usage of physical violence is accepted, or even encouraged. As such, displays of acceptable physical violence within policing impacts the perception of job competency.

Blumenfeld (1992) argued that men overemphasise masculinity in certain cultures because any suggestion of displaying traditionally 'feminine' traits, such as gentleness or sensitivity, encourages colleagues to brand themselves as feminine acting or non-heterosexual; whereas heterosexual women within policing feel pressured to demonstrate masculine traits to prove their abilities (Zimmer, 1987), and in contrast lesbians may feel the need to assert their femininity (Miller et al., 2003). Schneider (1989) and Martin (1980) stated that lesbians may feel the need to display their femininity in order to avoid hostile homophobic confrontations at work. Female officers, straight and gay, recognise that policing requires 'masculine' characteristics, such as assertiveness, strength and supposed competitiveness, and that acting in this way might confirm suspicions that they are lesbian (Burke, 1993; Pharr, 1988).

Miller et al. (2003) contend that because policing entails homosociality – which is gendered social interactions between males in police culture – any display of 'feminine' characteristics is perceived as threatening masculinity. This threat towards masculinity causes male officers to conform to macho models to compensate for any questions about their sexuality or gender presentation (Miller et al., 2003). These threats can be validated through the subordination of women, heterosexism, genderism, authority, control, competitive individualism, independence, aggressiveness and the capacity for violence (Connell, 1995; Messerschmidt, 1996), as illustrated by the lack of social acceptance of trans feminine, effeminate gay male identities and femininity in general.

Constant themes of masculinity, often called 'hegemonic masculinity', exist that are pervasive to police ideologies (Kappeler *et al.*, 1998). Hegemonic masculinity describes the idealised form of masculinity in the dominant form of male reinforcement of power in a cultural and collective domain (Connell, 1995; Messerschmidt, 1996), and the maintenance of it involves engaging in certain practices that validate one's masculinity. The concept of hegemonic masculinity draws upon the 'Gramscian concept of hegemony' (Rabe-Hemp, 2009: 116), which states that those in dominant positions in society work through ideological means: a consensus of values based on how the dominant group positions it, which is known and understood by those in subordinate groups. Therefore, hegemonic masculinity can only be practised by the few men who exist in a dominant position. When existing in this dominant position, during social construction, influence is exerted upon those in subordinate masculinities, like gay men, who are typically equated with femininity, and those who do not conform to gender ideologies of heteronormativity.

In the U.S.A. and the U.K., hegemonic masculinity through social construction can take different forms and can be validated through the subordination of women, heterosexism, genderism, uncontrollable sexuality, authority, control, competitive individualism, independence, aggressiveness and the capacity for violence (Connell, 1995; Messerschmidt, 1996). Hegemonic masculinity's social construction and manifestation in policing can be seen in the division of police work, which relegates female officers to 'women's issues' (Barlow and Barlow, 2000; Merlo and Pollack, 1995; Schulz, 1995), and in administrative policies that value competitiveness, aggressiveness, persistence and emotional detachment (Epstein, 1971). As such, it is a significant construct within policing. Additionally, hegemonic masculinity has a solidarity theme that is instilled within policing, which unfortunately can make it problematic to change attitudes and perceptions.

Connell (1995) further states that gay men present the dilemma about masculinity for men who are attracted to other men. It should be noted that hegemonic (i.e. exaggerated masculinity) masculine police ideology typically defines gay men as effeminate (Connell, 1995). As such, gay masculinity is a contradiction for a gender order structured by the way cultural systems exist, much like those who challenge gender roles within the transgender realm.

It could be argued that LGBT+ identities are the repository of whatever is symbolically expelled from hegemonic masculinity in patriarchal ideology within policing. Modern societies view heterosexual men as dominant and gay men as subordinate (Connell, 1995). Gay theorists and feminists share the perception that mainstream masculinity is fundamentally linked to power, organised for domination and resistant to change because of power relations (Connell, 1995). As such, the occupation of policing brandishes a tremendous amount of power over the citizens they are sworn to protect. With the increase in the feelings of empowerment, the groundwork for a negative macho culture magnifies, and those who display any signs of perceived femininity could face conflict when integrating into police culture.

Contemporary British and American societies view sexuality as dichotomised and perceive bisexuality as demonstrating that sexuality is unstable (Connell, 1995). This dilemma has grown to encompass and conflict with lesbianism and those who are transgender or refuse to be classified in stereotypical gender binaries. Further, bisexuality is viewed as an alternation between heterosexuals and gay connections (Connell, 1995). As with bisexuality, there exists psychological conflict with understanding and the classification of transsexuality. This conflict and polarity exists between the binary sexes, since society catalogues individuals as 'male' or 'female'; this can help to explain why some individuals have conflicting feelings about understanding and accepting transgender individuals, arguably within police ideology. As previously discussed, heterosexism within policing is closely connected with dominant forms of masculinity within policing.

## Structural constraints: 'police culture' and gender bodies in context

When examining policing, it would be remiss to address masculinity without exploring gender roles in respect to physical presentations of gender, especially when examining individuals who identify as genderqueer, gender neutral, butch/ femme gender, female masculinity and other transgender identities. As with previous gender researchers, I do not see gender as a fixed unit with clearly defined and set restrictions, but rather as a relational entity itself. Gender, as a concept, is a mixture of sexuality and identity; just because an individual possesses a more assumed masculine demeanour, it does not mean they would be better at working in masculine perceived police roles. Hence, it is important to examine those who do not clearly fit within stereotypical assumed binary roles and how they negotiate police culture. Revisiting earlier parts of this chapter, gender intersects and is entangled with concepts in organisational culture and many other analytical social categories.

In respect to police perceptions of analytical social categories, they are not universal. Yet they are dependent on respective contextual setting and exist as a construction of the interaction and performance between the two binary genders (male and female). As such, they can differ between time and space and can be altered throughout history, as well as geographic locations. For example, a 'masculine' perceived officer might be better at deemed 'feminine' job assignments, and vice versa. It should be noted that this can change over time and during a person's career.

Walklate (2001) stated that there is a lack of research with regard to the correlation between perceived gendered tasks and active policing assignments. This reinforces why this research is important when examining policing through the perceptions of trans officers. Trans officers, who may not conform to gendered binaries, can provide an insight into how expected gendered tasks are performed and how trans officers' policing assignments varied once their gender presentations and sexuality constructions were perceived as challenging masculinity within cop culture.

In policing, the perception is that masculinity is strong and tough, with femininity being weak, sensitive, subordinate and vulnerable. Typically, male officers equate female officers with feminine moral virtue, the domestic realm, social work, formal rules, administration, cleanliness and emotions. Male officers typically equate male officers with guns, crime-fighting, combative, confrontational, resistance to management, fighting, weapons and a desire to work in high-crime areas (Hunt, 1990). Additionally, masculinity within policing is associated with the offensive use of profanity (Morash and Haarr, 1995), anti-women remarks, the usage of affectionate terms, like 'hun' and 'sweetheart' (Martin and Jurik, 2006), and innuendoes about fellow females' sexuality (Heidensohn, 1992; Hunt, 1984, 1990). Those who do not fit within the perceived binary masculinity constructs can be perceived as a threat to the masculine character of a crime-fighting policeman (Hunt, 1990). The integration of perceived binary masculinity constructs, if not already socially introduced and constructed, typically begins with an officer's first policing experience when they start police academy.

Prokos and Padavic (2002) theorised that police academies possess a 'hidden curriculum', which encourages conformity to a hegemonic environment. Prokos and Padavic conducted participant observation in an American academy and found that masculinity is viewed as an essential requirement for policing and that women are perceived as not belonging. Further, they contend that a police academy, the first introduction into police culture, introduces masculinity that excludes women and 'feminine' recruits while exaggerating their gendered differences.

These differences are not just heightened in police academy; the process is continued after the completion of police academy, where officers are typically assigned to areas of patrol. Normally, an officer's choice of initial assignment is not taken into account and they will be assigned to general patrol duties. Immediate supervisors (i.e. sergeants) decide which area an officer is assigned to patrol within their zone, beat, district, etc. Determinedly, this is often first female and deemed weaker officers first witness aspects of male overprotection. If a female or deemed weaker officer is perceived as physically or mentally incapable of handling one area over another, then an officer's immediate supervisor may assign said officer to a lesser crime area within the zone, beat, district, etc., where they will potentially face less physical dangers. After negotiating patrol work for a few years, females or deemed weaker officers will usually be 'yanked off the streets' to fill a role within an administration position within their agency. This process can indirectly cause some female and effeminate officers to adapt to a more masculine role and presentation in order to conform and be viewed as capable of effective police work (Zimmer, 1987). Thus, after the first few years of policing from the academy on, females and effeminate males feel pressured to conform to the masculine occupational hierarchy that exists in police culture.

Whittle (2000) described how gender relations are perpetuated through social and cultural practices by the adoption of gender roles. These social and cultural practices in relationship to gender can affect career prospects within policing, with the expectation that women should be assigned to child abuse investigation units and domestic violence units over their more masculine viewed job assignments, such as firearm tactical response units and homicide units. Westmarland (2001) contends that police masculinity is connected to personal autonomy and a perceived ability to fight/aggressiveness, and femininity, which is synonymous with childbirth, is connected to police roles involving victims who are children or women. Westmarland describes this process as 'differential policing' (2001: 6). This is the concept that women are unable to choose certain career specialities while being manipulated into undertaking policing assignments that are concerned with empathy, families and sexual offences, which are associated with positions held by women.

## Chapter summary

This chapter has discussed sociological gender theories to better understand how perceptions of sexuality and gender might explain the nature of gender ideologies within policing. The purpose of doing so was to conceptualise how dominant constructions of gender, and more specifically how these are situated within police culture, can promote certain attitudes towards those who challenge binary gender perceptions. Societal expectations of how gender is performed are reliant upon perceptions of 'gender identity'. Therefore, how gender is perceived within police culture can influence social perceptions of trans identities.

Theoretically, this chapter also explored how gender theory and the concepts of binaried gender systems of 'masculine' and 'feminine' are socially derived from our assumptions about biological sex characteristics (i.e. male or female). By using components of gender theory, this chapter argued that genderism can exist in cultural systems where there exist connections between biological sex and a person's gender presentation. These connections can impact on how socialised perceptions are associated within genderist ideology. Yet, the ways that transgender individuals present their gendered selves are social constructs of what they perceive as 'masculine' and 'feminine'. Notably, questions still remain as to how gender theories can explain those who identify as gender variant, since they are perceived as not conforming to any socialised binary constructs.

Additionally, this chapter has explored how the performance of gender is connected to hypermasculinity. Hypermasculinity can manifest within police culture, which has similar gender expectations to military culture, as a repudiation of feminine aspects of one's self; in defence against gay sexual activities; and as a result of socialised parental influences (see Brown, 1988; Glass, 1984; Mosher and Sirkin, 1984). As discussed in Chapters Six, Seven and Eight, hypermasculinity within policing has a profound impact upon gender attribution actions and is the basis for heterosexism/genderism. Further, in respect to hypermasculinity, this chapter has also examined how the masculine/feminine perceptions of gender are attributed to policing-gendered spaces in communal and sex-segregated areas.

## Notes

1 This will be explored in the following section.
2 Refer to the following section on 'displayers' and 'attributors'.
3 I subscribe to the notion that while gender can be innate, the social pressures of gender conformity must not be overlooked in respect to embodiment. This will be revisited in Chapters 6 and 7.
4 Historically, these colours were chosen based on American marketing campaigns. In contrast, some store chains marketed the colour pink with boys and blue with girls. Yet, because the majority of the marketing campaigns chose blue for boys and pink for girls these 'gendered' colours became socialised in both American and British cultures.
5 In relationship to the concept of a subconscious sex and trans experiences, most transgender identities, specifically transsexuals, state that their subconscious sex is innate and cannot be changed at will, as this research discovered in its introductory phases. Most transsexuals in policing indicated that they need to medically transition, and it is something that they cannot escape or suppress; therefore, it is involuntary, yet natural in nature.
6 Notably, readers will find that throughout this book, I use quotation marks when mentioning binary gender categories. This is intentional as I do not personally adhere to stereotypical assumptions of binary genders.
7 Refer to the Introduction.
8 Please refer to the previous section discussing 'displayers' and 'attributors' (Kessler and McKenna, 2006). This will also be revisited again in Chapter 7.
9 This will be explored in further detail in Chapter 5.
10 The presence of breasts is often socially deemed a characteristic of womanhood.
11 Lucal (1999) states in her research that she is a woman who often gets mistaken for a man.
12 I intend to conduct future research on this argument in the near future.
13 This is explored in Chapters 5 and 6.

## References

Acker, J. 1990. Hierarchies, jobs, bodies: A theory of gendered organizations. *Gender and Society* 4(2), pp. 139–158.
Appier, J. 1998. *Policing women: the sexual politics of law enforcement and the LAPD.* Philadelphia, PA: Temple University Press.
Balkin, J. 1988. Why policemen don't like policewomen. *Journal of Police Science & Administration* 16(1), pp. 29–38.
Barlow, D. and Barlow, M. 2000. *Policewomen in a multicultural society: an American story.* Prospect Heights, IL: Waveland.
Bender-Baird, K. 2016. Peeing under surveillance: bathrooms, gender policing, and hate violence. *Gender, Place & Culture* 23(7), pp. 983–988.
Birdwhistell, R. 1970. Masculinity and femininity as display. *Kinesics and context: essays on body motion.* Philadelphia, PA: University of Pennsylvania, pp. 39–46.

Blumer, H. 1969. *Symbolic interactionism. Perspective and method.* Englewood Cliffs, NJ: Prentice Hall.

Blumenfeld, W. 1992. *Homophobia: how we all pay the price.* Boston, MA: Beacon Press.

Bornstein, K. 1994. *Gender outlaw: on women, men, and the rest of us.* New York: Routledge.

Brissett, D. and Edgley, C. 2005. *Life as theater: A dramaturgical sourcebook.* New York: Transaction Publishers.

Brown, G. 1988. Transsexuals in the military: flight into hypermasculinity. *Archives of Sexual Behavior* 17(6), pp. 527–537.

Brown, J. 1992. Changing the police culture. *Policing* 8(4), pp. 307–332.

Brown, J. and Heidensohn, F. 2000. *Gender and policing: comparative perspectives.* Basingstoke: MacMillan Press.

Browne, K. 2004. Genderism and the bathroom problem: (re)materialising sexed sites, (re)creating sexed bodies. *Gender, Place & Culture* 11(3), pp. 331–346.

Browne, K. 2006. 'A right geezer-bird (man-woman)': the sites and sights of 'female' embodiment. *ACME: An International E-Journal for Critical Geographies* 5(43), pp. 121–143.

Burke, M. 1993. *Coming out of the blue.* London: Continuum.

Bussey, K. and Bandura, A. 1999. Social cognitive theory of gender development and differentiation. *Psychological Review* 106(4), p. 676.

Butler, J. 1990. *Gender trouble: feminism and the subversion of identity.* New York: Routledge.

Butler, J. 1993. Critically queer. *GLQ: A Journal of Lesbian and Gay Studies* 1(1), pp. 17–32.

Butler, J. 1997. Critically queer. In: Phelan, S., ed. *Playing with fire: queer politics, queer theories.* New York: Routledge, pp. 11–29.

Butler, J. 2004. *Undoing gender.* New York: Psychology Press.

Cavanagh, S. 2010. *Queering bathrooms: gender, sexuality, and hygienic imagination.* Toronto: University of Toronto Press.

Chan, J. 1996. Changing police culture. *British Journal of Criminology* 36(1), pp. 109–134.

Chan, J., Doran, S. and Marel, C. 2010. Doing and undoing gender in policing. *Theoretical Criminology* 14(4), pp. 425–446.

Cockburn, C. 1988. *Machinery of dominance: women, men, and technical know-how.* New England: Northeastern University Press.

Colvin, R. 2012. *Gay and lesbian cops: diversity and effective policing.* London: Lynne Rienner Publishers.

Connell, R. 1987. *Gender & Power.* Berkeley, CA: University of California Press.

Connell, R. 1995. *Masculinities.* Berkeley, CA: University of California Press.

Crank, J. 1998. *Understanding police culture.* Cincinnati, OH: Anderson Publishing.

Cresswell, T. 1996. *In place-out of place: geography, ideology, and transgression.* Minnesota: University of Minnesota Press.

Cresswell, T. 1999 Embodiment, power and the politics of mobility: the case of female tramps and hobos. *Transactions, Institute of British Geographers* 24(2), pp. 175–192.

Devor, H. 1989. *Gender blending.* Indianapolis, IN: Indiana University Press.

Doan, P. 2010. The tyranny of gendered spaces: reflections from beyond the gender dichotomy. *Gender, Place & Culture* 17(5), pp. 635–654.

Doran, S. and Chan, J. 2003. Doing gender. In: Chan, J. with Devery, C. and Doran, S., eds. *Fair cop: learning the art of policing*. Toronto: University of Toronto Press, pp. 276–300.

Ely, R. and Meyerson, D. 2010. An organizational approach to undoing gender: the unlikely case of offshore oil platforms. *Research in Organizational Behavior*, 30(C), pp. 3–34.

Epstein, C. 1971. *Women's place*. Berkeley, CA: University of California Press.

Feinberg, L. 1993. *Stone butch blues: a novel*. Los Angeles, CA: Alyson Books.

Fielding, N. 1988. Competence and culture in the police. *Sociology* 22(1), pp. 45–64.

Fielding, N. 1994. The organizational and occupational troubles of community police. *Policing and Society: An International Journal* 4(4), pp. 305–322.

Fielding, N. and Fielding, J. 1992. A comparative minority: Female recruits to a British constabulary force. *Policing and Society: An International Journal* 2(3), pp. 205–218.

Foucault, M. 1977. *Discipline and punish: the birth of the prison*. Harmondsworth: Penguin.

Garcia, V. 2003. 'Difference' in the police department: Women, policing, and 'doing gender'. *Journal of Contemporary Criminal Justice* 19(3), pp. 330–344.

Gardner, C. 1989. Analyzing gender in public places: Rethinking Goffman's vision of everyday life. *The American Sociologist* 20(1), pp. 42–56.

Garfinkel, H. 1967. *Studies in ethnomethodology*. Upper Saddle River, NJ: Pearson.

Glass, L. 1984. Man's man/ladies' man: motifs of hypermasculinity. *Psychiatry* 47, pp. 260–278.

Goffman, E. 1959. *Presentation of self in everyday life*. New York: Penguin Books.

Goffman, E. 1977. The arrangement between the sexes. *Theory and Society* 4(3), 301–331.

Greed, C. 2003. *Public toilets: inclusive urban design*. Oxford: Architectural Press, Elsevier.

Greer, G. 1999. *The whole woman*. London: Doubleday.

Grosz, E. 1994. *Volatile bodies: toward a corporeal feminism*. Bloomington, IN: Indiana University Press.

Halberstam, J. 1998. *Female masculinity*. Durham, NC: Duke University Press.

Hale, J. 1996. Are lesbians women? *Hypatia* 11(2), pp. 94–121.

Heidensohn, F. 1992. *Women in control? The role of women in law enforcement*. Oxford: Clarendon Press.

Heidensohn, F. 1994. We can handle it out here'. Women officers in Britain and the USA and the policing of public order. *Policing and Society: An International Journal* 4(4), pp. 293–303.

Herman, J. 2013. Gendered restrooms and minority stress: The public regulation of gender and its impact on transgender people's lives. *Journal of Public Management & Social Policy* 19(1), pp. 65–80.

Hines, M. 2003. *Brain gender*. New York: Oxford University Press.

Hines, M. 2010. Sex-related variation in human behavior and the brain. *Trends in Cognitive Sciences* 14(10), pp. 448–456.

Hines, S. 2006. What's the difference? Bringing particularity to queer studies of transgender. *Journal of Gender Studies* 15(1), pp. 49–66.

Hines, S. 2007. *Transforming gender: transgender practices of identity, intimacy and care*. Bristol: Policy Press.

Horney, K. 1932. The dread of woman. *Psychoanalysis and Male Sexuality*, 13, pp. 83–96.

Hunt, J. 1984. The development of rapport through the negotiation of gender in fieldwork among police. *Human Organisation* 43(4), pp. 283–296.

Hunt, J. 1990. The logic of sexism among police. *Women and Criminal Justice* 1(2), pp. 3–30.

Jeffreys, S. 2003. *Unpacking queer politics: a lesbian feminist perspective.* Cambridge Malden, MA: Polity Press in association with Blackwell Publishing.

Johnson, K. 2012. Transgender, transsexualism, and the queering of gender identities: debates for feminist research. *Handbook of Feminist Research*, pp. 606–626.

Juang, R.M. 2006, Transgendering the politics of recognition. In: Stryker, S. and Whittle, S., eds. *The transgender studies reader.* New York: Routledge.

Kappeler, V., Sluder, R. and Alpert, G. 1998. *Forces of deviance: understanding the dark side of policing*, 2nd ed. Prospect Heights, IL: Waveland Press.

Kessler, S. and McKenna, W. 1978. *Gender: an ethnomethodological approach.* Chicago, IL: University of Chicago Press.

Kessler, S. and McKenna, W. 2006. Toward a theory of gender. In: Stryker, S. and Whittle, S., eds. *The transgender studies reader.* New York: Routledge, pp. 165–182.

Kohlberg, L. 1966. A cognitive-developmental analysis of children's sex-role concepts and attitudes. In: Maccoby, E., ed. *The development of sex differences.* Stanford, CA: Stanford University Press.

Loftus, B. 2008. Dominant culture interrupted: recognition, resentment and the politics of change in an English police force. *British Journal of Criminology* 48(6), pp. 756–777.

Loftus, B. 2010. Police occupational culture: classic themes, altered times. *Policing & Society* 20(1), pp. 1–20.

Lucal, B. 1999. What it means to be gendered me: life on the boundaries of a dichotomous gender system. *Gender & Society, 13*: pp. 781–797.

Mallicoat, S. and Ireland, C. 2013. *Women and crime.* Thousand Oaks, CA: Sage.

Manning, P.K. 2007. A dialectic of organisational and occupational culture. In: O'Neill, M., Marks, M. and Singh, A-M., eds. *Police occupational culture*, Vol. 8. Bingley: Emerald Group Publishing, pp. 47–83.

Martin, C., Ruble, D. and Szkrybalo, J. 2002. Cognitive theories of early gender development. *Psychological Bulletin* 128(6), p. 903.

Martin, S. 1980. *Breaking and entering: policewomen on patrol.* Berkeley, CA: University of California Press.

Martin, S. 1999. Police force or police service? Gender and emotional labor. *Annals of the American Academy of Political and Social Science* 561(1), pp. 111–126.

Martin, S. and Jurik, N. 2006. *Doing justice, doing gender: woman in legal and criminal justice occupations*, 2nd edn. Thousand Oaks, CA: Sage.

McCarthy, D. 2013. Gendering 'Soft' policing: multi-agency working, female cops, and the fluidities of police culture/s. *Policing and Society* 23(2), pp. 261–278.

Messerschmidt, J. 1996. Managing to kill: masculinities and the space shuttle Challenger explosion. In: Cheng, C., ed. *Masculinities in Organizations.* Thousand Oaks, CA: Sage, pp. 29–63.

Merlo, A. and Pollack, J. 1995. *Women, law and social control.* Boston, MA: Northeastern University.

Miller, S., Forest, K. and Jurik, N. 2003. Diversity in blue: lesbian and gay police officers in a masculine occupation. *Men and Masculinities* 5(4), pp. 355–385.

Morash, M. and Haarr, R.N. 1995. Gender, workplace problems, and stress in policing. *Justice Quarterly* 12(1), pp. 113–140.

Mosher, D. and Sirkin, M. 1984. Measuring a macho personality constellation. *Journal of Research in Personality* 18, pp. 150–163.

Munt, S. 1998. Butch and femme. *Inside lesbian gender*. London: Cassell.

Namaste, V. 2000. *Invisible lives: the erasure of transsexual and transgendered people*. Chicago, IL: University of Chicago Press.

Namaste, V. 2005. *Sex change. social change: reflections on identity, institutions, and imperialism*. Toronto: Women's Press.

Nolan, T. 2009. Behind the blue wall of silence: essay. *Men and Masculinities* 12(2), 250–257.

Pasciak, A. and Kelley, T. 2013. Conformity to traditional gender norms by male police officers exposed to trauma: Implications for critical incident stress debriefing. *Applied Psychology in Criminal Justice* 9(2), pp. 137–156.

Pharr, S. 1988. *Homophobia: a weapon of sexism*. Little Rock, AR: Chardon.

Prosser, J. 1995. No place like home: The transgendered narrative of Leslie Feinberg's Stone Butch Blues. *MFS Modern Fiction Studies* 41(3), pp. 483–514.

Prosser, J. 1998. *Second skins: the body narratives of transsexuality*. New York: Columbia University Press.

Prosser, J. 2006. Judith Butler: queer feminism, transgender, and the transubstantiation of sex. In: Stryker, S. and Whittle, S., eds. *The transgender studies reader*. New York: Routledge, pp. 257–280.

Prokos, A. and Padavic, I. 2002. 'There oughtta be a law against bitches': masculinity lessons in police academy training. *Gender, Work & Organization* 9(4), pp. 439–459.

Rabe-Hemp, C.E. 2009. POLICEwomen or policeWOMEN? Doing gender and police work. *Feminist Criminology* 4(2), pp. 114–129.

Raymond, J.G. 1980. *The transsexual empire*. New York: Teachers College Press.

Reiner, R. 2010. *The politics of the police*, 3rd edn. London: Oxford University Press.

Rubin, H. 1996. Do you believe in gender? *Sojourner* 21(6), pp. 7–8.

Rubin, H. 2003. *Self made men: identity, embodiment, and recognition among transsexual men*. Nashville, TN: Vanderbilt University Press.

Scheff, T. 2005. Looking-glass self: Goffman as symbolic interactionist. *Symbolic Interaction* 28(2), pp. 147–166.

Schilt, K. 2010. *Just one of the guys? Transgender men and the persistence of gender inequality*. Chicago, IL: University of Chicago Press.

Schilt, K. and Westbrook, L. 2009. Doing gender, doing heteronormativity: 'gender normals', transgender people, and the social maintenance of heterosexuality. *Gender and Society* 23, pp. 440–464.

Schneider, B. 1989. Invisible and independent: lesbians' experiences in the workplace. In: Stromberg, A. and Harkess, S., eds. *Women working*. Palo Alto, CA: Mayfield Publishing, pp. 132–152.

Schulz, D. 1995. *From social worker to crimefighter: women in United States municipal policing*. Westport, CT: Praeger.

Seelman, K. 2014. Transgender individuals' access to college housing and bathrooms: Findings from the National Transgender Discrimination Survey. *Journal of Gay & Lesbian Social Services* 26(2), pp. 186–206.

Seelman, K. 2016. Transgender adults' access to college bathrooms and housing and the relationship to suicidality. *Journal of Homosexuality* 63(10), pp. 1–22.

Serano, J. 2007. *Whipping girl: a transsexual woman on sexism and the scapegoating of femininity*. Berkeley, CA: Seal Press.

Skeggs, B. 2001. The toilet paper: Femininity, class and mis-recognition. In *Women's Studies International Forum* 24(3), pp. 295–307.

Skolnick, J. 1966. *Justice without trial*. New York: John Wiley & Sons Inc.

Skolnick, J. 2011. *Justice without trial: law enforcement in democratic society*. New Orleans, LA: Quid Pro Books.

Stryker, S. 1994. My words to Victor Frankenstein. *GLQ: A Journal of Lesbian and Gay Studies* 1(3), pp. 237–254.

Stryker, S. 1998. The transgender issue: An introduction. *GLQ: A Journal of Lesbian and Gay Studies* 4(2), pp. 145–158.

Tate, C., Youssef, C. and Bettergarcia, J. 2014. Integrating the study of transgender spectrum and cisgender experiences of self-categorization from a personality perspective. *Review of General Psychology* 18(4), p. 302.

Turner, B. 1984. *The body and society*. Oxford: Blackwell.

Uildriks, N. and Van Mastrigt, H. 1991. *Policing police violence*. Aberdeen: Aberdeen University Press.

Vade, D. 2002. Gender neutral bathroom survey. Unpublished report on file with author. Factsheet, p. 2012.

Vannini, P. and Waskul, D. 2013. Introduction: The body in symbolic interaction. In: Vannini, P., Waskul, D. and Gottschalk, S., eds. *The senses in self, society, and culture: a sociology of the senses*. London: Routledge, pp. 1–25.

Walklate, S. 2001. *Gender, crime and criminal justice*. Cullompton: Willan.

West, C. and Zimmerman, D. 1987. Doing gender. *Gender and Society* 1, pp. 125–151.

Westmarland, M. 2001. *Gender and policing: sex, power and police culture*. New York: Willan.

Whittle, S. 2000. *The transgender debate: the crisis surrounding gender identity*. Reading: South Street Press.

Wilchins, R. 1995. What's in a name? The politics of Gender Speak. *Transgender Tapestry* 74(46–7).

Zimmer, L. 1987. How women reshape the prison guard role. *Gender & Society* 1, pp. 415–431.

## Chapter 4

# My reflective exploration into police culture

## Reflective exploration

Reflective exploration, in research circles, allows the social sciences to expand the ontological, epistemological and axiological limitations that previous qualitative research had not allowed (Ellis and Bochner, 2000). Reflective exploration additionally allows approaches that acknowledge and accommodates subjectivity, emotionality and the researcher's influence on research as opposed to hiding these matters or assuming that they do not exist (Ellis *et al.*, 2011). Researchers have realised the benefits of reflection in regard to the positive response to critiques of canonical ideas about what and how research should be done (Ellis *et al.*, 2011). Specifically, researchers who fully and freely disclose their role as a researcher seek to concentrate on more constructive ways of producing meaningful, accessible, and evocative research. The benefits of being reflective is that: (1) it enhances cultural understanding of one's self and others; (2) it offers a more intimate perspective; (3) a properly constructed reflection expands and opens up a broader perspective of the observed; and (4) provides meaningful and useful insight by giving researchers the ability to record cultural experiences that may not have been properly recorded by quantitative and traditional qualitative measures (see Dauphinee, 2010; Ellis and Bochner, 2000; Sparkes, 1996). Using guidance from previous reflective pieces, such as those accounts presented by Sparkes (1996) and Dauphinee (2010), this section is presented as a series of readable reflective stories in a series of dialogues to highlight the difficulties of being LGBT+ within police cultures. Thus, for reflection, I have drawn from my own personal experiences to illustrate several critical incidents which can help explain how I constructed meaning from my participants' stories and how I interpreted my research data. In essence, the reason for including them in this book is because they fulfilled three main contributing factors. First, these reflective stories provide a rare glimpse into the socialisation aspects of negotiating police culture as a 'butch' lesbian, which is similar to some of my participants' stories. Second, they highlight my views and why I possess them, which might have an influence on how I conducted and analysed this research (this will be explored in the Chapter 5). Third, I aim to assist readers in further understanding the findings of this research by providing some type of visualisation on how these incidents occur in certain social spaces within police culture. Fourth, this chapter highlights how bias is confronted in various situations across three distinct career phases within policing: police academy stage, rookie stage and veteran stage.

I believe it is naive to assume that a researcher with insider knowledge is not beneficial in conducting objective research. As Popper (1945) argued, if science relied on individual scientists to be objective, it would never be so; because they 'have not purged themselves by socio-analysis or any similar method' (p. 217). Rather, I contend that all social science researchers possess some aspect of positionality in their research, which impacts how data is acquired and how it is analysed. Arguably, all researchers have an impact on what they are studying, and sometimes a strong connection to the subject that is being researched benefits knowledge production.

In the case of this research, I took every measure to ensure that the presented readable dialogues are true and accurate portrayals of my experiences and observations during my tenure as a police officer. The experiences, told in a series of reflective narratives, were taken from field notes in my second notebook, where I personally experienced and witnessed heterosexism and genderism while serving as a sworn police officer. Notably, these incidents were not recorded as a researcher and they were instead a type of personal occupational documentation. I collected these incidents and dialogues as a means to protect myself should there be an internal investigation into any claims of police unprofessionalism.

This common practice of personal documentation in the field of policing exists for officers to arm themselves when supervisors or fellow officers accuse them of minor or major occupational infractions. It is a record of what was said, how it was interpreted and who was present. This is often called the 'two-notebook rule'. Under the two-notebook rule, officers possess two notebooks, one for official police reports which contains victim(s) info, suspect(s) info, vehicle(s) info, crime scene drawings and any other essential information needed to construct an official police report; with the second notebook containing records of personal and occupational documentation of incidents. This note-taking practice is a typical routine in law enforcement to prevent lawsuits and complaints that are commonplace within policing circles, yet most criminological researchers are unaware of its common practice.

While these reflective narratives are presented in a series of readable dialogues they are not notably word-for-word verbatim. When these incidents occurred, I wrote down the conversations immediately after or even during my interaction with fellow officers to ensure their content accuracy. While recording these workplace incidents, I had no idea how much these experiences would influence my future role as a researcher. Notably, I have omitted names, ranks, locations and times to protect the confidentiality of those officers involved. These reflective narratives are divided based on historical occurrence, into the three phases of my policing career when my own police identity was being formed: as a police recruit, as a police rookie and earning my police veteran status. These stories shaped how I perceived police culture and how I negotiated it, much like my participants in this research.

Between the time periods of 13 February, 2001 to 21 August, 2012, I was employed with a major police department in the southern United States. During my tenure, I worked under the capacity of a sworn officer and was promoted to a Field Training Officer in 2003 and then to police detective in 2006. I held positions within patrol, training and investigations. I was assigned to narcotic units working in plain clothes/undercover capacities, burglary investigations, larceny investigations, aggravated assault investigations, aggravated battery investigations, domestic violence investigations and other general investigations. During this time period, I unknowingly collected police field notes on the dynamics of policing/gender itself from a cop's standpoint, my position in it, and observed the impact heterosexism and genderism has upon policing.

## Police academy stories

During police academy training, the first half of the day typically entailed physical training activities and the other half of the day involved academic aspects of the job. The physical training encompassed hand-to-hand defensive combat techniques, arrest techniques, physical conditioning and the usage of any level of force. The academic activities incorporated criminal laws, criminal procedures, stop-and-frisk and other various educational departmental policy training. As such, within the third week of training at the police academy, we received a total of 50 minutes of diversity training in dealing with members of the LGBT+ communities. The instructor was an openly 'out' serving supervisor within our department, who stated 'don't call anyone out there a "fag" guys; otherwise you will end up in some trouble'. The training was presented in a semi-formalised structure, which allowed fellow police recruits to ask questions within the last ten minutes of the training, but no one participated in this section of the training. As a police recruit, I viewed this in a conflicted way. First, I was impressed that my police department actually had LGBT+ specific training, even though there was no mention of trans identities. Yet, second, I was insulted by the lack of professionalism displayed by the training coordinator on the module. I assumed because she was a fellow lesbian, she would have invested more expressive thought into promoting LGBT+ awareness besides telling fellow officers which words are socially appropriate and which ones were not. Third, I had a glimpse into the future of some of the perceptions of fellow colleagues if everyone had to specifically be warned to not use the 'fag' word.

Based on my early police recruit experiences, I was terrified to reveal to my classmates that I was gay, despite the fact that most people assumed I was by my outward physical masculine appearance. I tried instead to focus on getting through police academy, as it was very demanding and there existed little time for extensive social interactions. In time, I came out to my classmates after feeling pressured to disclose my sexuality, since they had started taking an interest in my personal life.

Before I came out to my fellow female classmates, they had no issues with showering or changing clothing in front of me after our physical training. Notably, our changing facilities were open with limited enclosed privacy barriers and all the female recruits had to share a small area. Additionally, we were on a constant time-scale to change into our police recruit uniforms from our PT uniforms daily to complete formal uniform inspections. This time-scale typically consisted of 15 minutes to shower and to be inspection-presentable with parade shined shoes and creased uniforms according to regulations. Once I came out to fellow female classmates, they then began to show awkwardness around me and never changed in my presence again (often changing in a small private toilet stall). I immediately perceived this change of behaviour as an indication that they were uncomfortable sharing a public gendered space with me.

My female classmates, once talkative and very social with me, stopped socialising with me once I came out to them. Over time, some of my male colleagues even changed their behaviour too. Some male classmates started calling me signal '79' in the hallways and laughed when I walked by. Notably, signal '79' is short radio code for 'snatch thief'. Undaunted by some of the treatment I received, I assumed that once I left the academy, things would positively change in respect to my social acceptance within policing.

## Police rookie stories: learning police culture

After completing six months of successful academy training, I received my gun, uniform and badge and began my three rotations of shift training, commonly known as 'field training'. During field training, you are assigned to a veteran who is certified as a Field Training Officer (FTO), who monitors and guides you during the shift. Often this entailed responding to 911 calls while conducting daily routine patrol activities for a period of up to six weeks. During field training I had one FTO bluntly ask, 'you ain't one of those fags are ya?' Startled, I responded that I am a lesbian. From there our conversation continued:

MALE FIELD TRAINING OFFICER: So, we got a few of y'all on the department.

ME: Really, I was not aware of that.

MALE FIELD TRAINING OFFICER: Yep ... some of the best female cops we have on the department are gay. I know a few but I don't know any gay guys on the department. I know we got this one guy on the department who is going through the sex-change thing to become a woman you know.

ME: Really, where is she assigned?

MALE FIELD TRAINING OFFICER: They got the 'he-she' assigned in communications because of the hormones and how the general public may perceive a 6-foot-tall man with long hair who dresses as a woman. I think they are afraid of how the department will look, but to be honest with you when people need help they don't give a damn about how an officer may look. Sure, it's strange but who am I to judge.

ME: Do you think she needs to be on the street like us instead of buried some-where in communications?

MALE FIELD TRAINING OFFICER: I got no problem with the 'he-she' being out here like the rest of us, but I ain't gonna be friends with 'it' or meet 'it' for lunch.

ME: Why is that?

MALE FIELD TRAINING OFFICER: I just don't understand it I guess. I hope you don't think that is offensive or anything.

ME: Well … I really don't care how someone looks or acts, I always will have their back if they are in the same uniform and a good cop.

MALE FIELD TRAINING OFFICER: I guess you are right.

ME: But, just to let you know if she prefers to be addressed as 'she' you probably should address her as such. It takes a great amount of fortitude to face other officers while changing genders don't you think?

Over time, I realised that my FTO was an excellent patrol officer who policed without his personal bias getting in the way, but he was a product of the 'old-school' days of policing when sexuality and gender presentation outwardly appeared pretty clear cut and dry. It appeared that the attitudes he had towards the LGBT+ community was due to a lack of actual experience with members of the community and his perceptions were a by-product of stereotypical heterosex-ist and/or genderist society's views. Eventually, my FTO asked me a series of typical inquisitive questions about my sexuality without displaying any inten-tional outwardly heterosexist and/or genderist behaviour. I soon realised that he had limited experience with working in close quarters with LGBT+ officers and during my last day of training he apologised for using the 'fag' word because he did not understand how deconstructive it was to describe a member of the LGBT+ community. Arguably, by my FTO having more social interactions with me as a member of the LGBT+ community (i.e. his perception of a foreign concept of existence) he began to become more socially accepting and know-ledgeable of LGBT+ identities. In other words, LGBT+ identities began to 'nor-malise' and became less socially foreign for him within work settings.

After completing field training, I was assigned to my first patrol assignment where I encountered initially some offensive behaviour from fellow colleagues after I walked in on them making crude jokes about my sexuality. One of the younger officers in particular was quite crude about his comments saying 'we got another lezbo', 'she just ain't had the right dick yet' (while grabbing his crotch) and 'I know why she is a lesbian, she is just afraid of the dick'. This usage of heterosexist language perfectly demonstrates what underlies the domi-nation of hegemonic masculinity; reinforced by Meyers et al. (2004) who stated that police work is pervaded by heterosexism.

Undaunted by the comments, I stuck to my daily patrol and kept to myself most of the time, always backing up fellow officers when they needed help. Ini-tially, I felt very socially excluded and isolated from my fellow patrol officers but that soon changed over time. During one incident, one officer who made crude comments about me was involved in a physical fight with a suspect and a signal for an 'officer down' call came across the radio. Realising I was the closest responding officer, I responded as quickly and safely as I could and was able to place the fighting suspect into custody. After the suspect was secured in handcuffs, the young officer and I engaged in some controversial banter:

MALE OFFICER:  You know what, you faggots aren't too bad.
ME:  You know what, you homophobic red-necks aren't too bad either.

After a laugh, I explained to the officer that the word 'faggot' is offensive and he shouldn't use it anymore. The officer nodded and apologised for making crude comments about me and stated that he just 'didn't get it'. I told him I would be more than happy to explain it to him and in time I did, with the officer eventually becoming one of my dearest friends. Additionally, the officer disclosed that he felt the need to prove his masculinity by insulting my sexuality in the presence of other male officers, since he was not married and he was afraid by associating with me that he would be labelled gay himself.

Often, I felt unsure if the difficulties I had faced were because I was a woman, or if it was because I was a gay woman. It took close to two years before officers began 'sticking up' for me, when I was given my first official beat I was responsible for patrolling. One particular instance involved a younger colleague correcting a male in custody who was mouthing off inside the precinct.

MALE ARRESTEE:  Look at this bull-dyke. Looks like you need to be fucked by the right man baby, I would tear you up.
MALE OFFICER:  Hey man, shut the fuck up. She is family. Don't talk like that about her. How would you feel if someone talked about your sister like that?
MALE ARRESTEE:  Whatever … what are you gonna do about it faggot lover.
ME:  It's OK man (tapping my colleague on the back). I ain't paying him no attention.

For the most part, if I did encounter blatant heterosexism and/or genderism within policing, it was from officers stating their personal opinion due to lack of involvement with members of the LGBT+ community, as previously discussed. Particular instances involved responding to 911 LGBT+ domestic calls and officer's perceptions of LGBT+ couples. While walking up to the emergency call the following conversation with the assisting officer took place:

MALE OFFICER:  Dispatch advised that this is a gay domestic call, so heads up.
ME:  What does that mean?
MALE OFFICER:  Come on Panter, you know these gay domestic calls are violent. More violent than other domestic calls; I have seen guys pour bleach over their lover's clothes and cut them up with a knife. Hell, I have even seen

them stab one another and cut each other's shit up really bad. And you got to be careful because of AIDS.

ME: I guess I have never viewed it any different than any other domestic call.

MALE OFFICER: I am willing to bet that gay domestics are the most violent calls you will encounter in your career.

ME: Really? Lesbians too?

MALE OFFICER: Even more so, ain't nothing like two women scorned – know what I mean? There is a whole lot of oestrogen going on there.

At this point, I could only shake my head in disagreement as we approached the residence where the call originated, since I did not want the callers to overhear our conversation. It should be noted that after 13 years of policing, all domestic violence calls have the potential to be violent and I did not observe LGBT+ domestics occurring more frequently or more violently than their counterparts, as I had been commonly told.

Often, when observing fellow officers, as a back-up officer, they would roll their eyes and use terms such as 'man lovers', which had a negative contention focusing on the sexual activity between the couple; or use the word 'tranny' when referring to a member of the trans community. I also observed that some officers were much more likely to arrest members of the LGBT+ community on a domestic than a heterosexual one, regardless of the violence level of the call. As one senior officer told me '... you gotta lock them up no matter what! The drama level of a gay domestic is so high they will keep calling 911 and then your supervisor will get on to you'. In situations like these, particularly with senior officers, I would sometimes keep my head down and not object to what I had heard, opting to instead pick and choose my battles.

While I am embarrassed of doing so in my rookie days, I knew by not standing-up to every crude LGBT+ comment or stereotypical remark that I potentially perpetuated any bias attitude a fellow colleague might have possessed. In hindsight, I knew I had to choose my battles because I was afraid of some type of personal social rejection and/or I did not possess the courage to stand-up to an older officer. Therefore, I often found myself torn between wearing the uniform as a cop and living the life of an openly gay woman trying to set a good example of gay identities within policing. Burke (1993, 1994a, 1994b) refers to this as the 'dual persona' phenomenon.

Over time, I noticed officers increasingly began asking for my personal assistance on LGBT+ emergency calls because they physically appeared to be uncomfortable or afraid of being labelled homophobic if they decided to arrest an LGBT+ offender. As one officer told me, '... its OK if *you* arrest them, they can't claim you are homophobic since you are gay'. As such, often I felt a twinge of betrayal to fellow members of the LGBT+ community when other officers requested me to handcuff their offender. I also was frequently raised via radio to assist on calls involving transgender men and women in both pre-op and post-op stages, including those who identified as other types of gender variant.

I observed that some officers had a hard time asking members of the transgender community what their gender was for generic police forms. I commonly observed some officers ask 'so … do you have a penis or what?' before even getting a person's name. I tried my best to correct the improper language and behaviour when I observed it, especially in regard to a person's gender identification. Yet, at times I felt I wasn't doing enough.

One specific memorable incident where I felt torn between being a cop and being a member of the LGBT+ community, occurred when I arrested a transwoman in a club for punching a straight male patron after she was relentingly taunted and called a 'faggot' in front of other patrons. Notably, I am unsure why any person with LGBT+ bias would enter a gay establishment. Yet, in America it is an individual's constitutional right to use terms like 'faggot' and they cannot be charged with any crime for doing so. Since the transwoman committed the only criminal act of the incident, I had to arrest her. While placing her under arrest, she promptly called me an 'Uncle Tom' in reference to Harriet Beecher Stowe's 1852 novel, *Uncle Tom's Cabin*. By her comment, implying that I was a LGBT+ traitor, I felt guilt for preforming my duties. Buhrke (1996) found this occurs frequently within the LGBT+ policing community and it is how many LGBT+ individuals view LGBT+ officers, even though he does not mention the terms 'Uncle Tom' specifically. In Buhrke's (1996) explanation, fellow LGBT+ members perceive LGBT+ police officers as a form of social traitor and betrayer of LGBT+ rights. By being a member of the police, LGBT+ officers are seen as turning their back on years of oppression by the same agency they represent.

Besides issues with heterosexist and genderist terminology and actions, I observed major issues with officer discretion. During one particular casual discussion, an officer mid-way through his career told me how he used a prior legal ruling to his favour when investigating and using discretion on a robbery call:

MALE OFFICER: Want to hear a funny story?

ME: Sure man.

MALE OFFICER: I got a call a few years ago of a robbery to a residence involving a gay man. When I pulled up he was running down the street and looked like he was chasing someone. He told me that someone had stolen his New York police officer uniform that was made out of leather and $200 dollars. Right away I knew it was going to be some crazy shit. So, I relocated the 'victim' back to the incident location that was at his residence.

ME: Ya. Then what?

MALE OFFICER: Well, he finally started telling me the truth about what really happened. He told me that he met this guy and they came back to his house to have sex in some kinky role-playing cop thing and the suspect put on his custom leather New York City police officer's uniform and tied him up after having sex. The suspect then took the $200 dollars from his dresser and then ran out of the room. And can you believe it, the 'victim' said he had the suspect on video doing this and started to play it for me to show me what the guy looked like.

ME: Well, did he?

MALE OFFICER: Hell no, I didn't want to see that. I told him that it was a crime for two males to have anal sex and that it was a felony and if I saw the video, I would have to lock him up for it.

ME: But that law was taken off the books years ago man.

MALE OFFICER: I know, but he didn't know that. Hell, it got me out of having to do a robbery report.

ME: That's messed up man.

MALE OFFICER: (laughing) I know, but it sure was funny. Somewhere in (city name omitted) there is a gay man wearing a leather cop uniform and $200 dollars richer.

It should be noted that the officer who disclosed this story did so with a disgusting sense of honour and humour when other several officers were standing around comparing other 'war stories'. The other officers standing around with me just rolled their eyes and walked away in a disapproving manner.

## Earning my police veteran status

During the process of integrating into policing, there is a typical process of socialisation that occurs that can be connected to the concept of the 'blue wall of silence' (see Silverman, 1999; Walker, 2001). During recruit and rookie days you are told and adhere to 'keeping your mouth shut' when speaking to veteran officers and 'to mind your business'. Often group socialisation is non-confrontational and when you observe occupational bias, whether against you or towards others, you typically do not confront those displaying the behaviour. This is why it is so difficult for minority officers, particularly LGBT+ officers to make it through their rookie days while being non-confrontational and instead observing and learning from the environment they are thrown in.

Typically, it is not until officers begin to gain rank that they gain more fortitude by being more active in confronting officers who display bias. Depending on the force size and the amount of 911 calls handled, an officer transitions from a rookie status to veteran status after five years or more. Or, as they said in my previous department, 'you are a rookie until the first time you get sued or kill someone, then after that you become a veteran'.

During this process of transition to veteran status, you learn to stand-up more for yourself and for fellow colleagues. In essence, the fear that you used to possess in challenging police administrators or fellow veteran colleagues diminishes comparatively with the amount of police action or amount of social interaction you have had while being a police officer. You feel that you have already proven yourself as an officer in the field and inside the precinct, thus you become more socially independent and you lean more towards a less grey understanding of what is socially 'wrong' versus what is socially 'right'. This concept also explains why rookie officers, who are relativity socially unknown, face more negativity for 'rocking the boat' by reporting observed wrongdoings. This is how components of the 'blue wall of silence' are reinforced – or to borrow academic terminology, 'institutionalised'.

As a police veteran, the first time I actively stood-up for a colleague against my administration was when we had our first transgender officer on our department. After completing her surgeries, she was assigned to the same precinct I was assigned. Prior to her arrival, fellow officers discussed their feelings towards her without giving her any credit to her performance as an officer. Prior to her arrival among the negative hallway chatter, I noted a maintenance man installing a key lock on the public women's restroom in my precinct.

Curious, I asked the maintenance man why he was putting a lock on the women's bathroom door and not the men's. He told me 'I don't know, go upstairs and ask the bossman'. I assumed he was speaking about my commander at the time, so I walked upstairs to his office. I asked my commander, who was very kind to me and actively stood-up for me when I was the only gay person in the precinct, why was a lock being placed on the women's restroom. He stated that a female colleague had expressed concern over the transfer of a transwoman to our precinct and did not feel comfortable using the women's restroom if she used it and he was going to distribute keys to only 'female' officers in the precinct.

Stunned by his remarks, I asked if I could shut his office door because I was concerned who might overhear our conversation. I promptly told him that what I was going to tell him would prevent our department from being sued and possible negative media reporting over the incident. Visibly confused, he patiently listened to me. I went on to tell him that we are not the bathroom-gender police. I told my commander that if any person identifies as a woman she deserves to use the restroom as much as I do, to deny someone's rights (especially a fellow police officer) as a human being would be deplorable. I additionally told him that there are privacy stalls inside the restroom and the female officer who had an issue with her using the bathrooms had no grounds to complain about it.

During the conversation, I learned that the same female who had complained also had an issue with me as a 'butch' lesbian using the same facilities as her. The supervisor in question was known to be anti-LGBT+, extremely religious and had decorated her office with extensive bible quotes. So much so, a concerned fellow officer asked if the bible quotes offended me. I jokingly told my concerned colleague that the bible quotes don't burn my eyes anymore, as I have been accustomed to them being raised in the South since it is common knowledge that lesbians practice witchcraft and ride brooms. It was at this point, I realised that some officers do not have a sense of humour.

Back to the story, I pointed out to my commander that it was his sergeant who had the issues and not the other female staff members; he apologised to me and told the maintenance worker not to install the lock. To this day, there is still a hole in the women's restroom where the lock installation was never completed and my fellow trans colleague does not know about the incident, or the fact that I went to upper command. While none of the other females, notably non-LGBT+ stated anything about the incident, the female sergeant in question still complained to other colleagues about not banning our trans colleague from using the same toilets.

Besides standing-up for fellow colleagues, I also had to stand-up for myself when I made detective (Figure 4.1). Prior to my first day assigned to my narcotics team, typically eight officers per team, my new sergeant pulled all of my team members into his office and told everyone that the new team-member, me, was a lesbian. I found out about this from a female team-member who thought it was wrong, since he had not done the same for other team-members who were,

*Figure 4.1* Author during assignment to a narcotics warrant entry team.

e.g. Black, White or Asian. Once I found out, I went to the sergeant directly and discussed my disappointment about how he had disclosed information about me that might have impacted first impressions of me when I was trying to fit into my new team assignment. The sergeant laughed the incident off and said he was just trying to make sure that everyone was comfortable working with me because I was 'very gay'. In response, I told him 'you should be more concerned with how I tolerate bigots on this force'.

Before I even became a member of the team, I felt socially excluded by my colleagues and my supervisor. These experiences, with others, led me to begin to resent policing, police culture and my homophobic and transphobic colleagues with whom I was forced to spend up to 16 hours a day (in narcotics, most shift work lasts longer than eight hours).

## Chapter summary

First, this chapter has examined my reflective police experiences through three distinctive police career phases: police academy, rookie and veteran status. Through reflective stories, this chapter highlights how biases are encountered and addressed through different police career phases. Further, this chapter has demonstrated that gender and sexuality bias can manifest differently in various police assignments.

Second, this chapter aids in establishing more creditability to how I constructed this research. While I have faced more positive acceptance within police culture than negative, I believe it is important to point out why I pursued this research. I conducted this research because I have felt personally connected to it at times. Additionally, these experiences aided in a more in-depth understanding of the similar experiences that my participants disclosed; I believe research of this nature requires a specific and greater level of empathy. This empathy afforded me as a researcher, a more privileged position when building rapport with participants. Besides building rapport with participants, being an insider with similar experiences afforded me access to a marginalised group that has never been researched before. Notably, I believe by being open about my background and why I conducted this research, it demonstrates my intentions as a researcher of pursuing the empirical truth.

## References

Buhrke, R. 1996. *A matter of justice*. New York: Routledge.

Burke, M. 1993. *Coming out of the blue*. London: Continuum.

Burke, M. 1994a. Cop culture and homosexuality. *Police Journal* 65, pp. 30–39.

Burke, M. 1994b. Homosexuality as deviance: The case of the gay police officer. *British Journal of Criminology* 34, pp. 192–203.

Dauphinee, E. 2010. The ethics of autoethnography. *Review of International Studies* 36, pp. 799–818.

Ellis, C. and Bochner, A. 2000. Autoethnography, personal narrative, reflexivity. In: Denzin, N.K. and Lincoln, Y.S., eds. *Handbook of qualitative research*, 2nd edn. Thousand Oaks, CA: Sage, pp. 733–768.

Ellis, C., Adams, T. and Bochner, A. 2011. Antoethnography: An Overview. *Forum qualitative sozialforschung/forum: qualitative social research* [Online] 12(1). Available at: www.qualitative-research.net/index.php/fqs/article/view/1589/3095 [accessed: 7 November 2013].

Meyers, K., Forest, K. and Miller, S. 2004. Officer friendly and the tough cop. Gay and lesbians navigate homophobia and policing. *Journal of Homosexuality* 47(1), pp. 17–37.

Popper, K. 1945. *The open society and its enemies: volume II, Hegel and Marx*. London: Routledge & Kegan Paul.

Silverman, E. 1999. *NYPD battles crime: innovative strategies in policing*. University Press of New England.

Sparkes, A. 1996. The fatal flaw: A narrative of the fragile body-self. *Sociology of Sport Journal* 17, pp. 5–20.

Walker, S. 2001. *Police accountability: the role of citizen oversight*. Belmont, CA: Wadsworth Thompson Learning.

# Chapter 5

# Comparative research on the intersection of police culture and transgender identities

My methodological 'investigation'

Going into this research, I constructed my research questions based on my previous experiences as a police officer and on previous literature. I was consumed with trying to understand why lesbians, gay men and transgender officers are viewed differently within police culture, even though at times they share a socially stigmatised status. I knew from my previous experiences[1] what I wanted to ask and what evidential leads I wanted to explore in this investigation. Therefore, I drew upon my background as a police detective in how I conducted this research. Unlike my previous criminal investigations, this time what I was investigating was the answers to my research questions:

1   What are the perceptions of cisgender officers towards transgender officers, and what are the consequences of these perceptions?
2   What are the occupational experiences and perceptions of officers who identify as transgender within policing?
3   What are the reported positive and negative administrative issues that transgender individuals face within policing?

As a former police officer, there is no doubt that I know a great deal about policing and the working mechanics and components of police culture from first-hand experience. Notably, I share Blum's (2000)[2] and Baigent's (2001)[3] views that the world of academia is foreign and has remained difficult at times due to my previous background in policing. During the course of my methodological investigation, the evidence (my data/interviews) was used to answer my research questions. Additionally, to ensure the credibility of this research, I mimicked the same critical and ethical approach that I adopted as a police officer when I examined my empirical findings and theoretical themes.

Transitioning from policing to a researcher role is not a new phenomenon within criminology (see Dunnighan, 1995;[4] Holdaway, 1983; Niederhoffer, 1967; Waddington, 1999;[5] Young, 1991[6]). Holdaway (1983) was a former British police sergeant who engaged in covert research and participant observation for *Inside the British Police: A Force at Work*. Arguably, Holdaway's (1983) work could be criticised for his documented difficulty in exploring how he acknowledged or separated his police identity from his research. While ethnographic in nature, Holdaway's accounts and observations did not indicate if he used his investigative skills to aid him during the course of his research, nor did he acknowledge how his role in his research could have impacted his data. Another cop turned researcher, Niederhoffer (1967), had a lengthy (21-year) grounded history within policing. Niederhoffer, a former American lieutenant with the NYPD, wrote several books about police culture and police cynicism. In Niederhoffer's (1967) brilliant book *Behind the Shield: The Police in Urban Society*, he used his police experience and interviewing skills to research cynicism in American police culture. Much like Niederhoffer, I used my grounded police interviewing skills to lift up the 'blue curtain', as Niederhoffer puts it, with the aim of conducting research without complex sociological jargon, which instead presents the phenomenon through the eyes of those being researched. Like Niederhoffer, I found that during my research interviews, I benefited from my previous service within policing and the skills I learned as a detective.

## Issues in comparative policing studies

Fosdick (1915) provided the earliest example of examining policing across cultures by evaluating handbooks of evidence for both their similarity and their diversity. Jones (1985) stated comparative research has three major merits: 'a better understanding of the home environment; broader ideas and 'lessons from abroad'; and wider case material which can further 'the development of theoretical constructs' (p. 4). Mawby (1990) contributed further by stating comparative research can be classified into 'overall comparisons of two or more countries; a focus of policing in one specific country; and a comparison of particular issues related to policing two or more countries' (p. 6).

Cross-cultural comparative criminological research assists in the task of 'establishing the regularity, and possibly, the universality of experience' (Brown and Heidensohn, 2000, p. 19). In having considered adopting a comparative approach, the present study explored the potential to yield the following benefits associated with cross-cultural comparative criminal justice studies (Bayley, 1999, p. 6):

1    extending knowledge of alternative possibilities;
2    developing more powerful insights into human behaviour;
3    increasing the likelihood of successful reform;
4    gaining perspective on ourselves as human beings.

Obviously when conducting comparative research between the U.S.A., England and Wales, there are political and cultural contrasts the researcher should take into account (Heidensohn, 1992). These contrasts can become more apparent or less obvious, based on the narrowed focus of the subject area that is explored comparatively. For example, if I were to examine officer attitudes towards firearms there could be a discrepancy between U.S. and U.K. responses due to all American officers being required to carry a firearm. Comparative research is notably riddled with variables because the unit of comparative analysis is influenced by multifaceted dimensions within national borders, region or locale, which on their own may require a comparative approach (Panter, 2015, 2017). As Hudson (2008), Friedrichs (2011) and Van Swaaningen (2007) note, when undertaking critical criminological enquiries, researchers always compare: internationally, culturally or on a micro-level (Hudson, 2008; Friedrichs, 2011; Van Swaaningen, 2007). Yet, where there are well-established similarities (i.e. masculinity within police) the differences may become less prominent.

Brown and Heidensohn (2000), in their research on gender, highlight the pragmatic issue when conducting comparative policing research by stating:

> ... it is not practically possible to experiment with society by creating laboratory conditions in which all factors but the key variables are controlled, comparisons of parallel societies or structures provide the nearest equivalent.
>
> (p. 26)

There are notable key differences between the U.S.A., England and Wales. One of the more obvious differences is the carrying of firearms in the U.S.A. (police and non-police alike). Policing styles are also somewhat different, from variations of 'zero-tolerance' in portions of the U.S.A. to 'policing by consent' in the U.K. Further, there exists innumerable complexities of social, political and cultural patterns that are unique to the U.S.A. and the U.K. specifically.

Yet, there are significant similarities that would allow this type of comparative research to be conducted reasonably. First, all three countries serve as representative examples of how policing is conducted in modern Western societies (Colvin, 2012). When examining policing as performance and organisational issues specifically, McKenzie and Gallagher (1989) stated:

> ... superficially all police departments are the same. They have identical ... organizational philosophies; usually expressed in the form of an aim to prevent crime and preserve public tranquillity.
>
> (p. 3)

As such, the 'nature of police work' (Heidensohn, 1992: 200) is similar, regardless of geographical location, because police are exposed to similar situations and problems (see Skolnick, 2011). Skolnick (2011) refers to this as a 'police personality' that is a prominent feature of what the police role entails. Heidensohn (1992) also refers to this social phenomenon as a 'working personality', which is the result of social and political influences upon the expectation of the policing role itself. Newburn (2012) states that there exists a common characteristic that policing is more than 'just a job', and that police perceive that they are fulfilling a specific role within social societies. Remarkably, in the preliminary stages of this research, I discovered that officers seemed to share more similarities in who and how a 'working personality' is perceived than their respective geographical differences. In other words, police officers themselves subscribe to the social concept of a monolithic policing ethos (Panter, 2017).

Third, all three countries have faced concurrent timelines in respect to LGBT+ equality and LGBT+ political movements. Additionally, LGBT+ police associations emerged in all three countries at nearly the same time, with similar goals and agendas (Colvin, 2012). Notably if, in comparison, there were apparent empirical differences, I drew distinctions and considered them in presenting the results and theorisations.

Therefore, my comparative approach was rather a blend of a practitioner approach (taking a pragmatic view on what can be learned from individual, site, culture, and eventually, to an extent, national differences and similarities) and a theorist approach (attempting to explain practices and predict how to use the different types of comparisons to improve policies) (Mawby, 1990).

The purpose of conducting research on this topic comparatively in the way I have undertaken it, was to establish if expectations of how masculinity is performed within the policing ethos in American and British policing impacted upon those who challenge it (namely those who are transgender). During the early stages of this research, I was somewhat aware that perceptions of masculinity could impact on those who challenge these notions of masculinity. Yet, I was unsure if this phenomenon was restricted to American police culture based on my previous experiences within American policing. Therefore, I comparatively focused on whether English and Welsh police cultures had similar, as much as differing, sociocultural expectations of the performance of masculinity as American police cultures. By doing so, my examination started to shed light on the perceived failure of masculine performance within policing as being somewhat responsible for the unacceptance of those who overtly either challenge masculinity (MTFs), embrace it (FTMs) or reject gendered binaries altogether (e.g. gender queer, gender fluid, etc.). Notably, I was aware that I was viewing two related and simultaneously separate political and cultural systems to determine the importance of masculinity in forming the experiences of transgender police.

## Ontological and epistemological connections

Humans as social beings are self-interpreting. As such, we typically attach meanings to what we do, how we believe or how we are, thus creating issues with how to research certain attitudes and perceptions of human behaviour. Feminist epistemology includes the belief that knowledge is produced, not simply found, and that the conditions of its production should be critically studied and evaluated (Ackerly and True, 2010). There is no general agreement on what feminist methodology is; there are only certain principles which can be applied to the use of such a method. Allen and Walker stated that '... feminism is a perspective (a way of seeing), an epistemology (a way of knowing) and ontology (a way of being in the world)' (1992: 201). Further, Stanley and Wise (1993) stated that research:

> ... is a process that occurs through the medium of a person – the researcher is always and inevitably in the research. This exists whether openly stated or not.
>
> (p. 175)

Stanley and Wise (2008) in *Gender and Women's Studies* further stated:

> Feminist methodology matters because it is the key to understanding the relationship between knowledge/power and so it has epistemological reverberations. It also provides important tools for helping to produce a better and more just society, and so it has political and ethical reverberations too.
>
> (p. 222)

To expand, the feminist research paradigm ideologically connects to social inequality research because feminism occupies a critical point in politics while having an underpinning emancipatory aim (Talbot, 2010). When further examining this feminist paradigm, Stanley and Wise (1993) concluded that:

> Knowledge is necessarily constructed from where the researcher/theoretician is situated, and so feminist knowledge should proceed from the location of the feminist academic and work outwards from this ... all research contexts are grounded and specific, and therefore the knowledge-claims which feminist researchers make should be modest and recognize their particularity and specificity.
>
> (p. 223)

Therefore, in the context of recognising particularity and specificity, my epistemological and ontological position aligns within a semi-symbolic interactionist queer lens. As previously discussed in detail in Chapter 3, I believe that gendered identities (to an extent) are created and maintained with the interactions with others. Further, my ontological position leans towards the notion that the social reality of gender expectations does not exist is a fixed state. Instead, the social reality of gender presentation exists in a fluid, sometimes fragmented and unfixed state within society. Because a body interacts and responds to a social environment (i.e. gender expectations) they are performing in, gender itself is a fluid in a social container.

Pragmatically, the primary issues for feminist researching transgender identities is whether or not to claim if gender categories should be grounded in essentialist or social constructionist realms (Johnson, 2012).[7] Feminist poststructuralist Simone de Beauvoir (1953) stated 'one is not born a woman, but rather becomes, a woman', which called for feminists to recognise the argument that gender is socially manipulated. While some essentialist feminists politically rejected transsexualism, post-structuralists found that this epistemological challenge of gender was beneficial for researching transgender identities. Kessler and McKenna (1978) stated:

> ... the constitutive belief that there are two genders not only produces the idea of gender role, but also creates a sense that there is a physical dictomy ... gender is a social construction, that a world of two 'sexes' is a result of the socially shared, taken-for granted methods which members use to construct reality.

> (p. xi)

Further, Kessler and McKenna (1978) argued that practices of 'passing' contributed to the 'naturalisation' of gender. In struggles to 'pass' within a binary gender, transsexuals consciously have to present gender attributes, general talk and physical appearances (Johnson, 2012). Kessler and McKenna notably drew upon Garfinkel's (1967) work, who suggested that 'passing' is an ongoing social interaction process (Johnson, 2012).[8] Notably, I do not subscribe to essentialist arguments that transwomen cannot lay claim to the identity 'woman' because they will never feel or experience what it is to be a 'woman' (e.g. Jeffreys, 2003; Raymond, 1980). Further, my epistemological and ontological position, as a semi-symbolic interactionist, I agree with feminist post-structuralism, which stresses the importance of social influences and the complex social interactions required to 'do' gender.[9]

For this research, I relied upon the components of feminist standpoint theory. Feminist standpoint theory is contingent upon claims that being in a subordinate position, e.g. as women or LGBT+, allows for a more accurate, comprehensive and objective interpretation of the world because they are 'situated knowers' of social oppression (Collins, 2000). As 'situated knowers', feminist standpoint epistemology asserts that all knowledge is socially situated; it requires researchers to specify the location and contexts in which their knowledge is produced. Further, conceptualised knowledge is situated and relational, instead of objective truth (Smith, 1990).[10] Much like Adams and Phillips (2006), I do not interpret socially situated knowledge as defining, but instead differences in socially produced knowledge can create different epistemic landscapes which both hinders and facilitate access to different information and experiences.

Notably, Homfray (2008) argued that the advantage of adopting a feminist standpoint and being objective to positionality enables one to adopt a critical perspective with respect to many concepts that can be taken for granted in the 'straight' world. Therefore, I openly acknowledge that I know little of the personal experiences of identifying as transgender as a cisgender woman. Yet, due to my 'butch' identity, I am familiar with being a victim of gender policing,[11] as well as having personal experience of being a gay cop and being socially stigmatised. Further, I also worked with the first transgender officer in our department and observed both heterosexism and genderism directed towards her (see Chapter 4). Arguably, I believe my connection to the LGBT+ community allows me to acknowledge the challenges that LGBT+ individuals face within policing and the unique perspectives and socialisation within the LGBT+ policing community. This is similar to what Homfray (2008) and Letherby *et al.* (2012) refer to as 'LGBT+ standpoint epistemology with emancipatory aims'. Thus, I contend with Jones (2014) that LGBT+ individuals are in the best position 'to know' about similar experiences and similar working environments because they are LGBT+ and studying LGBT+ identities. Yet, my position as a former police officer places me in an even more specific position of 'knowledge' than previous researchers (e.g. Jones, 2014).

As such, as transparently as possible, I have openly disclosed my positionality in this research during all components of my research methodology. Second, the feminist style of reflection was embedded within the execution of this research design. I was at all times aware of the politics of empiricism and power dynamics that existed between me and my participants. By placing my experiences and how they contributed to this research at the core, I followed previous feminist-inspired LGBT+ standpoint research (Table 5.1).[12]

*Table 5.1* Previous LGBT+ standpoint researchers

| Researcher(s) | Implications shared with participants | Research |
|---|---|---|
| Adams and Phillips (2006) | Black–biracial, bisexual and disabled | Two-spirit lesbian and gay Native Americans |
| Haritaworn (2008) | Genderqueer identity | Intersection of queer politics and interracial families in Britain and Germany |
| Homfray (2008) | Gay male | Ethnographic study of gay and lesbian community activists in the north-west of England, largely concentrating on the cities of Manchester and Liverpool |
| Jones (2014) | Gay male | British lesbian and gay police |
| Lee (2008) | Gay male | British older gay men |
| Yip (2008) | Gay male | Intersection of LGBT identities and religion (British LGBT Christians and Muslims) |

## Objectivity

A large portion of this research relies upon my reflectivity coupled with 'strong objectivity'. Strong objectivity requires that the 'subject of knowledge be placed on the same critical, casual plane as the objects of knowledge' (Harding, 1993: 69). Therefore, 'strong objectivity' requires what is commonly known as 'strong reflexivity' (Harding, 1993). This occurs because who we are as a researcher impacts every stage of research: the selection of a research topic, the research method, the collection of data, the interpretation of data, decisions when to 'stop' research and so on. Therefore, objectivity-maximising procedures rely upon the researcher and their social situation (standpoint theory) and must be considered as part of the object of knowledge when maintaining the highest scholarly standards. This process entails examining and acknowledging one's positionality transparently while reflecting upon how this position influences how the research was carried out. Notably, my gender, my sexuality, my masculine female presentation and my experiences as a police officer connect me to components of this research while privileges (primarily through a positivist, empirical frame replicating the split between the 'knower' and the 'known') and discredits other ways of knowing. Therefore in the context of this research, 'strong objectivity' also refers to the politics of knowledge reproduction with a greater emphasis on the social situation of knowledge producers to produce a more transparent and thus potential ethical result required to uphold the rigor of scholarly standards (see Longino, 1993).

I acknowledge that my research can never be a true reflection of the culture, place or people I have studied. My ability to 'tell it the way it is' is complicated by my own personal experience, and therefore I acknowledge that my writing is not a transparent representation of culture, nor should it be (Clifford and Marcus, 1986). Therefore, my 'reality' and my perceptions have been constructed in my previous social settings through direct and indirect experiences which are influenced by the tools I used (see Chapter 4). By acknowledging this, I am able to present my findings as 'textual constructions of reality' (Atkinson, 2014), which are a product in part of a story-telling institution (Van Maanen, 1995). Hence, the claims made in this research must be interpreted within context, and readers should note 'the orientation of the researcher ... will be shaped by their socio-historical locations, including the values and interest that these locations confer upon them' (Hammersley and Atkinson, 1995: 16).

## Ethics and accountability

Procedurally, due to the sensitivity of the topic of LGBT+ identity and the participants' relationship to the police community, it was essential that all data was dealt with in an anonymous and confidential manner. The purpose of this research was not to single out specific departments or specific officers, but instead to focus on generalised policing in the U.S.A. and the U.K. Informed consent, maintaining the anonymity and confidentiality of the subject, and protecting my interviewees from harm and deception was obligatory (Lewis, 2003; Bryman, 2004). Keeping this in mind, written informed consent was obtained by all parties involved, and the research abided by the code of ethics laid down by the British Society of Criminology (BSC), the Data Protection Act 1998, the Freedom of Information Act 2000 and Cardiff University's research ethics committee. Further, all participants were given assurances that their details and their identity would remain anonymous. In relation to conducting interviews with serving LGBT+ officers, it was understood that the upmost confidence in non-disclosure of their information was arranged. All research data presented in this research was anonymised using researcher-created pseudonyms, and all participants were made fully aware of the intent of this research and were allowed the opportunity to withdraw at any point during the process.

## Research participants: sampling

The sampling I used was purposive or criterion-based, and not focused on non-probability (see Ritchie *et al.*, 2003; Silverman, 2010). Therefore, I examined similar themes within each interview, and reflected upon how specific features of each theme were significant to this study. By doing so, statistical representativeness was irrelevant, and the interviewees' subjective and individualised experiences were emphasised.

I chose to interview police officers/constables who have direct interaction with members of the transgender community and the LGBT+[13] policing community. Further, my sample included members of the transgender policing community and their colleagues. Table 5.2 differentiates my sample according to country, sexuality and/or gender identity.

During the interviews, I gave participants the choice of their preferred interview location, due to the perceived sensitivity of this research. Interviews took place in police training institutions, on patrol during police ride-alongs, at trans and gay PRIDE events, in police offices, at my research office and over the telephone. After each interview, I asked participants if they knew of any other colleagues who would like to participate in my research. Through these contacts provided by my interviewees, I solicited additional participants who might be interested in talking to me. I believe this 'snowballing' approach was successful and imperative in gaining LGBT+ participants, because they represent a 'hidden' and vulnerable population (Browne, 2005). Furthermore, the transgender population has been noted to be a hard-to-reach population for research (Office for National Statistics, 2009). Additionally, snowball sampling is extremely relevant and useful when the subject matter is sensitive and private and where individuals might not therefore participate readily because of social stigmas (see Biernacki and Waldorf, 1981).

During this snowballing process, initial participants forwarded my contact information to other potential participants. Transgender participants, specifically,

*Table 5.2* Participant demographics

| Participants | American | English/Welsh | Total |
| --- | --- | --- | --- |
| Cisgender heterosexual males | 8 | 3 | 11 |
| Cisgender heterosexual females | 2 | 1 | 3 |
| Cisgender lesbians | 3 | 4 | 7 |
| Cisgender gay males | 2 | 2 | 4 |
| Cisgender bisexual individuals | 0 | 0 | 0 |
| FTM | 1 | 2 | 3 |
| MTF | 4 | 4 | 8 |
| Genderqueer identity[1] | 0 | 2 | 2 |
| Cross-dresser identity[2] | 0 | 1 | 1 |
| Total | 20 | 19 | 39 |

Notes
1 Trans participants' sexuality identification was reliant upon disclosure. Therefore, those who identified as genderqueer did not identify with any type of sexuality because they did not associate with any type of gender (since sexuality is usually defined by gender, as discussed in Chapter Three).
2 My only cross-dresser participant identified as male and he firmly stated that his sexuality was heterosexual.

verified that I was a legitimate researcher and not a feared news reporter.[14] By vouching for me through this type of snowballing method, it assisted in a larger participation rate of trans-identified officers. Further, this snowball technique served as a procedural process of a verification to ensure that my participants were actually serving police officers. During the second stage of this verification process, I verified work e-mail addresses that were assigned to police institutions and used questions during the interview to further verify participants' officer status.

## Data collection

The interviewees chose the date and time that was convenient for them and their preferred method for conducting the interview. During the data collection stage, I made myself available at all hours of the day; some interviews were conducted at 2 a.m. or later due to time differences. This allowed for the interviewees to secure a comforting atmosphere to discuss any personal opinions they chose to disclose with me. One of the aims of my interviews was to offer participants a degree of control over the research process, which is part of the power-exchange process and encourages a more equal relationship between researcher and participant (see Rappaport and Stewart, 1997). I believed offering my participants a choice of how they could communicate with me was important due to the sensitive nature of my research. As a result of this research medium, my participants chose to be interviewed mostly via telephone, while a few chose to be interviewed in person.

## Telephone interviews

All interviews were recorded with a digital voice recorder for future transcription. Most of the interviews were conducted via telephone, which was the participants' choice, and yielded several benefits. These benefits included a greater sense of empowerment for the interviewee, accessibility, disclosure on sensitive topics and cost-savings. I believe these benefits were derived from my interview approach, which placed the needs of the interviewee at the centre of the research.

## In-person interviews

For in-person interviews, I allowed my participants to choose their location. The locations included a patrol car during a ride-along, transgender PRIDE events, a coffee shop and in two cases, my research office. By letting my participants choose their preferred location, I believe it helped rapport with them and also allowed them to disclose sensitive information in areas where they felt the most comfortable.

For the participants who chose an in-person interview, I made all attempts to ensure that they were in a convenient space which allowed for full disclosure without fear of other parties overhearing our conversation. When I conducted one interview during a police ride-along, there was only myself and the constable inside the patrol car, so what we discussed was not overheard. During transgender PRIDE events, I interviewed my participants in a secure location away from the crowds; Manchester police conveniently had a mobile office that they allowed me to use privately for some interviews. I also had one interview at a coffee shop, and I conducted the interview in the corner away from other patrons. For the two interviews that I conducted at my research office, I used a private room during the interviews. During all of the interviews, I did my best to ensure privacy and confidentiality by keeping my participants and what they were discussing in adaptable secluded locations. Thus, I do not believe that the location of the interviews had an impact on what or how things were disclosed to me.

## Unsolicited second notebooks

Two of my transgender participants electronically sent copies of their second notebooks/work diaries, which chronicled their experiences within policing. This information was analysed and used in this research. I used these work diaries in conjunction with what was disclosed to me during the participants' initial interviews, which I believed aided in the validity of the stories they had previously disclosed to me. Notably, some of the earliest sociologists acknowledged the value of unsolicited diaries. As Thomas and Znaniecki (1958, five volumes) wrote:

> We are safe in saying that personal life records, as complete as possible, constitute the perfect type of sociological material.
>
> (p. 1832)

Personal diaries provide personal accounts of experiences and beliefs and offer researchers a rare glimpse into a participant's social life. Thus, they are increasingly recognised as a valuable method in organisational and management research (Van Eerde *et al.*, 2005).

Both disclosed diaries had either photos, locations, dates, witnesses or other details which documented their experiences of trans bias within policing. Both of these participants stated that they believed that their personal work diaries gave better, detailed accounts of the claims that they had disclosed, which added more credibility to their occupational stories. To protect my participants' anonymity, when presented in this research, demographics are omitted along with names of persons present during the incidents described in their disclosed work journals.

Being a new academic, I often felt conflicted when I reviewed their submitted second notebooks/work diaries. I perceived these diaries as something that was meant to be personal and for the writer's eyes only; it felt intrusive at times looking through their personal words of their experiences. Notably, both officers expressed that they wanted others to hear their chronicled experiences, hence why they are included in this research. One officer in particular told me during our interview that what she had experienced at work was so upsetting that she could not talk about it without crying and instead told me to reference the incident in her work diary. I included this type of research participation as inclusive to the other types of interview data that I used. Therefore, data from these research journals are presented alongside interview data.

## Cisgender and conducting transgender research: the insider/outsider dilemma

### 'Cop turned researcher': qualitative interview skills on sensitive topics

As a 'cop turned researcher', I possess a specific skill set that was beneficial in conducting qualitative interviews on a sensitive topic. St-Yves (2013) highlighted specific basic interview skills that police officers utilise in investigations, these are keeping an open mind while remaining objective and building rapport. While keeping an open mind and remaining objective should be imperative in any academic and police interview, within policing it is instilled that first contact with an interviewee is often decisive. It is during this first contact that both parties (the interviewee and the interviewer) form initial opinions of one another (St-Yves, 2013). Therefore, this subjective perception has a strong influence upon how the interview unfolds. As such, who I am as a researcher has an impact on how and what was disclosed.

During this process, interviewers often engaged in an interview management process, which includes reciprocity, rapport-building and closure of an interview (St-Yves, 2013; Shepherd, 2007). First, typically when we receive something from someone we feel obliged to reciprocate by giving something back (Shepherd, 2007). This is the basis for conversation, relationship building, power sharing and constructive listening. It is during this process that knowing what to self-disclose is vital. When interviewing areas sensitive in nature, a mutual trust must be established for reciprocation to be successful and to foster a psychological bond. If an interviewee discloses something upsetting or personal, the interviewer must ensure that any conveyed emotion will not be exploited. For example, in one interview, I had a participant disclose his negative feelings about gay and transgender identities, yet I conveyed to the interviewee that I was not a judgemental listener. For example:

> I understand what you are saying, but could you tell me why you believe you feel this way.
>
> (Researcher field notes, 2012)

In a police interview it would be something like this:

> Nothing you can tell me will bother me ... I just want to get a better understanding of how and what happened.

This is a common tactic used by police investigators during interviews. If reciprocity fails during the interview, then what the interviewee further discloses will be censored. Therefore, to be a successful interviewer (in policing and research) on sensitive topics, one must cope with emergent anomalies, admissions, disturbing and distressing detail, without taking it personally.

## Process and strategy of interviewing: power sharing and constructive listening

Building rapport in police interviewing as well as qualitative interviewing is acquiring a delicate balance between what we desire to uncover and what the interviewee agrees to disclose. Prior to asking my questions, I asked for generic demographic information in my interviews. The demographic questions I asked beforehand entailed the individual's rank, age, length of service with the department and location of their respective department. I made sure not to ask any interviewees their gender identity or sexual orientation, since I discovered that officers almost immediately always freely disclosed their status without my inquiry. Also, due to issues that the transgender community has towards voice depth and gender association, I felt that, as a researcher, asking someone's gender over the phone, if not in person, could be perceived as insulting, and I did not wish to upset any of my participants. Further, I intentionally used gender-neutral pronouns while beginning questioning in an attempt not to offend and additionally to determine which pronoun my participant preferred to be addressed as. If I was unable to determine my

participant's preferred pronoun, I would address them by their rank and/or preferred disclosed name.

When I began the interviews, I explained the process of the interview and the
idea of a theme-based conversation and structured questions. I also reiterated the
importance of confidentiality and disclosure. I advised interviewees that I would
create pseudonyms for their names and their departments during my research.
Further, I stressed that I was less concerned with their actual demographics and
more concerned with their personal observations and experiences. During this
process, I used constructive listening.

During the process of constructive listening, I allowed participants to talk
about whatever they felt like[15] as long as it didn't stray too far away from my
structured research questions. Instead of filling voids of silence within our conversations with needless chatter, I often allowed a small void in silence, and then
continued with a question on what my participant had previously disclosed. This
is another interview tactic used within policing. Valentine (2007) refers to this
process of 'empathic distance'. Leaving a void in silence allows participants to
reflect briefly and compose thoughts more effectively where necessary. Valentine further stated that using this process demonstrates and confirms to participants that researchers are hearing and receiving what is being said.

During this constructive listening process, I also used the following tactics
which are frequently used in police interviewing: minimal interaction, para-
phrasing and identification of emotions (St-Yves, 2013). Minimal encouragement involves the moderation of encouragements given to the interviewee that
you are listening to what they are expressing without interruption (St-Yves,
2013). During interviews, I had to be aware of non-verbal cues that I expressed
to interviewees during disclosure of sensitive information. For example,
when interviewing about cisgender positive or negative opinions of trans identities I often would nod my head to indicate that I understood what was being
said. Then I would paraphrase what was disclosed and ask the interviewee to
expand on it further. This process assures the interviewee that what was
disclosed was understood and is vital to facilitate discussion and rapport
(St-Yves, 2013).

When participants disclosed either verbal (i.e. words/changes in verbal tones)
or non-verbal emotions (i.e. crying), I made my empathy very clear. Fisher and
Geiselman (1992) stressed that rapport is established by personalising the interview and showing empathy. If I sensed an interviewees tone changed when discussing an experience or event, I stated, 'I can tell that upset you, can you tell
me why you believed that upset you?' If the interviewee began crying, I
promptly stated, 'I can tell this is very upsetting for you, would you like to stop
the interview as I do not want to upset you'. If the interviewee wanted to continue I would follow with, 'how about we revisit this later and move on to
another question'. By giving the interviewee a perceived break from traumatic
disclosure, I was able to convey that I cared for their well-being which further
built rapport.

As such, questions were used that were intended to trigger the interviewees' narrative potential. Based on the response I received from my first initial structured intro question, I then determined which additional questions I pursued. If I perceived the respondent to speak easily and freely with responses, I then conducted the interview allowing for my respondents to speak freely at length about the structured questions and anything else they felt the need to disclose. This allowed for a more fluid type of conversation which elicited more details in responses. If I perceived the respondent as being restrictive in speaking with a lack of fluidity, then I stuck more formally to the structured interview style, which provided respondents with guidance during the conversation.[16] This explorative-interpretative approach allowed for the interviews I conducted to maintain an interactive structure and allowed for the allocation of power sharing between myself and the interviewee.

This allocation of power sharing, which is one of many tactics used within police questioning (Carter, 2011; Powell, 2002), allowed interviewees the opportunity to discuss concepts and issues they wished to share and explore in relation to my research. Additionally, it allowed for more self-personal disclosure of officer opinions and experiences. The concept of power sharing during my interviews was very important, because police officers are publicly viewed as having more power than any other professional groups in society. Therefore, when I conducted interviews I constantly was aware of this power dynamic. During the interview, I asked structured questions, but often I found that over the course of the interview, either some of the semi-set questions were not relevant and/or the interview focus shifted towards other topics surrounding my research. Regardless, I focused on the structured questions to maintain the possibility of analysis and comparability.

## Positionality in research and analysis of data

I believe that my experience of having been in policing for 13 years, 12 of which were at a local level and one at a federal level, considerably influenced and motivated this research. As such, my positionality is relevant to the components of my research, because I played a direct role in both data collection and analysis. During my research role, I took two different stances in relation to this approach.

When conducting my qualitative research on transgender constables, at times I felt I had to disclose my personal stance on heterosexism and genderism, which forced me to confront my own personal biases in relationship to this research. However, when interviewing non-LGBT+ officers, I kept my sexuality in the background. Yet, I was able to use my position as an in-betweener to gain participants and the trust of those who participated, which I believe contributed to a higher rate of disclosure on perceived 'sensitive topics' within policing. Unlike Young (1991) and Dunnighan (1995), both police officers who turned researchers, I do not perceive myself as belonging to a particularly dangerous breed due to my existing knowledge of the police or possessing any threatening power to make public the secrets of police work. Instead, by identifying as an in-betweener, I believe I was not perceived by my respondents as potentially being a police betrayer.

Notably, researchers conducting attitudinal and behavioural research only see what is presented to them. As such, police are more likely to disclose less about their behaviour if an outsider is viewing them. As Manning (1970) stated, cops are knowledgeable on how to play the public; how to manipulate their image for different audiences; when to show off; and when to be quiet and cover themselves. Therefore, I believe that my previous tenure as a police officer benefited this research on several levels. As such, this afforded me unique access to and trust from those who participated. In other words, what was disclosed was perceived by me to be more truthful and less politically correct. Second, I was able to use the skills I gained as a police officer/detective to conduct a more effective qualitative interview.

### Being an insider

Being an insider refers to researchers who conduct research with a participant group that they are members of (Kanuha, 2000), so that the researcher shares a group identity and language (Asselin, 2003). This allows researchers to gain greater acceptance from participants more rapidly. Therefore, often there is more openness, and there may be more data depth during interviews. Commonality affords access to groups which would be closed to outsiders (Dwyer and Buckle, 2009). I found, with this research, that access to participants would have been problematic, if not impossible, had I not been considered at points as an insider to this research. I often found myself during my interviews stating 'we' and 'fellow officers', despite the fact that I was a recently retired police detective no longer in law enforcement. I do not think being an insider made me either a good or inferior researcher; instead, it made me a different type of researcher in the field of criminology.

Two of my research participants, self-admitted homophobic and transphobic officers, felt free to discuss their opinions and views in person, despite the fact that they probably perceived that I was gay. I used my previous interview experience as a police detective to build rapport and trust without showing any disregard for or objection to their opinions. As with police interviewing, I conducted my research interviews the same way – it is not about my opinions, but about theirs. Thus, my ability to maintain neutrality during the interview was upheld by my researcher integrity. I acknowledge that I am a supporter of police officers, and I am aware of the negative attention they receive in academic and media realms. But, by acknowledging this bias outwardly and honestly, I believe it adds to the credibility of my research as an insider. This is consistent with what lies at the heart of feminist standpoint theoretical concepts.

### Being an outsider

During portions of this research, instead of being an insider, I considered myself an outsider. This occurred when I was researching transgender police officers and constables. As stated throughout this research, I do not consider myself to be an authoritative expert on the plight of transgender officers. Rather unexpectedly, I found that my role as an outsider, yet also as an insider at times, benefited the levels of disclosure in respect to my trans participants. Some trans officers felt obligated to 'take me under their wing' and show me a glimpse into their experiences while being supportive of my research. Additionally, due to my outsider status, I was able to observe and ask inquisitive questions that an insider to the trans community might overlook.

Often my attempts at trying to remain a detached emotional outsider were much more difficult than I had anticipated during the course of this research. I recall a perfect example of the conflict in my role as an insider-outsider researcher when I went to dinner with several trans constables after a PRIDE event in England. We visited a well-known chain restaurant, and immediately I noticed that the hostess sat us away from other patrons and in the corner of the restaurant in an attempt to socially exclude us, even though we were near the gay district. I observed some of the constables become frustrated, and upset, when other patrons began taking mobile-phone photos of us without permission. Additionally, we were denied proper table service that other tables were noticeably receiving. As one constable said: 'this is how some people treat us, like freaks; throw us in the corner and avoid us and maybe we might leave the establishment ... but the joke is on them. We are fighters'. As an outsider, this experience alone allowed me to see how hurtful and disrespectful people can be of the trans community. I had encountered social exclusion for being a 'butch' gay woman in the southern states, but I had never experienced anything like this. I found myself having to refrain from expressing my opinion towards the rude patrons and staff at the restaurant; I did so to remain objective and to observe how the trans constables responded to the incident. It was then that I found that sometimes I struggled in shifting from an outsider (being cisgender) to an insider (a member of the LGBT+ community and a retired cop). This is similar to that which Adler and Adler (1987) described as an 'ultimate existential dual role' (p. 73), in that some researchers struggle with the role of the in-betweener.

### Being an in-betweener

As previously discussed, who I am and what I have experienced had a huge impact on how I conducted this research, how I explored the topics, why I explored the topics and how I socialised with participants in my research. Without my previous experiences and interactions with the first transgender police officer in my department, I would not have had a passionate interest in exploring this research. Without my personal observations and experiences of being a 'butch' gay woman in a hypermasculine environment, I might have lacked empathy towards the experiences of trans officers when trying to explain the meaning of what I explored. Additionally, my role as an outsider to the trans community presenting non-threatening curiosity aided in more personal disclosure of experiences and opinions.

Thus, during this research, I perceived that I was an 'in-betweener', moving fluidly from an outsider to an insider during interviews and also during the analysis of this research. I openly acknowledge my awareness of the politics of empiricism and the intersectionality of power dynamics which may have existed between me and those I researched. This coincides with feminist thoughts on the importance of transparency and positionality in research.

### Southern charm: the benefits of having a unique accent when interviewing

Some participants disclosed that they participated in my research solely because they perceived me as being trustworthy, and also because they wanted to hear my southern American accent. Thus, the interview was perceived as fun and entertaining for them. As Amber, a British constable, stated:

> I have a family member who moved to the south and I have heard that southern women are not prone to lie, and are about as sweet as the tea they make there.[17]

Clair, another British constable, stated:

> I just love American southern accents; when I listen to your accent I feel like I am in the movies or something. There is something honest about a southern accent.

Even American participants stated that they found my accent trustworthy and 'charming'. As Jessie from an American northern department stated:

> I just don't know what it is about southern charming accents ... I could listen to you talk all day. We don't hear too many southern accents where I am at. I have always heard you can trust a southerner.

Sometimes my participants would laugh or comment that they enjoyed how I used words like 'y'all', 'ma'am', 'sir' and 'ain't' (very common regional vernacular). I believe that my non-threatening manner, the tone of my speech and my accent helped build additional rapport during interviews.

## Usage of humour: building research rapport when talking about sensitive topics

A significant amount of literature has focused on the importance of humour in communication (see Carter, 2011; Jefferson, 1979, 1984). Laughter, which may not necessarily be synonymous with humour, has been considered an important recurrent part of conversational interaction (Jefferson, 1979, 1984) by enabling open talk about personal issues (Jefferson, 1984), affirming relationships (Glenn, 1995) and creating familiarity between participants (Sacks *et al.*, 1974). From my years of police work, I learned very quickly how important laughter is when dealing with stressful, private or intimate details, for certain types of individuals. Brown and Levinson (1987) contended that laughter helps maintain social order by identifying and 'smoothing over' complaints and potentially embarrassing or offensive talk.

Goffman (1959) stated that humour can help people explore relationships by 'putting out feelers' (p. 191) and tests the social climate of acceptability of a situation. Often if I felt the participant was making jokes during our interview, I would exchange funny stories or make comments to encourage laughter if I deemed it appropriate. By doing so, I was better able to understand the boundaries of discussed topics and how not to cross them when speaking about sensitive issues. For example, if a lesbian transwoman was making jokes about her sexuality but not her gender identity, I knew it was safe to joke about sexuality topics but not about gender identity ones.

Additionally, I was able to use humour to emotionally diffuse talk about personal and sensitive information. For example, during an interview with one gay participant, he began to show signs of emotional distress when he discussed perceived social non-acceptance of gay and trans identities within policing. This reaction during our interview was quite an emotional shift, because earlier in the interview he was making jokes and had laughed frequently. Once I sensed that he was beginning to get emotionally upset, I told him:

> You know, I told a previous co-worker who treated me the same way that if straight people stopped having gay babies, this wouldn't be an issue.

Immediately, my participant laughed and his tone appeared more upbeat. This, in turn, made him feel more comfortable, and he opened up further dialogue without showing any further signs of emotional distress.

### Police interview skills and my sexuality disclosure: knowing when to bite my gay tongue

When interviewing members of the cisgender police population, I typically did not disclose my sexuality or my trans ally status unless asked. During the course of these interviews, all participants (cisgender and trans) freely disclosed their sexuality and/or trans status to me without my asking. As Johnson (2012) stated: 'when conducting research with or about trans-identified people, allowing participants to self-identify … be(ing) mindful of the way labels and labelling strategies reveal as much about our own positions, personally, politically, and theoretically, as they do about others' (p. 610). As such, I wanted to ensure that participants labelled themselves to examine why they assumed said labels.

Further, during the interviews, I learned that not presenting myself as threatening, never asking direct confrontational questions and offering an interviewee a way out, often led to more answer disclosure. If you make your interviewee feel special and allow them to detach from any discussed negative issues, it tends to open up the interviewee's narrative responses. Thus, I would often enquire about observed bias-type incidents without asking about their involvement with them. In essence, I would give my interviewees a way out of acknowledging personal responsibility for reported bias incidents, or emotional distance if the traumatic event happened to them. Notably, this was very beneficial when interviewing cisgender officers, especially self-confessed 'homophobic and transphobic' ones.

When interviewing the LGB cisgender population over the telephone, I only disclosed that I was lesbian after I was directly asked. I did this tactfully to ensure that participants could explain their perceptions and feelings to me in better detail. I did not want a participant to state, 'Well, you understand, you are gay'; I wanted to better understand how work experiences made them feel personally. An example of this is when I interviewed a gay constable who stated that he had been a victim of heterosexist abuse at work. When I asked the constable the specifics about the incidents, he replied:

> Well … there was the one time I was called 'gay boy' in front of co-workers; they used it in a joke.

I found this odd, because I have been called 'gay girl' or even worse during my police career and I did not perceive it as being traumatic. Notably, I didn't disclose to the participant that I was lesbian because he never asked. Therefore, I was able to let him disclose in his own words why this one incident was so traumatic for him within his context, which allowed me to better understand why he felt victimised by the incident.

When I interviewed transgender participants, I took a different approach. During my interviews, I operated with complete transparency. I found that disclosing more about myself, particularly that I was gay and a trans ally with trans friends, eased any apprehensions that my transgender participants may have had. This allowed participants to freely open up about what they disclosed. While building continuous rapport during the interview process, I never asked questions about their gender or their status during transition, or any medical questions. Based on my previous interactions with friends who identify as trans and my experience of being raised in 'the South' (i.e. states in the south-eastern part of the U.S.A.), I knew that some of these types of questions could be offensive.

Most participants disclosed after the interviews, that they enjoyed sharing their stories and talking with me. As one research participant stated: 'that was almost like therapy'. This is similar to Walls *et al.*'s (2010) suggestion that qualitative interviews may be perceived as cathartic and therapeutic when researching personal topics. Valentine (2007) stated that interviews can provide relief and reinforce participants' experiences, therefore creating a comfortable environment where they choose to disclose as much as they wish.

## Analysing data

Coffey and Atkinson (1996) suggest that data analysis is not a 'distinct stage' (p. 6) of research, but a 'reflective activity that should inform data collection, writing, further data collection, and so forth' (p. 6). My interviews collectively spanned eight months, with interviews carried out at different time intervals. During this time, I used what I had previously obtained to guide further interviews during the overall course of this research. Therefore, like Coffey and Atkinson (1996), I did not perceive analysis as the last stage of research. Instead, given that theorisation, data-gathering and -analysing, and data/theory integration is commonly applied within the domain of socio-criminological research (Bottoms, 2008), I perceived analysis as having fluidity during my collection of interview data, because I was categorising, thematically coding, thinking about and connecting disclosed responses throughout the entire research process.

During this fluid process of analysing my qualitative data, I used a thematic type of analysis. This is consistent with Tesch (1990), who stated that the process of analysing qualitative data involves the 'translation' of raw data, which places the researcher as an instrument in the process. Therefore, the researcher is required to engage on their own behalf, which results in a second-level data document, instead of perceiving analysis as an exact science (Tesch, 1990). As previously stated, I acknowledge the role that my identity and my experiences have upon how I analysed my data, hence why it was explored in detail. Therefore, I openly acknowledge that my own theoretical positions and values are embedded in all aspects of this research.

Notably, I do not subscribe to a naive realist view that researchers can simply 'give voice' (see Fine, 2002) to all research participants. As Fine (2002: 218) states 'giving voice' 'involves carving out unacknowledged pieces of narrative evidence that we select, edit, and deploy to border our arguments'. Consistent with arguments by Braun and Clarke (2006), I acknowledge that these decisions existed during the process of thematic analysis and I openly recognise them as decisions. Therefore, my thematic analysis relied upon my own inductive approach of recognising an important moment or experience that was disclosed and encoding it prior to the process of interpretation (Boyatzis, 1998). Since I relied upon my own inductive reasoning, the data that was identified as a theme was based on how I viewed its occurrence in frequency. In other words, I let the data guide me to determine what a theme was and what was not. Notably, the entire process was reliant upon how I interpreted the transcriptions of my interviews so the data was influenced by my own interpretation.

Despite acknowledging the impact that researchers have upon data during thematic analysis, I found that using thematic analysis possessed more benefits in this type of research than any of its perceived detriments. First, 'thematic analysis provides a flexible and useful tool, which can potentially provide a rich and detailed, yet complex account of data' (Braun and Clarke, 2006: 5). Following-up on Braun and Clarke (2006), Smith (2015) and McLeod (2011) state that thematic analysis has an increased capability to uncover rich data that other sources may not. Similarly, I found this to be true when examining individual experiences of my participants, their views and opinions, and the reasons why they felt the way they felt. Second, besides identifying and recognising themes within data, thematic analysis interprets various aspects of the research topic (Boyatzis, 1998; McLeod, 2011; Smith, 2015). Notably, I started this research with a focus on a specific concept: *the experiences of transgender police within police culture*. However, various other topics arose that turned out to be unexpected findings. In other words, I discovered several contributory findings that were not related to my original investigative intention.

Third, thematic analysis is not committed to any pre-existing theoretical framework and can be used within different frameworks. From an essentialist or realist method, thematic analysis can report experiences, meanings and the perception of reality of participants. From a constructionist method, thematic analysis can examine the ways in which events, realities, meanings and experiences are on the effects of a range of discourses operating within society (Braun and Clarke, 2006). Further, somewhere within the range of essentialism and constructionism (e.g. critical realism), thematic analysis encourages the ways individuals make meaning of their experiences and the broader social context impinges on those meanings (Braun and Clarke, 2006). During the construction of these meanings, focus can retain on these experiences and other limits of 'reality' (Braun and Clarke, 2006). Therefore, one of the most positive contributions thematic analysis can make is that it is a method which works to both reflect reality, while at the same time revealing and dissecting the surface of said reality.

During analysis, 'fracturing' (Strauss, 1987: 55) of my data into specific 'codes' occurred so 'individual pieces can be classified or categorized' (Babbie, 2009: 402) and situated within broader (theoretical) ideas and themes (Bottoms, 2007; Coffey and Atkinson, 1996). I established, identified and validated each specific theme while fluidly transitioning from collecting data to defining conceptual categories based on these themes. Subsequently, I clarified the links between the conceptual categories. Notably, I was not using data to obtain meaning; instead I used the recurring patterns in which certain themes emerged in interview transcripts to confirm their importance based on what a respondent disclosed. Themes that emerged during data-gathering and -analysis, were simultaneously used to, first of all, provide (increased) focus on collecting data and, second of all, theorising and connecting between the empirical reality and my view and experience of it.

Treating data and the coding of it in this way, enabled me to highlight possible problems, issues, concerns and matters of importance to my respondents.

By coding data by hand, I was able to prefect my coding categories. During this process, I was better able to organise the data. When I was coding the data by hand, I began to see the patterns that emerged because I was at all times close to the data. Therefore, I felt more connected to my research and the data itself.

## Chapter summary

This chapter has examined my methodological 'investigation' by examining why, with whom and how I conducted this research. During this process, I outlined the contested theoretical underpinnings of my methodology, the reason the data was chosen, the individuals I recruited to study and why my research took the path it did. Additionally, a large portion of this chapter explored how my own background and social position aided my research.

Although this chapter may increase the level of critical attention as to how I analysed my data, my aim is to openly acknowledge my role during this research in order to provide a transparent and honest account of my methodological process. In other words, I agree with Bourdieu's (1994) notion that being reflective is paved with good intentions and is a necessary precondition for scientific research within the social sciences. By providing an open and critical account of my history, my social position and my research practices, I am able to explore different and innovative knowledge claims. As Bourdieu (1994) acknowledged, reflexivity is not a means of underwriting scientific knowledge, but instead provides an epistemological basis for the production of social scientific knowledge.

Additionally, I believe it is naive to assume that a researcher with insider knowledge is not beneficial in conducting objective research. As Popper (1945) argued, if science relied on individual scientists to be objective, it would never be so; because they 'have not purged themselves by socio-analysis or any similar method' (p. 217). Rather, I contend that all social science researchers possess some aspect of positionality in their research, which impacts how data is acquired and how it is analysed. Arguably, all researchers have an impact on what they are studying, and sometimes a strong connection to the subject that is being researched benefits knowledge production. I would argue that my position as an in-betweener and using my position as a research instrument has produced a deeper understanding of my research topics, in turn making a valuable contribution to academia.

## Notes

1 See Chapter 4.
2 Blum (2000) worked in a shipyard and then moved on to do research about shipyards.
3 Baigent (2001) was a firefighter and then moved into academia researching masculinity within the fire services.
4 Dunnighan served as a police constable in the U.K.

5 Waddington served for three years as a police constable in the U.K.
6 Young served as a police officer in Australia.
7 My opinion on 'gender essentialism' is presented in Chapter 3.
8 This was discussed in Chapter 3 and will be revisited in Chapters 7 and 8.
9 This was discussed in Chapter 3, in detail.
10 Haraway (1988) referred to this as 'situated knowledges'.
11 This is covered at length theoretically in Chapter 2 and empirically when I discuss 'bathroom battles' in Chapter 7.
12 Notably, there are several researchers who have relied upon LGBT+ standpoint methodologies who defend emancipatory aims. Yet, these studies specifically addressed the benefits of conducting such research on LGBT+ communities, while reflecting upon how their LGBT+ identity plays a role upon data collection.
13 See Chapter 6 for cisgender participants' empirical data.
14 During the beginning stages of my interviews, I had some participants advise that they conducted a background check to verify that I was not a news reporter trying to exploit them.
15 Sometimes we talked about football (American and European), physical training, rugby, fashion styles, car chases, funny police stories, etc.
16 Refer to Appendix A.
17 After our interview, I gave Amber and others who inquired, my family sweet tea recipe.

# References

Ackerly, B. and True, J. 2010. *Doing feminist research in political and social science.* New York: Palgrave Macmillan.

Adams, H. and Phillips, L. 2006. Experiences of two-spirit lesbian and gay Native Americans: An argument for standpoint theory in identity research. *Identity* 6(3), pp. 273–291.

Adler, P.A. and Adler, P. 1987. *Membership roles in field research.* Newbury Park, CA: Sage.

Allen, K. and Walker, A. 1992. A feminist analysis of interviews with elderly mothers and their daughter. In: Gilgun, J. *et al.*, eds. *Qualitative methods in family research.* Newbury Park, CA: Sage, pp. 198–214.

Asselin, M. 2003. Insider research: Issues to consider when doing qualitative research in your own setting. *Journal for Nurses in Staff Development* 19(2), pp. 99–103.

Atkinson, P. 2014. *The ethnographic imagination: textual constructions of reality.* London: Routledge.

Babbie, E. 2009. *The practice of social research.* Belmont, CA: Wadsworth Publishing.

Baigent, D. 2001. Gender relations, masculinities and the fire service: a qualitative study of firefighters' constructions of masculinity and in their social relations of work. PhD thesis. Cambridge: Anglia Polytechnic University.

Bayley, D. 1999. *Patterns of policing: a comparative interactional analysis.* New Brunswick, NJ: Rutgers University Press.

Biernacki, P. and Waldorf, D. 1981. Snowball sampling: problems and techniques of chain referral sampling. *Sociological Methods & Research* 10(2), pp. 141–163.

Blum, J. 2000. Degradation without deskilling: twenty-five years in the San Francisco Shipyards. In: Burawoy, M. *et al.*, eds. *Global ethnography: forces, connections and imagination in a postmodern world.* Berkley, CA: University of California Press, pp. 106–136.

Bottoms, A. 2008. The relationship between theory and research in criminology. In: King, R. and Wincup, E., eds. *Doing research on crime and justice*. Oxford: Oxford University Press, pp. 75–116.

Bourdieu, P. 1994. *In other words*. Cambridge: Polity Press.

Boyatzis, R. 1998. *Transforming qualitative information: thematic analysis and code development*. Thousand Oaks, CA: Sage.

Braun, V. and Clarke, V. 2006. Using thematic analysis in psychology. *Qualitative Research in Psychology* 3(2), pp. 77–101.

Brown, J. and Heidensohn, F. 2000. *Gender and policing: comparative perspectives*. Basingstoke: MacMillan Press.

Brown, P. and Levinson, S. 1987. *Politeness: some universals in language use*. Cambridge: Cambridge University Press.

Browne, K. 2005. Snowball sampling: using social networks to research non-heterosexual women. *International Journal of Social Research Methodology* 8(1), pp. 47–60.

Bryman, A. 2004. *Social research methods*. New York: Oxford University Press.

Carter, E. 2011. *Analysing police interviews: laughter, confessions and the tape*. London: Continuum International Publishing Group.

Clifford, J. and Marcus, G. 1986. *Writing culture: the poetics and politics of ethnography: a School of American Research advanced seminar*. Berkeley, CA: University of California Press.

Coffey, A. and Atkinson, P. 1996. *Making sense of qualitative data: complementary Perspectives*. Thousand Oaks, CA: Sage.

Collins, P. 2000. *Black feminist thought: knowledge, consciousness, and the politics of empowerment*. New York: Routledge.

Colvin, R.A. 2012. *Gay and lesbian cops: diversity and effective policing*. Boulder, CO: Lynne Rienner Publishers.

de Beauvoir, S. 1953. *The second sex*. London: Jonathan Cape.

Dunnighan, C. 1995. 'Hello, Hello, What's going on 'ere then?' The dilemmas encountered in researching a sensitive topic. In: *British Criminology Conference*. Loughborough: Loughborough University, pp. 18–21.

Dwyer, S. and Buckle, J. 2009. The space between: on being an insider-outsider in qualitative research. *International Journal of Qualitative Methods* 8(1), pp. 54–63.

Fine, M. 2002. *Disruptive voices: the possibilities for feminist research*. Ann Arbor, MI: University of Michigan Press.

Fisher, R. and Geiselman, R. 1992. *Memory enhancing techniques for investigative interviewing: the cognitive interview*. London: Charles C. Thomas.

Friedrichs, D. 2011. Comparative criminology and global criminology as complementary projects. *Comparative Criminal Justice and Globalization, 463*, p. 163.

Fosdick, R. 1915. *European police systems*. Reprint 1969. Montclair, NJ: Patterson Smith.

Garfinkel, H. 1967. *Studies in ethnomethodology*. Upper Saddle River, NJ: Pearson.

Glenn, P. 1995. Laughing at and laughing with: negotiations of participant ailments through conversational laughter. In: Have, P. and Psathas, G., eds. *Situated order: studies in the social organization of talk and embodied activities*. Washington DC: University Press of America, pp. 43–56.

Goffman, E. 1959. *Presentation of self in everyday life*. New York: Penguin Books.

Hammersley, M. and Atkinson, P. 1995. *Ethnography*. London: Routledge.

Haraway, D. 1988. Situated knowledges: The science question in feminism and the privilege of partial perspective. *Feminist Studies* 14(3), pp. 575–599.

Harding, S. 1993. Feminist epistemologies. Rethinking standpoint epistemology: what is strong objectivity? In: Alcoff, L. and Potter, E., eds. *Feminist epistemologies*. London: Routledge, pp. 49–82.

Heidensohn, F. 1992. *Women in control? The role of women in law enforcement*. Oxford: Clarendon Press.

Holdaway, S. 1983. *Inside the British police: a force at work*. Oxford: Blackwell.

Homfray, M. 2008. Standpoint, objectivity, and social construction: reflections from the study of gay and lesbian communities. *Sociological Research Online* 13(1).

Hudson, B. 2008. Difference, diversity and criminology: The cosmopolitan vision. *Theoretical Criminology* 12(3), pp. 275–292.

Jefferson, G. 1979. A technique for inviting laughter and its subsequent acceptance declination. In: Psathas, G., ed. *Everyday language: studies in ethnomethodology*. Hillsdale, NJ: Erlbaum, pp. 79–96.

Jefferson, G. 1984. On the organization of laughter in talk about troubles. In: Atkinson, J. and Heritage, J., eds. *Structures of social action: studies in conversation analysis*. Cambridge: Cambridge University Press, pp. 346–369.

Jeffreys, S. 2003. *Unpacking queer politics: a lesbian feminist perspective*. Cambridge Malden, MA: Polity Press in association with Blackwell Publishing.

Johnson, K. 2012. Transgender, transsexualism, and the queering of gender identities: Debates for feminist research. In: Hesse-Biber, S., ed. *Handbook of Feminist Research*. Los Angeles, CA: Sage, pp. 606–626.

Jones, C. 1985. *Patterns of social policy: an introduction to comparative analysis* (Vol. 296). London: Taylor & Francis.

Jones, M. 2014. Cultures of difference: examining the career experiences and contributions of lesbian, gay and bisexual police officers post-Macpherson. PhD thesis, Cardiff University.

Kanuha, V. 2000. 'Being' native versus 'going native': Conducting social work research as an insider. *Social Work* 45(5), pp. 439–447.

Kessler, S. and McKenna, W. 1978. *Gender: an ethnomethodological approach*. Chicago, IL: University of Chicago Press.

Letherby, G., Scott, J. and Williams, M. 2012. *Objectivity and subjectivity in social research*. London: Sage.

Lewis, J. 2003. Design issues. In: Ritchie, J. and Lewis, J., eds. *Qualitative research practice: a guide for social science students and researchers*. London: Sage, pp. 47–75.

Longino, H. 1993. Essential tensions – phase two: feminist, philosophical and social studies of science. In: Antony, L. and Witt, C., eds. *A mind of one's own: feminist essays on reason and objectivity*. Boulder, CO: Westview, pp. 257–272.

Manning, P. 1970 Talking and becoming: a view of organizational socialization. In: Jack D. Douglas, ed. *Under-standing everyday life*. Chicago, IL: Aldine, pp. 239–258.

Mawby, R. 1990. *Comparative policing issues. The British and American experience in international perspective*. London: Unwin Hyman.

McKenzie, I. and Gallagher, G. 1989. *Behind the uniform: policing in Britain and America*. New York: Harvester Wheatsheaf.

McLeod, J. 2011. *Qualitative research in counselling and psychotherapy*. London: Sage.

Newburn, T. 2012. *Handbook of policing*. London: Routledge.

Niederhoffer, A. 1967. *Behind the shield: the police in urban society*. Garden City, New York: Doubleday & Company, Inc.

Office for National Statistics. 2009. *Trans data position paper*. Newport: ONS.

Panter, H. 2015. Heterosexism and genderism within policing: a study of police culture in the US and the UK. Doctoral dissertation, Cardiff University.

Panter, H. 2017. Pre-operative transgender motivations for entering policing occupations. *International Journal of Transgenderism* February, pp. 1–13.

Popper, K. 1945. *The open society and its enemies: volume II, Hegel and Marx*. London: Routledge & Kegan Paul.

Powell, M. 2002. Specialist training in investigative and evidential interviewing: Is it having any affect on the behavior of professionals in the field? *Psychiatry, Psychology and Law* 9(1), pp. 44–55.

Rappaport, J. and Stewart, E. 1997. A critical look at critical psychology: elaborating the questions. In: Fox, D. and Prilleltensky, I., eds. *Critical psychology: an introduction*. London: Sage, pp. 301–317.

Raymond, J. 1980. *The transsexual empire*. New York: Women's Press.

Ritchie, J., Lewis, J. and Elam, G. 2003. Designing and selecting samples. In: Ritchie, J. and Lewis, J., eds. *Qualitative research practice. A guide for social science students and researchers*. London: Sage, pp. 77–108.

Sacks, H., Schegloff, E. and Jefferson, G. 1974. A simplest systematics for the organization of turn-taking for conversation. *Language* 50, pp. 696–735.

Skolnick, J. 2011. *Justice without trial: law enforcement in democratic society*. New Orleans, LA: Quid Pro Books.

Shepherd, E. 2007. *Investigative interviewing*. Oxford: Oxford University Press.

Silverman, D. 2010. *Doing qualitative research*. London: Sage.

Smith, D. 1990. Women's perspective as a radical critique of sociology. *Sociological Inquiry* 44(1), pp. 7–13.

Smith, J. 2015. *Qualitative psychology: a practical guide to research methods*. London: Sage.

Stanley, L. and Wise, S. 1993. *Breaking out again: feminist epistemology and ontology*. London: Taylor and Francis.

Stanley, L. and Wise, S. 2008, Feminist methodology matters! In: Richardson, D. and Robinson, V., eds. *Gender and women's studies*. Basingstoke: Palgrave Macmillan, pp. 221–243.

Strauss, A. 1987. *Qualitative analysis for social scientists*. Cambridge: Cambridge University Press.

St-Yves, M. 2013. The psychology of rapport: five basic rules. In: Williamson, T., ed. *Investigative interviewing*. Abingdon: Routledge, pp. 87–106.

Talbot, M. 2010. *Language and gender*. Cambridge: Polity Press.

Tesch, R. 1990. *Qualitative research: analysis types and software tools*. New York: Falmer.

Thomas, W. and Znaniecki, F. 1958. *The Polish peasant in Europe and America* (5 volumes). New York: Dover Publications.

Valentine, C. 2007. Methodological reflections attending and tending to the role of the researcher in the construction of bereavement narratives. *Qualitative Social Work* 6(2), pp. 159–176.

Van Eerde, W., Holman, D. and Totterdell, P. 2005. Editorial: special section on diary studies in work psychology. *Journal of Occupational and Organizational Psychology* 78(2), pp. 151–154.

Van Maanen, J. 1995. *Representation in ethnography*. Thousand Oaks, CA: Sage.

Van Swaaningen, R. 2007. Naar een kosmopolitische criminology [Towards a cosmopolitan criminology]. In: Bunt, H., Spierenburg, P. and Van Swaaningen, R., eds. *Drie perspectieven op sociale controle* [Three perspectives on social control] (pp. 17–66). The Hague: Boom Juridische Uitgevers.

Waddington, P. 1999. Police (canteen) sub-culture: an appreciation. *British Journal of Criminology*, 39, pp. 287–309.

Walls, P., Parahoo, K. and Fleming, P. 2010. Issues and considerations when researching sensitive issues with men: examples from a study of men and sexual health. *New Researcher* 18(1), pp. 26–34.

Young, M. 1991. *An inside job*. Oxford: Clarendon Press.

## Chapter 6

# 'A man who cuts his penis off will never be a woman'

## Cisgender police perceptions of transgender officers

This chapter is structured around two major themes that emerged during my analysis of the interview data: (1) categorisations of heteronormative and gender ideologies and (2) the consequences of their (mainly negative) perceptions of their LGBT+ colleagues and the occupational environment more broadly. First, this chapter starts by examining problematic perceptions that make transgender acceptance within policing difficult for members of the cisgender police population. The highlighted subthemes that are examined in this section are hegemonic masculinity, perceptions of gender normality and how gender is categorised.

Aimed at an advancement of previous research on masculinity and gender role ideologies within policing (see Chapters Two and Three), this chapter expands upon theories of how the performance of gender (see Butler, 1990; Connell, 1995; Messerschmidt, 1996; Westmarland, 2001) can influence acceptance within social groups (see Allport, 1954; Tajfel and Turner, 1979). The chapter theorises that acceptable[1] masculinity, regardless of LGBT+ status, equals to perceived competency in performing police tasks. Furthermore, this perceived competency influences integration into police cultures. By advancing further understanding of how these perceptions exist and the consequences associated with these beliefs, it is theorised that recommendations can be made for administrative improvements within policing to encourage the acceptance of those who display less desirable 'feminine' traits (i.e. trans feminine and gay identities).[2]

Conceptually, this chapter also explores how cisgender rigid expectations of 'maleness' are perceived to be connected to ownership of male genitalia. This 'maleness' acceptance is further expressively understood when examining 'female' unacceptance within police cultures as previous research (see Berg and Budnick, 1986; Brewer, 1991; Heidensohn, 1992) has highlighted. Further, previous researchers have disclosed that perceptions of 'female' identities are connected to incompetency, promiscuity and lesbianism (see Berg and Budnick, 1986; Brewer, 1991; Heidensohn, 1992; Westmarland, 2001). While social advances towards gender equality and improvements in diversity have occurred since these previous studies, I contend here that 'feminine' identities are still associated with social undesirability within police cultures. Hence, it is further theorised that those who challenge 'maleness' (i.e. trans feminine and gay identities), face specific integration barriers in police cultures.[3] This 'cultural devaluation' (Schilt 2010: 157) of 'maleness' within a masculine work environment can lead to more hostile treatment than those who are perceived as 'culturally embracing' masculinity (i.e. trans masculine and lesbian identities). To further explore this further, this chapter examines cisgender perceptions of those who are perceived as 'culturally devaluing' and 'culturally embrace' heteronormative gender systems. As such, the demographics of cisgender participants are highlighted in Table 6.1.

## Perceptions of officers

### Hegemonic masculinity within police culture

As previously discussed in Chapter 3, historically, policing has been perceived as an occupational culture that is infused with hegemonic masculinity, with a distinction drawn between the men's work of crime fighting and the women's work of social service activities (Fielding, 1994). Policing, as a masculine profession, adopts the notion that there are 'socially gendered perceptual, interactional, and micro-political activities that cast particular pursuits as expressions of masculine and feminine "natures"' (West and Zimmerman, 1987: 126). This binary gendered division permeates the expectations of those who wear the uniform and their perceptions of performance abilities in relation to police work. These entrenched binary gender-role stereotypes and assumptions of 'masculine' and 'feminine' have been used to exclude women and those who associate with 'femininity' from job assignments to upper management positions (see Westmarland, 2001). Some researchers even state that the mere presence of women (i.e. femininity) can symbolically undermine the traditional masculine ethos of policing and be perceived as a threat to masculinity itself (Fielding and Fielding, 1992).

With the police masculinity ethos or 'working personality', danger and authority are interdependent elements in policing and individuals must conform to the adoptive culture (Martin, 1980). Martin (1980) found that women adapt to policing by either emphasising their femininity (e.g. portraying themselves as

*Table 6.1* Cisgender participants

| Participants | American | English/Welsh | Total |
| --- | --- | --- | --- |
| Heterosexual males | 8 | 3 | I I |
| Heterosexual females | 2 | I | 3 |
| Lesbians | 3 | 4 | 7 |
| Gay males | 2 | 2 | 4 |
| Bisexual individuals | 0 | 0 | 0 |
| Total | I 5 | I 0 | 25 |

weak and passive in the presence of male officers) or accentuating the masculine aspects of their personality (e.g. portraying themselves as strong). This masculinity ethos creates a dichotomous relationship between gender ideologies of male and female identities within policing (see Fielding, 1994; Garcia, 2003) and can arguably lead to binary assumptions about sexuality and gender. Therefore, assumptions about masculinity and femininity can conflict and influence perceptions of 'male' and 'female' identities alongside assumptions about non-binary identities. As Frank, an American officer, best summed up all of my participants' responses, stated:

> Police are supposed to be viewed as masculine and tough as nails ... so the more manly you are, the better you will be on the job.

Another American officer, Fred, stated:

> You have to be masculine to do the job. You have to fight, be assertive and be commanding. If you do not assert your strengths, this job will eat you alive.

Luke, an American officer, stated:

> Masculinity is a requirement for the job. If you don't show it or express it, then you will fail at being a cop.

As Frank, Fred, Luke and others disclosed, there is a perception that if you are not masculine enough, then you will not be viewed as a competent officer. This is consistent with Hunt (1990), who has suggested that those who do not fit within the perceived masculinity constructs can be perceived as a threat to the masculine character of a crime-fighting policeman. Further, this perception that masculinity, i.e. non-femininity, is a requirement within policing was consistent across American, English and Welsh participants. Simon, a British constable, stated:

> Policing requires you to be masculine; it doesn't matter if you are a man or a woman. You can't be weak and passive; you have to be tough and strong mentally and physically.

Peter, another constable, stated:

> You can't be weak. It benefits you to be as masculine as possible regardless of your gender.

Further, as participants indicated, there is a perception that effective policing requires adherence to typically 'masculine' characteristics, such as being strong and tough, whereas officers socially associated with 'feminine' characteristics, such as being weak, sensitive, subordinate and vulnerable, are not viewed as being capable of the job. As Tom, an American officer, stated:

> Transwomen? ... Nope, they want to be as feminine as possible. I don't think they can handle the job.

Tom was not alone in his perception that transgender women portray themselves as unmasculine and are inadequate to perform policing. As Peter, a British constable, stated:

> They may have the strength because they used to be a man, but since they are trying their best to not be masculine anymore they are ... viewed as not competent.

Once again, as the above quotes highlight, being trans feminine equates to a perception of the rejection of embracing a desirable policing 'working personality' (i.e. masculinity). Further, masculinity is perceived as a measurable performance within the culture of policing. Notably all heterosexual cisgender participants, American and British, disclosed that they believed that trans women (those who are perceived as expelling masculinity) would be less competent within policing due to being, as Tom best summed it up, as 'feminine as possible'. When explored further, participants disclosed that there is a perception of different levels of heteronormative masculinity. As John, an American officer, stated:

> Most lesbian women that serve tend to be more 'manly', for lack of a term, while gay men and transsexuals tend to be more passive. This is not a job where you can be passive – you need to be the one in charge. If you can't appear as an authority, nobody on the street is gonna take you seriously.

Another American officer, Thomas, stated:

> We are just now getting used to gay and lesbians within policing, let alone transsexuals.... Lesbians are great to work with, but if you are not masculine enough, then you might not make it.

Jason, another American officer, stated:

> Police are supposed to be viewed tough as nails ... I am unsure if a transsexual woman would be able to do this job.... Gay men are not tough enough to do the job, since they are pretty weak ... Lesbians are alright since I have worked with a few of those and they are like one of us. They can talk about women, don't get offended by stupid stuff, and can handle their own in a fight.

Mirroring Jason's comments, Fred, an American officer, stated:

> Policing is a tough culture to work in. If you are lesbian, gay or transgender, you will have to face obstacles that straight people don't have to face. I don't have a problem with them in policing as long as they are tough enough to do the job ... I mean, they gotta fight when it comes time to fight – you know, people's lives are on the line. You can't be weak or you will fail as an officer.

Fred further stated:

> Lesbians are tougher and are able to do the job better than gay men, because gay men are not tough ... I think transwomen would also be weak too, but I have never worked with one of those before.

Like their American counterparts, English and Welsh constables also pointed out that lesbians are perceived as more masculine than gay men and that passivity and femininity is connected to a failure to do a job properly. Kelly stated:

> I think the stereotype of a gay female who is very masculine versus gay and transgender individuals fits better with the perceptions of what is needed in policing. You have to be tough or you will not make it.

Another British constable, Peter, stated:

> You have to be tough. If you are perceived as challenging what is needed for the job, like being gay or transgender, then they think you are not strong enough to do the job.

Based on participants' responses, there is a perception that masculinity is pervasive within police culture, much like previous researchers found (see Kappeler *et al.*, 1998). Masculinity exists in occupational settings due to the social and historical context of how it is constructed (i.e. 'hegemonic masculinity') (see Connell, 1995). Further, masculinity is dominant in the male reinforcement of power in both a cultural and collective form. Therefore, masculinity is deconstructed, constructed and reinforced in a regulatory capacity uniquely within policing. Due to the fact that there is an expectation of a higher level of masculinity, masculinity itself becomes more magnified by those existing in a hypermasculine environment.

Uniquely, some LGBT+ gender identities and sexualities are perceived in this hypermasculine environment as having different levels of desirable masculinity. Revisiting John's, Thomas's, Jason's, Fred's, Kelly's, Peter's and other heterosexual cisgender responses, there appears to be a suggestion that police masculinity is relevant to women, and that unlike gay men and transwomen, lesbians are perceived as more likely to display more accepted forms of masculinity. This coincides with Burke (1994a, 1994b), who argued that it is easier for lesbians within the occupational culture of policing because of the stereotypical assumptions of female masculinity and the perceived connection to lesbianism. Further, Connell (1995) stated that patriarchal culture interprets gay men as lacking masculinity; this interpretation is linked to the assumption that American and British culture makes about the mystery of sexuality that opposites attract (i.e. heteronormativity). Notably, not all lesbians are masculine of centre and masculinity can range, at times interchangeably, across LGBT+ identities. As such, this phenomenon is explored further throughout this chapter and the following two chapters.

## Masculinity, femininity and job assignments within policing

Theoretically, masculinity's manifestation in policing can be seen in previous research on the division of police work that relegates effeminate officers to 'women's issues' (Barlow and Barlow, 2000; Merlo and Pollack, 1995; Schulz, 1995), and in administrative policies that value competitiveness, aggressiveness, persistence and emotional detachment (Epstein, 1971). Therefore, this 'cultural devaluation' of heteronormative gender systems as Schilt (2010) describes it, is connected to perceptions of desirability of police performances alongside desirability of gender performances. As such, participants disclosed that hegemonic masculinity not only influences perceptions of masculinity, but also impacts perceptions of who will be deemed more successful at certain job assignments within policing. Jason, an American officer, stated:

> If you are real macho, then you can join SWAT or a warrant execution team. They only accept the toughest.

Another American officer, Frank, stated:

> Everyone knows you have to be tough for the job, but there are higher expectations in SWAT because of the macho-ness of it all. A lot of officers want to go to these units because your fellow officers view you as a badass, you know?

What Jason, Frank and my other American participants disclosed indicates that there is a perception that certain positions within policing have different masculinity performance expectations. All American respondents stated that in units like SWAT and in tactical teams, you had to display extra degrees of masculinity to perform the job successfully.

Much like American participants, all English and Welsh participants disclosed that specialised units like firearms and traffic require heightened masculinity than that typically required within policing. Ian, a British constable, stated:

The macho officers work firearms or traffic. I haven't seen anyone assigned to those units be sissy. You have to be even tougher to be there.

Kelly, a lesbian British constable, disclosed:

Look at the firearms department ... I think the stereotype of a female gay fits better with the perceptions of macho police officer roles ... even the profession of policing. And I think it is a shame. I have heard people, well, my experience is that there is more openly out gay women than openly out gay men on the force.... It is easier for a gay woman.... Perhaps in the fire-arms department there is a perception that there are less visible gay men and it is easier for masculine gay women.

Kate, another lesbian British cisgender constable, stated:

On the firearms department which is kind of, for us, one with a culture of a kind of macho-ism.

When I asked Kate and others why certain units are deemed more masculine than others, and why certain more masculine individuals are perceived as being better at these assignments, Kate best summed up other participants' responses:

It is kind of certain jobs come in and ... you don't get an opportunity if you do not fit a certain kind of physical profile. Lesbians fit in better in certain assignments because you kind of roll your sleeves up, and I suppose that is seen as some type of imitation. See how you respond and you do have to be seen as getting stuck in the masculine sort of, kind of role.

Westmarland (2001) described a similar process to that which my participants disclosed, indicating how heteronormative gender relations are perpetuated through social and cultural practices and through the adoption of gender roles. These social and cultural practices of heteronormative gender can affect career prospects within policing, as women are typically assigned to more 'feminine' assignments, and males are assigned to more 'masculine' assignments (West-marland, 2001). Westmarland referred to this phenomenon as 'differential polic-ing'. This occurs when a disproportionate number of women are employed in domestic violence units, sexual assault units and youth units ('feminine' units) within policing; and alternatively, a disproportionate number of male officers are often found in homicide units, vice units and tactical teams ('masculine' units) (Brown and Heidensohn, 2000; Martin and Jurik, 2006; Schulz, 2004). Contrib-uting to previous research (Brown and Heidensohn, 2000; Martin and Jurik, 2006; Schulz, 2004; Westmarland, 2001; Whittle, 2000) on the intersectionality of binary gendered expectations and police assignments, as highlighted above, this research found that some women are an exception. This research found that lesbians, if perceived as possessing more stereotypically 'butch' masculine traits, are more associated with and accepted within 'masculine' police assignments than their gay and trans feminine counterparts.

Just like their American counterparts, English and Welsh constables disclosed that there are different masculinity perceptions within police culture and police assignments. As Helen, a heterosexual British constable, stated:

> I am not tough enough to be on the firearms unit or traffic, you have to be very aggressive to be assigned to those units ... I do not believe that a woman transsexual or a gay man could do any better, they wouldn't be tough enough.

Kelly, a British constable, stated:

> Certain jobs come in and certain people are sent to them and you don't get an opportunity if you don't fit a desirable physical profile. That still happens.... It is easier if you are more masculine when trying to fit into more masculine roles within the constabulary.

What all cisgender participants disclosed (American and British) could be explained by Corsianos (2009). Corsianos contended that the feminisation of certain specialised units, coupled with the lack of physical action, high-speed chases and the lack of 'big arrests', perpetuates perceptions that officers assigned to those units are more important and thus further ostracises officers assigned to feminine units. Thus, I contend with Westmarland (2001) that masculinity is connected to personal autonomy and a perceived ability to fight/aggressiveness, and femininity, which is synonymous with childbirth, is connected to police roles involving victims who are children or women. Westmarland (2001) described this process as 'differential policing' (p. 6), in which women are unable to choose certain career specialties while being manipulated into undertaking policing assignments that are concerned with empathy, families and sexual offences ('feminine' units). Thus, cis-women, transwomen and effeminate men who do not appear masculine enough may not be given the opportunity to enter into 'macho' units like firearms or traffic.

Consistent with Westmarland's (2001) research, there was a perception among all respondents that certain units were deemed more masculine than other assignments within the police service. Further, Westmarland suggests that femininity can be devalued in environments where there are hierarchical gender assignments. As discussed in Chapter 3, Butler (1990) initially described this phenomenon as a 'heterosexual matrix',[4] which maintains inequality between men and women. Connell (1987) and Schippers (2007) stated that inequality between men and women is hierarchical and that there is a higher value on masculinity than femininity. Therefore, those who challenge this hierarchy disrupt heteronormative perceptions of gender. Since masculinity is perceived as a necessary trait in policing, certain police assignments are more desirable than others. This reinforces a 'heterosexual matrix' (Butler, 1990), which emphasises heteronormative ideological perceptions of acceptable femininity and acceptable masculinity within police culture. Furthermore, I contend that with the fostering of masculinity in a 'heterosexual matrix' coexisting with the rejection of femininity, this results in the foundational groundwork of bias and social unacceptability of LGBT+ identities within policing.

## Cisgender normality: moral discourses on gender and sexuality

Much like previous research (Colvin, 2012; Jones and Williams, 2013; Lyons *et al.*, 2008), I found that LGBT+ bias is still very apparent within policing, despite social progression of LGBT+ rights. For example, I had one participant, Jay, who engaged in e-mail exchanges with me. He objected to the morality of my research and LGBT+ existence within policing. Jay, a self-confessed Christian and police officer, sent direct quotes from Leviticus 18:22, Leviticus 20:13, 1 Corinthians 6:9–11 and Romans 1:26–28, with a little additional dialogue, to my university e-mail. I sent an e-mail back to Jay with an attached consent form and thanked him for his interest in my research, stating that I would love to hear more from him and his opinions about my research. I also notified Jay that by having further contact with me he was consenting to my research, and that what he disclosed from then on would be used for my study. Jay promptly responded with an additional e-mail (Figure 6.1).[5]

Similar to Jay's e-mail comments, several American, English and Welsh officers stated that they still have issues with LGBT+ identities within policing. Fred, an American officer, stated:

Date: 06/26/2013 11:55PM
Subject: Re: Re: STUDY

Actually, I already know what its all about, its a subject that you are covering because you want answers to your own life because you dont even know who you are?
And i do NOT agree with gays or any other disgusting lifestyle, yet alone working along with law enforcement. Big mistake. Working with a homosexual is uncomfortable, annoying, and disturbing.
Homosexuality disrupts, and causes children in this world to be confused. Gays are a bad example to all, and are a disgrace to mankind.
Take notes in your research and do youself a favor, just stop wasting your time trying to justify your lifestyle, when you know it is wrong. Realize that you are wrong and need to change your ways.
I dont candy coat anything, so if you did not like this reply, or if you are offended by this, than do not ask for information from real people anymore.
You can be fake as long as you want, but one day, you will realize that u are actually corrupting and contaminating the world, and not making it a better place. Your only making it worse.
The truth hurts...but its the truth that will set you free..."

*Figure 6.1* Screen-shot of e-mail from an American participant.

> If you are lesbian, gay or transgender you will have to face obstacles that straight people don't have to face. I don't have a problem with those people[6] being in policing, I just don't want to know about it.... It's weird, you know? ... I just hate it when they cram it down your throat.

Notably, Jay spent a considerable amount of time discussing his attitudes towards the 'gay agenda' as he described it. As he further stated:

> I mean why does it have to constantly be in your face, dancing at PRIDE with leather chaps on and stuff. It ain't about rights, it is about being a sick pervert, a pedo,[7] or a he-she. No one wants to see that, just keep what you do in the bedroom.

Jason, another American officer, stated:

> You can be gay, transgendered or whatever ... but policing is not a friendly environment for those people, they are not welcome ... I know some officers who wouldn't work alongside one of 'em.

Helen, a heterosexual British constable with 26 years' police experience, stated:

> Gay men tend to go to the more feminine side, so they are not viewed as being as good as the other males.... They face the same type of social exclusion that us women face within policing. But transwomen? ... I just don't understand that. I mean, can you imagine on a flight to Singapore and you got someone on there who is transgender and you got 400 passengers and you got this man with a bra on, there is an appropriateness of when it can be used. I mean imagine, your pilot, on your way to Hong Kong and the pilot walks in with a bra – you would get off the plane, wouldn't ya? You would, you would say turn around folks, let's go back. There is an element of confidence behind it.... There is a professionalness that needs to go with it.... That is why transgender people shouldn't be in policing.

As with other cisgender interviewees, there appeared to be a connection between being trans and being socially unacceptable and 'unprofessional' due to perceptions of a failure to adhere to socialised gender role ideologies. This perception of unprofessionalism due to having a trans identity is similar to Connell's (2010) findings of transgender individuals' experiences in non-police occupational roles. Mirroring some of Connell's (2010) findings, Hill and Willoughby (2005) found that perceptions of cisgender individuals towards transgenderism were not correlated with perceptions of masculinity and femininity; instead, perceptions were associated with traditional or dichotomous gender role beliefs. Similarly, Tebbe and Moradi (2012) found that trans bias and gender role beliefs were strongly correlated with each other. Tebbe and Moradi (2012) suggested that the relationship between traditional gender role beliefs and attitudes towards both sexual and gender minorities 'may reflect a perceived overlap (or conflation) of sexual orientation with gender identities and perceptions eschew traditional sex-types gender role prescriptions' (p. 252). This is similar to previous studies which have linked relationships between gender roles and attitudes towards gay sexualities (see Basow and Johnson, 2000; Swank and Raiz, 2010).

Whitley (2001) suggested those who express higher displays of 'masculinity' possess more negative attitudes towards homosexuality. Further, Whitley (2001) found that participants' sex and traditional gender role perceptions predicted both attitudes towards LGBT+ individuals, heterosexism and genderism. These studies, similar to what some participants disclosed, suggested that sexual minorities are perceived as threatening traditional gender role beliefs, much like those who exist outside gender binaries (i.e. transgender individuals). Thomas, an American officer, disclosed:

> I don't think my co-workers would be open to a transgender officer ... Lesbians though are viewed in a more positive light than gay males because they are feminine acting.

Mirroring American responses, Ian, a British constable, stated:

> I think lesbian women are more acceptable than gay men in general because of the sexuality aspect of it.... That is why men are uncomfortable with it.... Men look at the homosexual side of males and transsexuals differently because they have sex between males.... For me it is repulsive.

Peter, a British constable like Ian, disclosed:

> The gay and trans thing is kinda gross if you think about it, you know? Not to sound too harsh, but I guess that is why they are not accepted as well within policing. Also gay men and people who cross-dress are viewed as not being masculine enough.... You have to be tough to be taken seriously in this profession.

As highlighted above, cisgender male participants disclosed that female sexuality was as Thomas stated 'sexy' and perceived as more acceptable, and gay male and transgender sexualities were viewed as 'gross', 'seedy', 'unacceptable' and 'repulsive'. Further, some participants disclosed that these perceptions have a direct impact on acceptance within policing. As Fred, from the American east coast, with 15 years' experience, stated:

> I don't think that policing is ready for transgender officers in policing. I know myself and other officers think it is weird and strange, but there is also the safety concern.... If someone doesn't bond, other officers may not have your back, you know?

Frank, another American officer, recalled:

> We had a transsexual female on our department and she was a hard worker, yet she met a lot of flak from fellow officers. They wouldn't back her up on calls because they thought she was a 'weirdo' and didn't fit in with the rest of us. It was pretty messed up.

What Fred and Frank are describing in the context of social acceptance could partially be explained by the social identity theory. Discrimination, stereotyping and bias reflect, respectively, people's cognitive, affective and behavioural reactions to people from other groups (e.g. LGBT+ police officers) (Fiske, 1998). As proposed by social identity theory, individuals identify themselves based on similar characteristics, such as age, gender, and race or, in the context of this research, non-LGBT+ identity. Social identity theory (Tajfel and Turner, 1979) refers to an individual's self-concept in relationship to others. Therefore, based on the assumption that social hierarchies exist within society, different groups are perceived to stand in power and status compared with others (Tajfel and Turner, 1979). The premise of this theory is that these groups provide members with a social identity. As such, the in-group will discriminate against the out-group to enhance their self-image (Tajfel and Turner, 1979). Further, members of an in-group will seek to find negative aspects of an out-group, thus further enhancing their self-image and distancing themselves from the out-group. Herein lies the conflict, as some groups can be perceived as more socially accepted than others. Those who are not viewed as part of the more dominant and more socially prevalent in-group will face social resistance because they are perceived as an out-group identity.

As such, even in occupational environments, people typically seek out other people to socialise with whom they perceive to be similar to themselves (Fiske, 2002). Individuals identify more with those whom they believe share characteristics (i.e. the in-group) than with those who are perceived as less similar (i.e. the out-group) (Tajfel and Turner, 1979). Thus, the potential applicability of this theory in the context of this research resides in non-LGBT+ officers (in-group) and LGBT+ officers (out-group); non-lesbian officers (in-group) and lesbian officers (out-group); non-gay officers (in-group) and gay officers (out-group); or cisgender officers (in-group) and trans-identified officers (out-group). This is how intergroup(s) and out-group(s) can form within the culture of policing.

Additionally, intergroup cultures within policing enable an in-group of individuals to socialise and discuss similar feelings of bias without fear of disclosure of exhibiting biased behaviour. Within policing, this fear of disclosure would be the fear of reported biased language and behaviour to upper administration or an internal affairs unit. Officers socialising in an in-group would not want to betray the group as a whole; if they did, then they would be cast out into an out-group. Notably, intergroup members are not only motivated to protect the group to preserve their social status, but feel compelled to justify their group behaviour (dominant or subordinate) through a hierarchical system.

As with other sociological groups, being considered an out-group identity has consequences. In an occupational subculture which prizes solidarity, this can have profound safety implications that are policing specific. For example, by showing undesirable 'feminine' emotional vulnerability and being perceived as not 'fitting in', can lead to ostracism from the same officers who may have to provide back-up assistance during patrol. This process is commonly referred to as 'blackballing' in police slang and is an example of treatment towards those who do not conform to the dominant 'police persona' through the process of dis-association. Colvin (2009) referred to a similar process, which he entitled a 'weak link' (p. 89), in which an officer might be more likely to have their safety compromised due to a reduction of overall group cohesion among officers.

### Intersectionality of LGB sexuality and perceptions of masculine gendered identities

Some heterosexual cisgender officers perceived that any individual (deemed members of an out-group) who challenged stereotypical gender role perceptions of femininity and masculinity was classified as transgender, regardless of their sexuality. Tom, an American officer, stated:

> I always thought that gay people were just born in the wrong body, you know? I mean ... a lesbian obviously wants to be a man and a gay man wants to be a woman. So, I guess someone being transgender is not as weird as a gay guy acting sissy, you know? I know it sounds bad, but I think that is what the whole gay thing is, they are confused about their gender or something.

While heterosexual cisgender participants disclosed various degrees of non-acceptance of LGBT+ identities within policing, alarmingly, members of the LGB policing community expressed that they had similar issues with social acceptance of transgender identities in general. Ann, an American cisgender lesbian, stated:

> You know what the T in LGBT stands for, don't ya? It means tagged on.... Transmen are different than us, obviously.... They are often perceived as butch women trying to grow a penis. Some transmen still come to the gay bars and try to pick up women. Me and my butch friends are like, 'Why are you here? You don't belong here'.

Ann's statements were mirrored by other American cisgender lesbian officers I spoke to. As Tiffany stated, some lesbians have a hard time understanding transmen:

> I just don't get it; you can be a butch woman and still be accepted within policing. I guess I just don't understand the transman thing. It is odd for me

since they still want to associate with 'butch' lesbian culture.... They are nothing like us, though.... It really confuses straight officers; you know?

Tiffany, a self-identified 'butch' lesbian, described how she has been compared to a transman in the past:

> It is insulting when people ask me if I am trans; I am not. I am a woman and I love being a woman. I think transmen damage butch identities.... They bring us down when we are trying to portray positive lesbian identities within policing ... I mean, I don't have a problem with them; it is just I don't know if they belong in policing due to their lack of acceptance from non-gay officers.

When examining perceptions of transmen, much like their American counterparts, English and Welsh cisgender constables who identified as lesbian stated they possessed socialised conflict when accepting transgender identities. As Zoe, a British constable, stated:

> I hate it ... I mean, they say they are separate than us and get defensive when you use the wrong pronoun. I had to tell a colleague, 'Listen – I have known you for years as a she; it is going to take a while to get to know you as a he'. I just don't get why they come to the bars and still associate with gay women if they want to be seen as men.... You know, it is also insulting sometimes when people assume I am trans because I am butch. I mean, I am a woman. I am not confused about my gender and I belong in policing.

Beth, like Zoe, stated it is common for 'butch' officers to be associated with trans masculine identities:

> I have had co-workers in the past ask if I am trans because I am butch. I am not. It is a little insulting, because most straight people just don't get that there is a difference between gender identity and someone's sexuality.

As highlighted by Zoe, Beth, Ann and Tiffany, most lesbian participants disclosed conflict in their perceptions of trans masculine identities.

### 'Girls have vaginas; boys have a penis': perceptions of anatomy during transitions

Garfinkel (1967) presented a case study of 'Agnes', a patient of his who wished to obtain a sex reassignment surgery. 'Agnes' presented herself as male until the age of 17; then at the age of 19 she began presenting herself as female. Garfinkel used her case as an 'occasion to focus on the ways in which sexual identity is produced and managed as a "seen but unnoticed", but nonetheless institutionalized, feature of ordinary social interactions and institutional workings' (Heritage, 1984: 181). The 'Agnes' case study illustrated how the working of what we perceive as gender is a social practice within a binaried gendered culture. In the 'Agnes' case study, Garfinkel disclosed that there are distinctions between the possession of a penis and/or a vagina as a biological event and a cultural event in which either genitalia are possessed (Kessler and McKenna, 1978). Socially, genitalia can be perceived as being possessed physically or can be perceived culturally if the person feels entitled to it and/or is assumed to have it (Garfinkel, 1967). Therefore, not only is gender socially constructed in certain circumstances, but socially 'male' and 'female' categories are also socially constructed. As such, social perceptions of genitals and gender attribution is reflective (Kessler and McKenna, 2006). Often gender is 'proved' (Kessler and McKenna, 2006: 174) by which genital is socially attributed through this gender attribution process.

As such, Bornstein (1994: 46–50) reformulated Garfinkel's (1967) notion of the primary components of social attitudes towards gender as:

1   Genitals are perceived as the sign for gender (males have a penis; females have a vagina).
2   There is a social perception that there are two, and only two, genders (male and female).
3   One's gender is invariant; if you are female/male, you always were female/male and you will always be female/male.
4   Exceptions to these social perceptions of gender will not be taken seriously (seen as jokes, pathology, etc.).
5   There are no transfers from one gender to another.
6   Socially, everyone is classified as a member of one gender or another (there are no cases in which gender is attributed).
7   Males and females exist independently of criteria for being male or female.
8   Membership, or association, in one's gender or another is socially perceived as 'natural'.

What Bornstein (1994) referred to as 'natural' refers to socialised perceptions that gender is perceived as binary as 'a natural matter of fact', and any deviation from socialised perceptions of such are regarded as 'strange' (Garfinkel, 1967: 123–124). As Bornstein (1994) stated, 'it has little or nothing to do with vaginas. It's all penises or no penises' (p. 22). Therefore, perception of gender could equate to an absence of a penis to the defining characteristic of a female. Kessler and McKenna (1978) found that:

> ... the presence of a penis is, in and of itself, a powerful enough cue to elicit a gender attribution with almost complete (96 per cent) agreement. The presence of a vagina however does not have the same power. One third of the participants were able to ignore the reality of the vagina as a female cue.
>
> (p. 151)

Much like Bornstein (1994), Garfinkel (1967) and Kessler and McKenna (1978), all of the participants discussed possessing a penis as being a primary characteristic of 'maleness'. Prior to this research, I had expected a finding of this nature, but what I did not anticipate was that LGB participants held similar perceptions towards transmen as did heterosexual cisgender males. As Stuart, a British constable, stated, sharing views similar to those held by all of my gay cisgender participants:

> ... don't get me wrong, I respect transmen. Hell, some of them are kinda hot, but they are not real men.

When I asked Stuart why transmen are 'not real men', he further stated:

> They don't have a penis; they were not born with one.... Just because someone says they are a man, doesn't make them a man. I mean ... I should be more supportive, but they are just one step above a butch woman.

Tim, a gay American officer, stated:

> Transmen, while some may look good, are not real men. They don't have a penis; you know ... that is why I would never date one. They don't have normal working male anatomy, you know?

Luke, another American officer, stated:

> I think it is all weird. I mean, I don't understand why gay men get dressed up as women and think they are women. I have heard stories about some men cutting their penis off and getting boob jobs ... just like transwomen will not be real women, transmen will not be real men.

Notably, all cisgender American male participants (regardless of their sexuality) disclosed difficulty in deciphering the difference between 'butch' lesbian identities and trans masculine identities. As Fred, whose statements aligned with other American cis-male participants, stated:

> Is there such a thing as a transman? I thought that was just a butch lesbian.

Here Fred, like all cisgender male participants, associates 'butch' lesbians with trans masculine identities. Levitt and Ippolito (2014) described this phenomenon as the 'transgender rubric (e.g. cross-dresser, transman, transwoman, butch lesbian)' (p. 1); those who challenge the social perceptions of gender are perceived as being similar, regardless of gender presentation. Fred's sentiments were echoed by others. As Thomas, an American officer, stated:

Do transmen have a penis? ... I mean, I just don't know.... How can you be a man if you don't have a penis? ... Seems to me that you are just a really butch woman if you don't have a penis.

Peter, a British constable, much like all of my participants, stated that unlike transmen, transwomen are perceived as gender mutilators:

What kind of guy cuts his penis off? Doesn't he know he will never be a real woman? I just don't get it. I don't have a problem with lesbians, but a man who cuts his penis off ... I just don't get.

Helen, a British constable, disclosed:

If you cut off your penis, you are abandoning your manhood ... but you are not a woman, a real one that is, and you definitely are not a man anymore.

Some constables stated that they had issues with understanding the difference between gay men and transwomen. Simon, a British constable, stated:

I don't think there is much difference between a gay man and a transsexual, because they are both biologically male and act feminine.

Like Simon, Peter, a British constable, stated:

I think transgender women are just like gay men. They just take it up another level.

While gay sexuality could be considered socially conflicting in respect to the social ideology of dichotomous gender roles, participants indicated that transgender identities are more commonly perceived as gender betrayers compared with LGB identities. Further, some American, English and Welsh officers disclosed a social repulsion towards trans feminine identities based on the perception that they alter their male genitalia, a gender taboo. So once again, like their American counterparts, English and Welsh constables disclosed that they perceive the possession of certain 'male' or 'female' genitalia as a defining characteristic of a person's gender, regardless of their gender identity. With the betrayal or, in this case, the physical altering, of genitalia assigned to an individual at birth, they are perceived as a gender traitor. Therefore, this threatens perceptions of heteronormativity and binary gender ideology. As a result of these categorisations, it is reasonable to conclude that there are consequences of these perceptions.

### Feminine gender categorisations: 'dykes or bikes'

Cis-female participants disclosed significant difficulties in expressing so-called 'femininity' on the job. All of these officers disclosed that women in general, or anything associated with femininity, were viewed more negatively within police culture. Ellen, an American lesbian, summed up what almost all female cisgender participants disclosed:

> You are either a dyke or a bike.... It is hard to be a woman in policing, let alone being a gay woman. Christ, I cannot imagine what it is like to be a transwoman.

Ellen, like other cisgender females, stated that the choice for women officers seems to be portraying yourself as either a masculine gay woman or a hyper feminine straight woman (potentially giving the impression of sexual promiscuity). As Ellen continued:

> I think straight women have to sleep around to prove that they are not gay to fellow officers. I know some women who hoe around to gain advancement, which is tragic.... If you sleep with the right person, you will not get a bad job assignment, but if you are a gay woman they will typically leave you on the streets longer or give you an assignment to SWAT if you are tough enough.

Helen, a British constable, stated:

> You have to be five times tougher and stronger to make it as a female cop. When you do, you also remind the blokes that you like men also, since most women in policing are perceived as being lesbian.

Ellen's and Helen's quotes were a very familiar theme in this research, persistent across American, English and Welsh participants. Consistent with Miller et al. (2003) 'out' lesbians disclosed that on the job they felt that masculinity is expected of them. Further, Corsianos (2009) and Miller et al. (2003) found that lesbians who display masculinity within policing perceive that it benefits them instead of being detrimental to them.

Martin and Jurik (2006) found that lesbians felt that they had to make extra efforts to prove themselves as competent officers, and sought social acceptance by separating themselves from 'typical' (heterosexual) female officers while proving that they are 'tough crime fighters' (p. 74). Vic, a heterosexual American female officer with 10 years' experience, stated:

> I made detective because I worked hard and fought. I didn't sleep around like the other straight women around here. I hear the quote all the time: 'You are either a dyke or a bike'. But I am neither, which is rare in policing. I can be a tough woman and a good cop despite who I sleep with.

This finding is similar to previous research on gender typologies within police culture (see Berg and Budnick, 1986; Brewer, 1991). Anthony (1991) stated that there is a double-edged sword in policing where women are demanded to be masculine, while at the same time, female officers who display equal prowess are trapped 'safely in the pigeon hole of lesbianism' (p. 4). Gender typologies within police culture tend to be similar and consist of two types of perceptions of policewomen: those mentioned in this common quote (called 'pseudo-masculine' by Berg and Budnick, and 'Amazons' by Brewer); and policewomen who are viewed as traditionally feminine (called 'feminine' by Berg and Budnick, and 'Hippolyte' by Brewer). Heidensohn (1992), interestingly enough, did not use any typology, but instead referenced a policewoman's quote when she was describing how she was perceived by male colleagues:

> There are two stereotypes for women; the hooker and the dyke. There is no good stereotype for women and both are sexual.
>
> (p. 140)

Based on the responses of my participants, either being hyper feminine (e.g. sexually promiscuous) or being a masculine gay woman, is a defining binary characteristic of police 'femaleness'. Tragically, despite social advances towards gender equality and the progress of time between previous studies, the perception of female police identities as 'dyke or bike' still holds true today according to cisgender participants.

## Consequences of perceptions

### Gay and transgender hard targeting: bias patrolling of LGBT+ identities

This section examines general perceptions that heterosexual cisgender participants disclosed about collective LGBT+ identities. By examining how straight cisgender individuals perceive LGBT+ identities outside policing, conceptually we can better understand attitudes towards acceptance and how they can translate into occupational acceptance of transgender police identities. Previous research on police perceptions of LGB identities has focused on shared perceptions within the workplace (Colvin, 2009). Therefore, shared perceptions build on the notion that individuals' perceptions are often communicated to other people both inside and outside of the organisation (Colvin, 2009). Therefore, an individual's perceptions are also shared and influenced by an individual's membership in specific groups (Bolton, 2003).

Perceptions of the workplace have been considered for different researched groups, for example Black officers (Bolton, 2003; Essed, 1991; Leinen, 1984), Black and Asian female officers (Holder et al., 1999) and Latino officers (McCluskey, 2004). Therefore, individual perceptions may impact cohesive group perceptions in monolithic police environments (Colvin, 2009). Further, if perceptions towards the LGBT+ community are shared, it can have a dramatic effect on the culture, mission, operations and productivity of an organisation (Colvin, 2009). This 'dramatic effect' that Colvin (2009) discussed was noticeable when participants discussed the concept of LGBT+ hard targeting.

Officers on patrol or those assigned to specific units have the freedom to choose who, what and when they wish to engage in proactive enforcement. In policing circles, this is called 'selective enforcement' (i.e. 'hard targeting'). Hard targeting often occurs within policing because policing itself relies heavily on discretion. If police have a specific bias towards certain groups of people, they have the freedom to target them for discretionary enforcement (Buist and Lenning, 2015). Contact between LGBT+ individuals and police is often dictated by a need to enforce what is perceived as 'normative' sexual behaviour. Hard targeting can occur when enforcing public sex offences, while dismissing heterosexual public sex offences or through illegal stops of LGBT+ identities (Stotzer, 2014). Hard targeting also involves the frequent police raids of gay bars and establishments (see Chauncey, 1994; Loughery, 1998) to enforce public order violations while not targeting non-LGBT+ communities for similar violations. In respect to transgender identities, Greenberg (2012) found that trans identities viewed selective enforcement not as means to prevent crime, instead it is used as a means to assess one's sex, or as Greenberg (2012) called it, 'gender checks'. Dwyer (2011) indicated that police often try to assess sexuality based on ideology constructs of masculinity, femininity and gender performance. Often transgender, specifically trans feminine identities, are assumed to be engaging in acts of prostitution by some members of the policing community due to reports of being disproportionately targeted for prostitution for 'walking while trans' (see Bailey-Kloch et al., 2015; Daley et al., 2000; Edelman, 2014; Wurth et al., 2013). Notably, this concept of hard targeting can lead to allegations of bias and discrimination towards the LGBT+ community, and more specifically, the transgender community (see Dwyer, 2011).

Similar to previous research, American heterosexual cisgender participants disclosed that they had mixed feelings over patrolling members of the LGBT+ population. Most officers disclosed that they have observed the gay and trans feminine community being specifically aggressively targeted by fellow colleagues because they are LGBT+, as Thomas, an American officer, said:

> Everyone has seen someone do it; now I haven't, but I know other officers who do.

Robert, an American officer, stated:

> Gay and transsexual people are often targeted by officers because they engage in certain public acts at night. If you do things in public, like the gay and trans people do, then you are much more likely to be targeted.

Robert, like others, disclosed that they perceived gay sexualities and trans identities as more likely to violate public sex laws, and that is why they are heavily targeted by the police. As Thomas stated:

> I know in (region omitted to protect anonymity) they target them because they hook up in their cars. It is not the best idea to do that with kids around, so those guys enforce and look for them.

Jason, an American officer, stated:

> It is pretty well known that gay and transgendered people go to public parks to have sex. Here in (a major city) it still goes on. You don't want kids to see that stuff.... They use the internet to post where they are meeting up and then they have random sex in public. I know not all gay and transgendered people sleep around like that, but I believe a majority do.

Like their American counterparts, some English and Welsh heterosexual cisgender participants also revealed that they still engage in hard targeting of LGBT+ identities while on patrol. Tony, a British constable, stated:

> Gay men are somewhat promiscuous and you have to patrol those areas more ... where they have public sex or at the bars. And most transwomen you see walking around are also prostitutes.

Tony further disclosed a story from when he previously worked for the London Met patrolling areas frequented by gay and transgender individuals. Tony further stated:

> There was a big issue with underreporting of male rape going on in London in general ... so there was a big drive towards going to the communities and exposing that so we could find out the true extent of what was going on. But there was also an issue with a lot of gay sort of ... um ... sections of the community that was raping straight males, so there was that type of competing imbalance going on.... Because of that, I still feel obligated to patrol those areas.

Here Tony believed that LGBT+ targeting within London[8] was conducted to protect straight victims from sexual assault committed by gay suspects. Burke (1993) in *Coming out of the Blue* mentioned this briefly when he examined how LGB constables negotiate police culture while being taxed with patrolling cottaging areas. Notably, Scarce (2001) contends that the fears typically associated with gay-on-straight rape are greatly exaggerated within society. Tony, who is now working with a different constabulary in the U.K., Tony went on to say:

There is a lot of male activity and transsexual activity, which I deem as quite seedy. Because instead of being like you know with a normal partner … there were a lot of extreme levels of public … um … sexual activities going on with males and people dressing up as females.

Tony further stated that he felt compelled in the past to use more proactive enforcement of areas frequently used by members of the gay and trans feminine community:

I think men look at the homosexual side of males differently because they have sex between males…. The same goes for transsexuals. For me that is repulsive. I can't see why those sections of the gay and transgender community go into toilets and cottage. I can't see going into parks where kids play and give each other blow jobs or have intercourse. I don't understand that.

Here, Tony is comparing gay and transgender sex and seeing them as similar in nature, and to him it is 'repulsive'. Tony's feeling of 'repulsion' could be explained by previous studies of other self-confessed 'homophobic' individuals.

Adams et al. (1996) found that self-confessed 'homophobic' individuals might claim that gay sex acts were repulsive, but that such claims proved not to be consistent with their physiological reactivity. Adams and colleagues exposed 'homophobic' participants to sexually explicit erotic stimuli of heterosexual and LGB videotapes while they were wearing a mercury-in-rubber (MIR) circumferential strain gauge.[9] They found that 'homophobic' men showed an increase in penile erection to male homosexual stimuli, unlike their 'non-homophobic' counterparts. They theorised that 'homophobic' individuals perceive gay sex as repulsive because it is a threat to their own homosexual impulses, causing repression, denial or reaction formation.[10] Notably, towards the end of our 3-hour interview, Tony stated:

Gay men fancied me … I questioned myself as to whether or not … you know … if perhaps I was gay myself.

Tony went on to tell me how he targeted public toilets at night to arrest gay and trans feminine individuals:

I would go up there and they wouldn't stop. I literally had to pull them apart. There is nothing worse than one bloke with his ass and another being semi-erect having his trousers around his ankles and the other bloke cross-dressing and looking at me, like, 'What the fuck are you gonna do about me?' I would just pull them apart and lock them up.

I asked Tony why he previously targeted the areas where he knew 'cottaging' activities took place since he found gay men and trans feminine identities 'sick', 'seedy' and 'disgusting', and he stated that he felt obligated to enforce public indecency laws and to prove to colleagues that he wasn't gay himself. Tony further stated that witnessing and enforcing these incidents of public indecency affected his perception of gay and trans communities which led to resentment. When I asked Tony why he believed he was, as he described it, 'homophobic', he stated that it was not police culture that made him feel that way; instead it was due to his previous negative encounters with members of the gay and trans communities while on patrol.

Despite Tony's personal opinions on why members of the gay and trans feminine communities are specifically targeted by the police, some constables also disclosed that gay and transgender targeting is still commonplace, and in the past it was a constabulary policy in some forces. As Peter, a firearms commander, stated:

> For example, five years ago one of our policies, it was horrendous, was to target toilets used by gay males and transgender individuals and try to go catch them potentially having sex in the toilets. Some constables still target them despite the changes in our policies.

Further, Peter stated that his constabulary had an issue with a prostitution 'cruise house', and his force recently started using the same type of enforcement practice in areas frequented by gay and trans feminine individuals. Peter stated that his constabulary enforces lewd behaviour crimes by 'policing them from the outside'. As Peter stated:

> If we got any issues in those areas we use CCTV and have appropriate cars that deal with LGBT+ people, because we don't want to be offensive.... It is the same for prostitutes as well.

Peter's comparison of LGBT+ public sex activities with prostitution was not unique. Several participants disclosed that their encounters with the gay and trans community were often associated with prostitution offences. As Fred, an American participant, stated:

> Most, if not all the, transwomen I see on patrols are prostitutes ... and if you see a gay man standing by himself on the corner, he is probably a prostitute too.

This finding is consistent with previous research (see Grant et al., 2011; Lombardi et al., 2001; Stotzer, 2014; Xavier, 2000),[11] as participants disclosed that LGBT+ identities are more likely to engage in acts of prostitution than heterosexual identities.

Interestingly, a New Zealand study indicated that police have learned to read visible bodily cues identifying a body as LGBT (Praat and Tuffin, 1996), and thus they target them. Police ($n=8$) stated that they read gay male bodies as 'effeminate' in terms of 'an effeminate way of speaking, an effeminate way of walking and standing (swinging the hips and bending the wrist)' (Praat and Tuffin, 1996: 61), and closely aligned these bodies with sexual deviance (sadism and masochism, paedophilia, promiscuity). Several police also disclosed similar comparisons. Simon summed up other British constables' statements:

> Gay men and transvestites typically engage in more obvious acts of prostitution. It is well known that most transvestites and transsexuals you see on the street are prostitutes.... It is easy to spot a transgender because they stand out.... When it comes to gay men you can tell by the way they move or talk sometimes ... you know ... kind of feminine acting.

Previous research on heterosexual officer attitudes indicates that bias exists within policing towards LGB individuals (Bernstein and Kostelac, 2002; Bernstein and Swartwout, 2012; Buhrke, 1996; Burke, 1993, 1994a, 1994b; Colvin, 2009, 2012; Jones and Williams, 2013; Leinen, 1993; Lyons et al., 2008; Miller et al., 2003). Yet, some participants indicated that officers also target the transgender community alongside the LGB community.

### Changing perspectives: after-effects of working with trans cops

A majority of my American participants stated that they have never worked with transgender officers; however, two currently disclosed that they work alongside a transgender colleague. Richard, an officer from the West with ten years of police experience, stated that transgender officers are accepted within his department because there are two with his agency alone. Richard stated:

> No one bothers either one and takes them as seriously as they would other officers; it is pretty much a non-issue.

Although a very small sample, it was notable that officers, like Richard, who work closely with a trans-identified officer seemed to have a better understanding of trans identities and existence than those who did not. As John, an American officer, stated:

> We are more acquainted with their lifestyle, I suppose. People tend to reject and fear what they don't understand – we understand it.

As described in Richard's and John's interview quotes, a better understanding of transgender identities was attributed to direct interaction with a member of the transgender community, specifically with a fellow officer. This could be further explained by notions of Allport's (1954) intergroup contact theory.

Allport (1954) theorised that positive effects of intergroup contact occur in group situations where there is equal group status within the situation, common goals, intergroup cooperation and the support of authorities, law or custom. These positive effects change intergroup relationships through the changing of behaviour, by generating affective ties and through in-group reappraisal. In other words, by working alongside a transgender colleague, officers can generate affective ties. Therefore, a social group that was unfamiliar becomes more familiar. This social familiarity allows for a better understanding of social rights, thus making social acceptance easier, since the affected group is not deemed as a foreign concept anymore. Notably, familiarity does not remove bias; instead, it leads to more social familiarity, which over time can change a person's social perceptions. When looking at the culture of policing as a subgroup, much of the intergroup cohesiveness that makes up the solidarity culture that officers have towards each other could be connected to Allport's (1954) intergroup contact theory.

Previous research (see Eskilson, 1995; Herek and Capitanio, 1996) found that the intergroup contact theory is very applicable to surrounding members of the non-policing LGB community, but there has only been one examination of whether the theory applies to transgender individuals (Walch et al., 2012). As such, this theory has been consistent across other subgroups (see Anderson, 1995; Drew, 1988; Pettigrew, 1998; Smith, 1994) and is also relevant within the context of police culture. Further, the intergroup contact theory has been supported with diverse research methods yielding supportive results in the field (Meer and Freedman, 1966; Ohm, 1988), archive (Fine, 1979), survey (Jackman and Crane, 1986; Pettigrew, 1997a, 1997b; Robinson, 1980; Sigelman and Welch, 1993) and laboratory (Cook, 1978, 1984; Desforges et al., 1991).

Belkin and McNichol (2001), Miller et al. (2003) and Meyers et al. (2004) contributed valuable research on the inclusion of lesbian and gay identities within law enforcement, which could be connected to intergroup contact theory. Further, research on the attitudes and beliefs of heterosexual officers about LGB counterparts continues to grow (Bernstein and Kostelac, 2002; Lyon et al., 2008). Lewis (2003) stated that attitudes and beliefs about LGB individuals suggest that familiarity with LGB individuals is highly correlated with positive perceptions. In other words, a social connection to an LGB person reduces stigmas held against them. Yet there exists minimal research on heterosexual cisgender perspectives of transgender individuals, and no research on their perspectives within policing.

Just like their American counterparts, most English and Welsh constables who disclosed that they worked alongside a transgender colleague stated that they had a better understanding of transgender identities than those who did not. Simon stated:

> Honestly, I didn't understand much about transgender identities until I worked with (constable name omitted), which is pretty sad because I am a

gay man. Once I worked with her, and the more time I spent with her, the more I understood it. They face much different obstacles than we do, you know?

Simon was not the only British constable to disclose that he had learned more about transgender identities because he worked alongside one. Tony, who worked alongside the first transgender constable on his force, stated:

> Because I spent more time with that constable, I was curious about why he feels the need to change genders. I realised that in his mind he felt that he has to wear women's underwear. Right, whatever his desire was he felt he needed to wear a bra. As a woman wears a bra, he felt he had to wear it too. And that is the way it is. There has to be a place along the line for some people to … like that particular officer to feel as his body is. If that bucks the system, so be it, but how do we accept that and move forward in the force? Because even to this day I do not know. But I have definitely become more aware of transgender identities because of my encounters around that particular officer. So, I think that is a good thing about how transgender identities are now existing within policing.

Notably, Tony, unlike my other American, English or Welsh participants who disclosed that they had worked with a transgender colleague in the past, admitted that he was 'homophobic in the past'. Tony, a British constable who supervised a trans employee, disclosed a story in which his colleagues didn't accept a transgender colleague. Tony stated he had to address a constable who was wearing women's underclothing prior to transitioning because other constables were making fun of and saying negative things directed towards the constable. Tony stated that he told the constable that he[12] could not wear women's underwear underneath his uniform as it was visible underneath the white patrol shirt. When confronted, the trans constable countered that 'female counterparts wear a white shirt to where you see a white bra underneath it'. Tony told the constable that he isn't a woman, but agreed with the constable's point and addressed the issue with his upper administration. During this time, Tony disclosed that other constables were addressing the trans constable with derogatory terms like 'he-she' and 'freak'. Tony further stated:

> I really felt sorry for this particular officer. Not because of what he decided to be but … or what he is … but because of the way he was treated by his peer group. And I didn't know how to deal with it myself, and I laughed at him when he told me because I thought he was winding me up.

Tony continued:

> He was basically a laughing stock. Right, he would wear ladies' thongs into work, right, there were a few issues surrounding it. He was quite feminine

in his approach; he would pluck his eyebrows, and do all the things that would be consistent with a gay man, or what a woman would do.... He took the openness element of I am allowed to be trans and cross-dressing at work, to the next level.

Yet, Tony, on a positive note, stated that currently he has become more 'understanding' of trans identities through working alongside a trans officer. Therefore, personalised socialisation with a fellow trans colleague could arguably lead to a better, as Tony described it, 'understanding' of transgender identities.

### Backlash of categorisations

English and Welsh constables, unlike American officers, disclosed that there was more perceived negative visibility of LGBT+ identities within constabularies. Notably, while most constables expressed civil rights support for LGBT+ identities, a few disclosed that they did not approve of how constabularies publicly display their support of the LGBT+ rights movement. While there appeared to be a higher level of LGBT+ acceptance compared with American counterparts, straight constables disclosed that they were supportive as long as it wasn't too visible to fellow colleagues. In fact, straight cisgender constables who participated in this research stated that the visible presence of LGBT+ identities within police culture can potentially lead to further social isolation, which reinforces the construction of out-group identification in respect to the social identity theory. As Peter stated:

> You know when we are flying PRIDE flags outside the station they are not taking, you know, when I saw that I felt insulted by it because it flew below our police flag. For me the flag and the emblem for the police represents that anyways ... it undermines the police service, I think.

Simon, much like Peter, stated:

> I am fine with it as long as it isn't too much in my face. If you are too out and proud then I don't think it reflects the force properly.... It is okay to be trans or gay, but just don't shove it down our throats, ya know?

When I explored Peter's, Simon's and other similar statements further, there appeared to be an inner conflict between accepting LGBT+ constables who participate in PRIDE events, and seeing this, through the public's eyes, as reflecting unprofessionalism in the police. As Tony stated:

> Why do we celebrate this? Ya, I accept that there are gay people out there ... yet I see all the comments on social media about how they (the public) perceive (constabulary name omitted) to be. Like one comment that summed

it up for me was that '(constabulary name) is bent'. So the perception of the community is then that the police officers with (constabulary name) are bent. It makes us look unprofessional.

English and Welsh interviewees versus American interviewees gave rise to more negative views about LGBT+ visibility within policing for two arguable reasons. First, there exists more English and Welsh legal protections for LGBT+ identities within employment than in U.S. institutions (Mogul *et al.*, 2011). For example, being LGBT+ in America is not a protected class and therefore you can lose your job for being so.[13] In contrast, in England and Wales, LGBT+ individuals may feel more comfortable engaging in more visible advocacy roles (i.e. flying a PRIDE flag and marching in PRIDE parades) because their job is protected. With increased visible advocacy roles, LGBT+ identities are made more apparent to those who previously might not have been exposed to them.

Second, new changes within employment rights can in turn create a ripple effect across political, sociological and cultural ideologies. With this ripple effect, public negative opinions can become highlighted or expressed. Often coined the 'mere exposure effect', mere exposure to something new leads to more liking for stimuli that are novel and neutral in connotation, yet repeated exposure of something that has a negative attitude associated to it will strengthen negative affective reactions (Crisp *et al.*, 2009). Unfortunately, this mere exposure effect backlash could arguably be applicable to current LGBT+ identities within policing. This has occurred because more LGBT+ identities are more noticeably visible within policing compared to 20 years ago. In other words, with familiarity breeds content. Notably, this is an area I wish to explore further in future studies, for confirmation.

Additionally, English and Welsh constables disclosed perceived occupational incidents of LGBT+ favouritism, which was not mentioned by their American counterparts. Within an occupational construct, this was disclosed to occur when LGBT+ individuals use a 'gay card' or 'trans card' to their advantage. This advantage results in perceived assumptions of positive discrimination within policing. As Peter, who best summed up statements from other constables, stated:

> Officers who are gay, lesbian and transgender, it would seem that promotion is there.... If you are not employing minority groups, you appear prejudiced.... It seems that if you are a member of that network you are more likely, you are more successful in any selection or progression ... I heard a sergeant say you are white, British, heterosexual male, you don't have a card to play.

Peter further explained that he feels that if a constable is up for promotion who is not LGBT+, they will not get the job. When I enquired about this type of police occupational discrimination and how it is permissible, Peter stated:

There are hidden stats that no one gets to see. I know the stats are there on the process. Everyone says it is equal, but we all got the ability, but if you have two ideal candidates, one may be a particular minority or network over one who is a white British male.

Peter further stated:

No one has the balls to say, you know what, I don't think the recruitment process – I don't think you gave an equal opportunity. I think you gave the job to him because he is gay or she is trans. No one will ever say that, because they will go, well here is evidence that he or she scored higher than you when they really didn't.

Interestingly enough, no English or Welsh cisgender female participants ($n=5$) shared the same observation of LGBT+ positive discrimination. I believe this could be explained by the social obstacles that cisgender females have to face throughout their life prior to their employment within policing (see Westmarland, 2001) and also from their treatment within policing due to integrated masculinity components within police culture. In other words, since cisgender females exist as a stigmatised minority within policing, they may be more occupationally sympathetic towards other stigmatised individuals.

## Chapter summary

To recap, the research question of this chapter was:

What are the perceptions of cisgender officers towards transgender officers, and what are the consequences of these perceptions?

This question was answered by examining the way participants categorise heteronormativity and gender role ideologies while examining the consequences of these categorisations. Data indicated that heteronormative perceptions of masculinity influence perceptions of gender role ideology. Further, sexual minorities are perceived as threatening traditional gender role beliefs, much like those who exist outside gender binaries (i.e. transgender individuals). Participants disclosed that monolithic masculinity within policing impacts perceptions of gender and how gender is performed. Those who do not conform or perform 'conventional' gender within policing are more prone to experience social rejection within police culture in the form of heterosexism and genderism. Due to socialised perceptions of gender roles, those who deviate from these roles are more prone to be susceptible to cisgender anti-LGBT+ prejudice.

Data suggested that police perceptions of masculinity and femininity influence how gender and sexuality are perceived, and reveal how it is socially situated. It was theorised that police, who are both shaped by and continue to shape a highly masculine occupational subculture, view those who present themselves as masculine are more socially acceptable than deemed feminine identities (i.e. cisgender women, gay, and trans feminine identities). American, English and Welsh[14] police disclosed that there are different levels of social acceptance and perceptions of occupational performance between gay men, lesbians, trans feminine identities and trans masculine identities. For example, officers who are perceived as challenging social expectations of 'maleness' (i.e. transwomen) were more likely to be socially rejected within policing compared with officers who were perceived as challenging 'femaleness' (i.e. masculine and/or lesbian women).

Contributing to previous research, this chapter has highlighted that cisgender participants perceive masculinity as an important resource and commodity within police work. Masculinity increases the likelihood of acceptance, which may allow some masculine women the opportunity to overcome concepts of 'differential policing', as described by Westmarland (2001). Consequently, participants disclosed that masculine lesbian women are considered to be more accepted within policing than gay men and transgender identities. Accordingly, this research uniquely revealed a higher level of social rejection of trans feminine identities specifically among American, English and Welsh officers. As theorised, this can be interpreted as indicative of a perceived threat to monolithic masculinity and gender ideologies within policing, which in turn could be seen as a disruption to a fundamental aspect of a police 'working personality' itself. Trans feminine identities offer an explicit challenge to police culture because they 'offend' or complicate monolithic perceptions of masculinity, reinforcing the social divide between in-group officers and out-group officers.

Cisgender heterosexual participants also disclosed that there is a sliding scale of female masculinity acceptance within policing. Beliefs about 'lesbian female masculinity' and 'gay male femininity' muddied the waters of how some officers perceived trans identities. For example, all of my participants felt that gay men and trans feminine identities were less masculine than lesbian and trans masculine identities, much like Connell's (1995) work on LGB identities. More feminine officers who are integrating into police culture will arguably face more social obstacles compared with officers deemed to be more masculine. Further, participants disclosed that their perception of 'maleness' was associated with genital constructs, such as the perception that there are two, and only two, opposite sexes, which are determined by one's genitals. It follows, then, that most transwomen will never be perceived as 'female' due to their lack of 'biological' vaginas, and most transmen will not be perceived as 'male' because they do not possess a 'biological' penis. This finding was consistent across all participants regardless of sexualities.

This chapter examined two major themes – cisgender perceptions of gender and sexuality, and the consequences of these perceptions for fellow colleagues and the workplace environment more generally – to better understand why biased behaviour exists within policing. This chapter theoretically contributed to existing literature by exploring how generating effective ties can lead to social acceptance for those who challenge normative masculinity. Therefore, this chapter confirmed: the applicability of Allport's (1954) intergroup contact theory to police cultures in respect to masculinity; and increased socialisation with those who challenge masculinity (i.e. gay and transfeminine identities) within police cultures may lead to advancements in some social acceptance. The following two empirical chapters examine transgender specific experiences within policing to appreciate the impact of these harmful perceptions on the functioning of the police workplace.

## Notes

1 This is explored in the following sections.
2 This is followed up in Chapters 7 and 8.
3 This is explored further in Chapters 6 and 7.
4 See Chapter 4.
5 The e-mail is a direct cut-and-paste of the e-mail that was sent to me on 26/06/2013. I have not altered the spelling, grammar or presentation.
6 Notably, terms like 'those people' can be indicative of a perception of hierarchy or social distance. In other words, often this phrase is used by those who have some degree of bias towards the group they are referring to.
7 Referring to Chapter 2, LGBT+ identities have been historically viewed as sexual deviants within policing. Further, often LGBT+ identities are associated with paedophilia despite empirical data indicating that they are the least likely to engage in paedophilia.
8 Tony was responsible for patrolling the area of Clapham Common. As Burke (1993) stated, this area historically has been a known area for gay male cruising and cottaging.
9 This is the same instrument used to measure sexual offenders' responses while in prison, and during their probation, to ensure they do not have a sexual arousal response to child pornography.
10 To quote one participant: 'Where there is smoke, there is fire'. Empirically, studies are currently also showing that some LGB identities (before coming out) engage in homophobic slurs to distract others from their own internal issues with their sexuality.
11 This was examined previously in American officers' responses in this section. Chapter 3 explores this at length, and it will be revisited in the conclusion of this chapter.
12 Tony addressed the constable as 'he'.
13 As of this writing, several 'religious freedom' laws have been passed in America, which allows individuals to legally discriminate and refuse to provide any type of service to those whose identity conflicts with their religious ideologies. It is anticipated that these state laws will be challenged in the Supreme Court, but until that time these laws feasibly allow for Christian and Muslim doctors to legally refuse to medical treat LGBT+ patients, business owners can legally refuse to serve LGBT+ patrons, private religious colleges can legally refuse LGBT+ students, etc. Further, several states in America are right to work states, in which you can be terminated without explanation unless it is due to a protected characteristic.
14 As discussed in detail in Chapter 5, the purpose of conducting a comparative piece between America, England and Wales was to determine if perceptions towards transgender identities within policing is monolithic. The reasons for choosing a comparison between America, England and Wales is because their police cultures are somewhat similar. The comparative differences and similarities will be further revisited in Chapter 9.

# References

Adams, H., Wright, L. and Lohr, B. 1996. Is homophobia associated with homosexual arousal? *Journal of Abnormal Psychology* 105(3), pp. 440–445.

Allport, G. 1954. *The nature of prejudice*. Reading, MA: Addison-Wesley.

Anderson, L. 1995. Outdoor adventure recreation and social integration: a social-psychological perspective. PhD thesis, University of Minnesota.

Anthony, R. 1991. Homosexuality in the police: an investigation of the requirement for the Metropolitan Police Service to include the words 'sexual orientation' in its statements of equal opportunities policy. MA thesis, University of Exeter.

Bailey-Kloch, M., Shdaimah, C. and Osteen, P. 2015. Finding the right fit: disparities between cisgender and transgender women arrested for prostitution in Baltimore. *Journal of Forensic Social Work* 5(1–3), pp. 82–97.

Barlow, D. and Barlow, M. 2000. *Policewomen in a multicultural society: an American story*. Prospect Heights, IL: Waveland.

Basow, S.A. and Johnson, K. 2000. Predictors of homophobia in female college students. *Sex Roles* 42(5–6), pp. 391–404.

Belkin, A. and McNichol, J. 2001. Pink and blue: outcomes associated with the integration of open gay and lesbian personnel in the San Diego Police Department. *Police Quarterly* 5(1), pp. 63–95.

Berg, B. and Budnick, K. 1986. Defeminisation of women in law enforcement: a new twist in the traditional police personality. *Journal of Police Science and Administration* 14(4), pp. 314–319.

Bernstein, M. and Kostelac, C. 2002. Lavender and blue: attitudes about homosexuality and behavior towards lesbians and gay men among police officers. *Journal of Contemporary Criminal Justice* 18(3), pp. 302–328.

Bernstein, M. and Swartwout, P. 2012. Gay officers in their midst: heterosexual police employees' anticipation of the consequences for coworkers who come out. *Journal of Homosexuality* 59(8), pp. 1145–1166.

Bolton, K. 2003. Shared perceptions: black officers discuss continuing barriers in policing. *Policing: An International Journal of Policing Strategies & Management* 26, pp. 386–399.

Bornstein, K. 1994. *Gender outlaw: on men, woman and the rest of us*. New York: Routledge.

Brewer, J. 1991. Hercules, Hippolyte and the Amazons – or policewomen in the RUC. *British Journal of Sociology* 42(2), pp. 231–247.

Brown, J. and Heidensohn, F. 2000. *Gender and policing: comparative perspectives*. Basingstoke: MacMillan Press.

Buhrke, R. 1996. *A matter of justice*. New York: Routledge.

Buist, C.L. and Lenning, E. 2015. *Queer criminology*, Vol. 13. London: Routledge.

Burke, M. 1993. *Coming out of the blue*. London: Continuum.

Burke, M. 1994a. Cop culture and homosexuality. *Police Journal* 65, pp. 30–39.

Burke, M. 1994b. Homosexuality as deviance: The case of the gay police officer. *British Journal of Criminology* 34, pp. 192–203.

Butler, J. 1990. *Gender trouble: feminism and the subversion of identity*. London: Routledge.

Chauncey, G. 1994. *Gay New York: gender, urban culture, and the making of the gay male world, 1890–1940*. New York: Basic Books.

Colvin, R. 2009. Shared perceptions among lesbian and gay police officers: barriers and opportunities in the law enforcement work environment. *Police Quarterly* 12(1), pp. 86–101.

Colvin, R. 2012. *Gay and lesbian cops: diversity and effective policing*. London: Lynne Rienner Publishers.

Connell, C. 2010. Doing, undoing, or redoing gender: learning from the workplace experiences of transpeople. *Gender and Society* 24(1), pp. 31–55.

Connell, R. 1987. *Gender & Power*. Berkeley, CA: University of California Press.

Connell, R. 1995. *Masculinities*. Berkeley, CA: Stanford University Press.

Cook, S. 1978. Interpersonal and attitudinal outcomes in cooperating interracial groups. *Journal of Research and Development in Education* 12, pp. 97–113.

Cook, S. 1984. Cooperative interaction in multiethnic contexts. In: Miller, N. and Brewer, M., eds. *Groups in contact: the psychology of desegregation*. Orlando, FL: Academic, pp. 291–302.

Corsianos, M. 2009. *Policing and gendered justice: examining the possibilities*. Toronto: University of Toronto Press.

Crisp, R., Hutter, R. and Young, B. 2009. When mere exposure leads to less liking: The incremental threat effect in intergroup contexts. *British Journal of Psychology* 100(1), pp. 133–149.

Daley, C., Kulger, E. and Hirshman, J. 2000. *Walking while transgender: Law enforcement harassment of San Francisco's transgender/transsexual community*. San Francisco, CA: Ella Baker Centre for Human Rights/TransAction.

Desforges, D., Lord, C., Ramsey, S., Mason, J., Van Leeuwen, M. 1991. Effects of structured cooperative contact on changing negative attitudes toward stigmatized social groups. *Journal of Personality & Social Psychology* 60, pp. 531–544.

Drew, B. 1988. Intergenerational contract in the workplace: an anthropological study of relationships in the secondary labor market. PhD thesis. Rutgers University of New Brunswick, NJ.

Dwyer, A. 2011. 'It's not like we're going to jump them': how transgressing heteronormativity shapes police interactions with LGBT young people. *Youth Justice* 11(3), pp. 203–220.

Edelman, E. 2014. Walking while transgender. Necropolitical regulations of trans feminine bodies of colour in the nation's capital. In Haritaworn, J., Kuntsman, A. and Posocco, S., eds. *Queer necropolitics*. Abingdon: Routledge, pp. 172–190.

Epstein, C. 1971. *Women's place*. Berkeley, CA: University of California Press.

Eskilson A. 1995. *Trends in homophobia and gender attitudes: 1987–1993*. Presented at the 90th Annual Meeting of the American Sociological Association, Washington DC.

Essed, P. 1991. *Understanding everyday racism: an interdisciplinary approach*. Newbury Park, CA: Sage.

Fielding, N. 1994. Cop canteen culture. In: Newburn, T. and Stanko, E., eds. *Just boys doing business? Men, masculinities and crime*. London: Routledge, pp. 46–62.

Fielding, N. and Fielding, J. 1992. Police attitudes to crime and punishment: certainties and dilemmas. *British Journal of Criminology* 31(1), pp. 39–53.

Fine, G. 1979. The Pinkston settlement: an historical and social psychological investigation of the contact hypothesis. *Phylon* 40, pp. 229–242.

Fiske, S. 1998. Sterotyping, prejudice, and discrimination. In: Gilbert, D, *et al.*, eds. *Handbook of Social Psychology*, 4th ed,, Vol. 2. New York: McGraw-Hill, pp. 357–411.

Fiske, S. 2002. What we know about bias and intergroup conflict, the problem of the century. *Current Directions in Psychological Science* 11, pp. 123–128.

Garcia, V. 2003. 'Difference' in the police department: women, policing and 'doing gender'. *Journal of Contemporary Criminal Justice* 19(3), pp. 330–344.

Garfinkel, H. 1967. *Studies in ethnomethodology*. Upper Saddle River, NJ: Pearson.

Grant, J., Mottet, L., Tanis, J., Harrison, J., Herman, J. and Keisling, M. 2011. Injustice at every turn: a report of the National Transgender Discrimination Survey. *National Center for Transgender Equality and National Gay and Lesbian Task Force* [Online]. Available at: www.thetaskforce.org/downloads/reports/reports/ntds_full.pdf [accessed: 7 November 2017].

Greenberg, K. 2012. Still hidden in the closet: Trans women and domestic violence. *Berkeley Journal of Gender, Law & Justice* 27, p. 198.

Heritage, J. 1984. *Garfinkel and ethnomethodology*. Cambridge: Policy Press.

Heidensohn, F. 1992. *Women in control? The role of women in law enforcement*. Oxford: Clarendon Press.

Herek, G. and Capitanio, J. 1996. Some of my best friends: intergroup contact, concealable stigma, and heterosexuals' attitudes toward gay men and lesbians. *Personality and Social Psychology Bulletin* 22, pp. 412–424.

Hill, D. and Willoughby, B. 2005. The development and validation of the Genderism and Transphobia Scale. *Sex Roles* 53(7/8), pp. 531–544.

Holder, K., Nee, C., Ellis, T. 1999. Triple jeopardy? Black and Asian women police officers' experiences of discrimination. *International Journal of Police Science & Management* 3(1), pp. 68–87.

Hunt, J. 1990. The logic of sexism among police. *Women and Criminal Justice* 1(2), pp. 3–30.

Jackman, M. and Crane, M. 1986. 'Some of my best friends are black …': interracial friendship and whites' racial attitudes. *Public Opinion Quarterly* 50, pp. 459–486.

Jones, M. and Williams, M. 2013. Twenty years on: Lesbian, gay and bisexual police officers' experiences of workplace discrimination in England and Wales. *Policing and Society: An International Journal of Research and Policy* 25(2), pp. 1–24.

Kappeler, V., Sluder, R. and Alpert, G. 1998. *Forces of deviance: understanding the dark side of policing*, 2nd edn. Prospect Heights, IL: Waveland Press.

Kessler, S. and McKenna, W. 1978. *Gender: an ethnomethodological approach*. Chicago, IL: University of Chicago Press.

Kessler, S. and McKenna, W. 2006. Toward a theory of gender. In: Stryker, S. and Whittle, S., eds. *The transgender studies reader*. New York: Routledge, pp. 165–182.

Leinen, S. 1993. *Gay cops*. New Brunswick, NJ: Rutgers University.

Leinen, S. 1984. *Black police, White society*. New York: New York University Press.

Levitt, H. and Ippolito, M. 2014. Being transgender: the experience of transgender identity development. *Journal of Homosexuality* 61(12), pp. 1727–1758.

Lewis, G. 2003. Black-white differences in attitudes towards homosexuality and gay rights. *Public Opinion Quarterly* 67, pp. 59–78.

Lombardi, E., Wilchins, R., Priesing, D. and Malouf, D. 2001. Gender violence: Transgender experiences with violence and discrimination. *Journal of Homosexuality* 42, pp. 89–101.

Loughery, J. 1998. *The other side of silence. Men's lives and gay identities: a twentieth century history*. New York: Henry Holt & Company.

Lyons, P., DeValve, M., Garner, R. 2008. Texas police chiefs' attitudes towards gay and lesbian police officers. *Police Quarterly* 11(1), pp. 102–117.

Martin, S. 1980. *Breaking and entering: policewomen on patrol.* Berkeley, CA: University of California Press.

Martin, S. and Jurik, N. 2006. *Doing justice, doing gender: woman in legal and criminal justice occupations*, 2nd edn. Thousand Oaks, CA: Sage.

McCluskey, C. 2004. Diversity in policing. *Journal of Ethnicity in Criminal Justice* 2(3), pp. 67–81.

Meer, B. and Freedman, E. 1966. The impact of Negro neighbors on white house owners. *Social Forces* 45, pp. 11–19.

Messerschmidt, J. 1996. Managing to kill: masculinities and the space shuttle Challenger explosion. In: Cheng, C., ed. *Masculinities in Organizations.* Thousand Oaks, CA: Sage, pp. 29–63.

Merlo, A. and Pollack, J. (1995).*Women, law and social control.* Boston, MA: Allyn & Bacon.

Miller, S., Forest, K. and Jurik, N. 2003. Diversity in blue: Lesbian and gay police officers in a masculine occupation. *Police Quarterly* 11(1), pp. 102–117.

Mogul, J., Ritchie, A.J. and Whitlock, K. 2011. *Queer (in)justice: the criminalization of LGBT people in the United States*, Vol. 5. Boston, MA: Beacon Press.

Meyers, K.A., Forest, K.B. and Miller, S.L. 2004. Officer friendly and the tough cop: Gays and lesbians navigate homophobia and policing. *Journal of Homosexuality* 47(1), pp. 17–37.

Ohm, R. 1988. Constructing and reconstructing social distance attitudes. PhD thesis, Arizona State University.

Pettigrew, T. 1997a. Generalized intergroup contact effects on prejudice. *Personality and Social Psychology Bulletin* 23, pp. 173–185.

Pettigrew, T. 1997b. The affective component of prejudice: empirical support for the new view. In: Tuch, S. and Martin, J., eds. *Racial attitudes in the 1990s: continuity and change.* Westport, CT: Praeger, pp. 76–90.

Pettigrew, T. 1998. Intergroup contact theory. *Annual Reviews in Psychology* 49, pp. 65–85.

Praat, A. and Tuffin, K. 1996. Police discourses of homosexual men in New Zealand. *Journal of Homosexuality* 31, pp. 57–73.

Robinson, J. 1980. Physical distance and racial attitudes: a further examination of the contact hypothesis. *Phylon* 41, pp. 325–332.

Scarce, M. 2001. *Male on male rape: the hidden toll of stigma and shame.* Cambridge, MA: Perseus Publishing.

Schilt, K. 2010. *Just one of the guys? Transgender men and the persistence of gender inequality.* Chicago, IL: University of Chicago Press.

Schulz, D. 1995. *From social worker to crimefighter: women in United States municipal policing.* Westport, CT: Praeger.

Schulz, D. 2004. Invisible no more: A social history of women in US policing. In Price, B. and Sokoloff, N., eds. *The criminal justice system of women: offenders, prisoners, victims, & workers*, 3rd edn. New York: McGraw-Hill, pp. 483–494.

Schippers, M. 2007. Recovering the feminine other: Masculinity, femininity, and gender hegemony. *Theory & Society* 36(1), pp. 85–102.

Sigelman, L. and Welch, S. 1993. The contact hypothesis revisited: black-white interaction and positive racial attitudes. *Social Forces* 71, pp. 781–795.

Smith, C. 1994. Back to the future: the intergroup contact hypothesis revisited. *Sociological Inquiry* 64, pp. 438–455.

Stotzer, R. 2014. Law enforcement and criminal justice personnel interactions with transgender people in the United States: A literature review. *Aggression and Violent Behavior* 19, 263–277.

Swank, E. and Raiz, L. 2010. Attitudes toward gays and lesbians among undergraduate social work students. *Affilia* 25(1), pp. 19–29.

Tajfel, H. and Turner, J.1979. An integrative theory of intergroup-conflict. In: Austin, W. and Worchel, S., eds. *The social psychology of intergroup relations.* Monterey, CA: Brooks/Cole, pp. 33–47.

Tebbe, E., Moradi B. 2012. Anti-transgender prejudice: A structural equation model of associated constructs. *Journal of Counseling Psychology* 59, 251–261.

Walch, S., Sinkkanen, K., Swain, E., Francisco, J., Breaux, C. and Sjoberg, M. 2012. Using intergroup contact theory to reduce stigma against transgender individuals: impact of a transgender speaker panel presentation. *Journal of Applied Social Psychology* 42(10), pp. 2583–2605.

West, C. and Zimmerman, D. 1987. Doing gender. *Gender and Society* 1, pp. 125–151.

Westmarland, M. 2001. *Gender and policing: sex, power and police culture.* New York: Willan Publishing.

Whitley, B. Jr. 2001. Gender role variables and attitudes toward homosexuality. *Sex Roles, 45,* 691–721.

Whittle, S. 2000. *The transgender debate: the crisis surrounding gender identity.* Reading: South Street Press.

Wurth, M., Schleifer, R., McLemore, M., Todrys, K. and Amon, J. 2013. Condoms as evidence of prostitution in the United States and the criminalization of sex work. *Journal of the International AIDS Society* 16(1).

Xavier, J. 2000. *The Washington DC Transgender Needs Assessment Survey, final report for phase two.* Washington DC: Administration for HIV/AIDS of the District of Columbia Government.

## Chapter 7

# 'We're the ugly child of the LGBT world'

## Trans police occupational experiences within police culture

This chapter is structured around the four major themes that emerged from my analysis of the interview data: (1) visual gender cues and trans status disclosure; (2) genderqueer identities within policing; (3) perceptions of masculinity/femininity and 'purging' transgenderism tendencies; and (4) transgender cultural subdivisions within policing. The first theme, trans status disclosure, examines how some transgender police choose or are forced to 'come out of the closet' or remain hidden. The second theme examines genderqueer identities within policing and trans perspectives towards genderqueer identities. The third theme, perceptions of masculinity/femininity and 'purging' transgenderism tendencies, examines why trans feminine individuals are more likely to be drawn to policing as a profession.[1] The fourth theme, transgender subdivisions, focuses on my observation of a new phenomenon I have labelled as the inter-trans feminine hierarchy.[2] I have provided a theoretical analysis of this hierarchy, which involves different levels of social acceptance of different trans feminine identities within police culture.

Aimed at advancing existing literature on transgender decisions of whether to 'come out of the closet' or 'hide in the closet', this chapter specifically examines the issues that transgender police face when choosing to openly transition within police cultures. While previous research has scantly examined the occupational ramifications for coming out as transgender within work cultures, this research uniquely contributes by examining the specific ramifications for doing so within police cultures. As such, this chapter refers to the theoretical underscoring which was highlighted in Chapters 2 and 3 which examined the performance of gender. Additionally, this chapter contributes to existing literature by examining genderqueer identities within police culture and how they challenge current Butlerian theories of gender performance.[3] By conceptualising how those, who do not adhere to binaried expectations of gender, negotiate a masculine environment where 'maleness' is embraced and 'femaleness' is viewed as undesirable (see Chapter 6), this chapter highlights how rigid gendered binaries exist within police cultures.

Besides examining why some transgender identities enter a known binary gendered hostile work environment, this chapter also contributes to a better understanding of how social rejection exists within trans feminine police cultures on a micro-level. This contributing theory, labelled the *inter trans feminine hierarchy concept*, describes how within trans feminine police cultures[4] there exists conflicting micro-relationships. In other words, within this trans feminine police culture, there exists social exclusion and isolation towards other transgender identities due to the rigid enforcement of gendered binaries. It is theorised that this occurs because trans feminine identities in policing exist in an environment where gendered differences are magnified, thus some transgender expressions are more accepted than others.

For this study, five American transgender officers and nine English and Welsh transgender constables participated ($n = 14$). The participants' ages ranged from 26 years to 65 years. Tables 7.1 and 7.2 detail the American, English and Welsh police who participated in this research. Trans identification is how each participant freely classified themselves; I never asked any participant to identify their sexuality or gender identity.[5]

## Transgender visual cues and trans status disclosure

Criminology researchers, who have empirically neglected transgender identities, have theorised that lesbian and gay men in policing represent a threat to gendered characteristics of police work, which has an emphasis on physical strength,

*Table 7.1* American transgender officer participants

| Pseudonym | Policing tenure | Trans ID | Region |
| --- | --- | --- | --- |
| Dave | 18 years | FTM | Rural |
| Holly | 35 years | MTF | Urban |
| Jessie | 33 years | MTF | Urban |
| Liv | 19 years | MTF | Urban |
| Josie | 27 years | MTF | Urban |

*Table 7.2* English and Welsh transgender constable participants

| Pseudonym | Policing tenure | Trans ID | Region |
| --- | --- | --- | --- |
| Erin | 15 years | Genderqueer | Urban |
| Tom | 30 years | FTM | Urban |
| Sarah | 2 years | MTF | Urban |
| Amber | 7 years | MTF | Urban |
| Addison | 15 years | Genderqueer | Urban |
| Elizabeth | 8 years | MTF | Urban |
| Clair | 17 years | MTF | Urban |
| Ellie | 35 years | MTF | Urban |
| Gareth | 11 years | Transvestite | Urban |

mental strength, aggression and authority (see Burke, 1993, 1994; Leinen, 1993; Colvin, 2012; Rumens and Broomfield, 2012). Yet, the intersection between visual gender cues and transgender status of officers who have transitioned or are in the process of transitioning is relatively unknown within police culture. Notably, there are transgender police whose newly acquired gender is never questioned, and their LGBT+ status may never be known. Therefore, some transgender officers are often faced with the daunting decision of having to choose between disclosing their transition and not disclosing if they enter policing post-op.[6] For some, there are gradual visual indicators of a transition status before, during and after transition that make disclosure an involuntary process. As Liv, an American officer, put it:

> I think it is a lot easier to be the first LGB versus a T, because a T is a big difference for people. When you come out gay or lesbian, you don't really physically change anything; it doesn't impact on the people you work with per se, because they don't see you with your partner. But when you transition, they have to deal with it for a restroom issue, locker room issues, the pronoun issue, etc. They physically see you different.

Yet, most transgender police disclosed that some members of the transgender community have an easier time transitioning within policing because they do not possess certain visual cues of being transgender. As Clair, a British constable, stated:

> You can spot a pre-op trans woman easily, but for some post-op transwomen it is much more difficult, which is why pre-op women and cross-dressers have to put up with a lot. Transmen, on the other hand, pass easier than transwomen. They can grow a beard and gain muscles quickly because of the test.

'Pass' or 'passing' as participants described is similar to how Stone (1991: 296–297) defined it:

> The most critical thing a transsexual can do, the thing that constitutes success, is to 'pass'. Passing means to live successfully in the gender of choice, to be accepted as a 'natural' member of that gender. Passing means the denial of mixture. One and the same with passing is effacement of the prior gender role, or the construction of a plausible history....

As Tom, a British constable, stated:

> Because I am now bald, most people do not question if I am a man or woman because of the test. The only notable thing that people may question is my short height and my smaller hands, but there is nothing they can do about that.

As Clair's and Tom's statements illustrate, some post-op individuals may not possess the visual cues to identify them as trans, and thus their trans status may be unknown. But for others, there are certain visual cues that might identify someone as transgender post-transition to people who have knowledge of medical transitioning. Dave, an American officer, stated:

> You are not as easily recognised if you are a post-op transman versus a post-op transwoman, so you have the ability to hide within society. Some transmen might have the phalloplasty, in which they take forearm skin to create a penis. If they use that method, then you will always be able to see scars around a transman's forearm … but unless you know how to spot things like that, most cisgender people aren't going to 'out' you.

Visual signs such as the noticeable presence of a laryngeal prominence (commonly referred to as the Adam's apple), variations in height, variations in muscle structure and surgical scarring may be a visual indication of post-trans status; however, often cisgender individuals are unaware, or unobservant, of these slight physical variations. Often to overcome these slight variations trans individuals will have a chondrolaryngoplasty (commonly called 'tracheal shave') to remove the visible appearance of a laryngeal prominence, have hormone replacement therapy (HRT) to alter muscle structure, and/or cover up or tattoo the forearm areas where a phalloplasty scar may be located to avoid further visual attention to any trans stigmas. As Dave continued:

> I know a few guys who have the scars on their forearm from surgery, and because it is a big scar and very noticeable, some transmen will either wear a forearm athletic sleeve or get tattoos to cover it up. You are trying your best to just fit in and look normal; it makes sense to not draw any extra attention to an area that might let others know that you are trans.

All English and Welsh participants, except for one, disclosed that they had transitioned during police employment. As Ellie stated:

> You can't hide when you transition. Everyone can see the changes.

The visual cues of changing gender presentation may force transgender individuals to face coming out of the closet, but those who identify as a cross-dresser do not typically undergo visual bodily changes. Therefore, officers who identify as a cross-dresser can hide their identity from their co-workers, whereas those who undergo surgical or hormonal procedures cannot. As Holly, an American officer, stated:

> Cross-dressing is much more common in the cis-male population than most people think, particularly within policing. I know of several males who

have secretly told me that they are cross-dressers.... They can hide, unlike most of us.

Mirroring Holly and other officers' statements, Elizabeth, a British constable, stated:

> Cross-dressers can hide ... but MTFs can't. Because we transition or have transitioned, other employees who don't know can see the little things that suggest that someone is trans ... for MTFs it might be height, jawline, facial hair, etc. For FTMs it might be small hands, short height and the typical NHS forearm scar if they have had bottom surgery.

Here Elizabeth, like all the other MTF participants, is indicating that despite most transitions, there are or will be permanent visual indicators that someone is transgender. Yet, members of the cross-dressing community (who may or may not identify as trans)[7] do not possess visual indicators of trans status. This visual and social differentiation between cross-dressers and transsexuals will be revisited in this chapter.

### 'Hiding in the trans closet'

Some officers, who were employed post-op or post-transition, stated that they have chosen not to disclose their trans status as a means to protect themselves while working in policing. Holly, an American officer, explained that her first policing job resulted in an unwarranted termination pre-transition, because at the time she identified as a male cross-dresser and disclosed this to her agency. Holly then took time off from law enforcement after her termination:

> I took time off from policing, because initially I was assessing if I should stay in law enforcement since they don't want me. They basically felt that it was incumbent on them to weed the people out who were gay, lesbian or transgender. Basically I took the year off and decided, you know what, that they didn't need to know, and if I could find a department where they didn't ask or didn't care, I would try there, so I did.

After her transition, Holly re-entered policing without disclosing her trans status out of fear that she would be fired again. When I asked Holly why she didn't disclose her status to her new agency, she stated:

> Self-protect, self-preservation ... ya know ... trying to also live the life and protect my family.

Holly was not alone in feeling that she needed to hide her transition status. Jessie, another American officer, disclosed that when she entered police academy, she had a chin-length bob haircut and wore a 'male' short-haired wig on top of her feminine hairstyle. Jokingly, Jessie stated that the wig made her look like Donald Trump: 'I mean, I look back on it, and, I mean, what did they think?' Jessie further stated:

> I am not sure what they thought.... They had to know something was up when I was hired as a male ... I was so afraid to show everyone who I really was.

When discussing her transition in policing, Jessie, like other American trans officers, felt that they were torn between giving up a career they loved and being true to their inter-self:

> I mean, at that point, you know, I had two tensions. I really loved my job. I really loved policing and I also knew that, or I thought that, if I transitioned it meant that I would have to give that up.

Holly, Jessie and others chose to live in the closet and not disclose their trans status during different points of their police career. This is similar to Burke's (1993, 1994) research on lesbian and gay officers in respect to workplace disclosure.

Notably, transgender existence can be just as much of an invisible minority existence as being a closeted LGB individual. For example, they become a visible minority member once they disclose their transgender status post-op or when they begin the process of transitioning. Since there is some form of a social disclosure, or visual indicators that someone is transitioning, socially they shift from one perceived social status to another. As previously stated, this disclosure process is a very unique social phenomenon, as their social stigma moves from having an invisible stigma to having a visible stigma, and (for some) back to having an invisible stigma again, making some transsexual individuals a *social stigma chameleon* over time, per se.

### 'Coming out of the trans closet'

When examining post-op transgender identity development, foundational research on transgender identities outside of policing has documented the unique struggle that individuals' face when deciding to disclose their status (see Budge *et al.*, 2010; Devor, 2004; Gagné *et al.*, 1997; Levitt and Ippolito, 2014). These struggles manifest through different conflict stages of identity development (Devor, 2004). These stages, as described in psychological studies, include feelings of interpersonal discomfort, anxiety, confusion and exploration of identities which support variation in forms of gender presentation (e.g. lesbian or gay male identities) (Devor, 2004; Levitt and Ippolito, 2014). Additionally, these stages involve evaluation of how they perceive they will manage social stigmas and discrimination, how they will integrate into their new identities, and, for some, how they will engage in some form of advocacy (Levitt and Ippolito, 2014) when disclosing their identities to colleagues.

Besides evaluating repercussions for disclosing post-transition status, often the decision to disclose trans status to colleagues is influenced by internalised beliefs about gender roles and heterosexuality (Gedro, 2009). When choosing to disclose trans status, post-op police are often forced to make a decision that compromises their personal integrity, which can include maintaining a false heterosexual (or homosexual) identity or avoiding discussing issues surrounding sexuality, family or personal home life altogether, which is similar to gay sexuality disclosures (see Colvin, 2012). Notably, transgender disclosure is not expected nor anticipated in occupational environments, and the action of disclosure is reliant upon personal choice, much like disclosure of sexuality.

Creed and Scully (2000) described reasons for LGBT+ individuals to 'come out of the closet': claiming (owning the stigmatised identity as a matter of fact), educative (providing clarity or inviting questions) and advocacy (illuminating injustices or inequalities). Notably, these motivations are not mutually exclusive and can rely upon several different factors occurring independently or in tandem (Law *et al.*, 2011). For example, an officer may disclose because they want to be authentic (claiming), due to a need to address misconceptions of being transgender (educative), and/or because of a need to expand diversity policies to include protection for gender identity (advocacy) (Law *et al.*, 2011).

Of the police interviewed, most of the participants transitioned during their police employment, so they were hired pre-op. Therefore, those who were pre-transition were forced to disclose to their agencies that they were going to medically transition. In addition to medical leave reasons or for administrative paperwork reasons (i.e. name changes), officers disclosed that they felt a need to disclose to maintain their personal integrity, and they wanted to be honest with themselves, their colleagues and their supervisors. As Holly, an American officer, stated:

> I didn't want to lie to anyone ... I was being honest with myself and I didn't want to lose trust from others.

Here Holly is 'claiming' her transsexual status, much as Creed and Scully (2000) described. Dave, another American officer, stated:

> I wanted to be honest with everyone since I respect them.

Yet, some trans police took a more educative and advocacy stance on why they disclosed their transgender status pre-transition. Sarah, a British constable, best summed up what others stated:

> I kept the same patch from when I was a male officer because I hold the perception that the only way members of the public, other police officers, etc.

will get used to it is if they see it and get educated. And it will be difficult for me, but if anyone should follow in my footsteps in the future ... in a few years' time ... maybe those trailblazing direct ideas will make it easier for them. Now ... I have faced some discriminatory and trans prejudice things within society and within the force itself.

Sarah, like others, owns her desire to create visibility for trans individuals within policing as a means to actively affirm her identity for other potential closeted trans officers and towards the citizens in the community she patrols. As Stone (1991) and Stryker (1994) argued, the necessity of 'coming out' to gain recognition of transsexual subjectivity can be interpreted as empowering. To frame this in reference to Creed and Scully (2000), Sarah feels that she is fulfilling an advocacy role by letting others know that she is trans and that she has transitioned. By doing so, she believes she is standing up for transgender identities within the community and within policing while educating others. This is similar, in some aspects, to Humphrey's (1999) and Clair et al.'s (2005) findings of motivations for sexuality disclosure in LGB individuals. With further reference to Creed and Scully (2000), Holly and Sarah's disclosure was based on wanting to own their transgender status and to be authentic; they wanted to claim their transgender status to those they work with.

Yet for some transgender police, the ability to come out of the closet on their own terms is denied. As Ellie, a British constable, stated:

You can't hide when you transition. Everyone can see the changes.... You are forced out without the luxury of having the option of choosing to come out on your own terms.

Holly, an American officer, stated:

We live in a society where gendered looks define you. Gay and lesbians and cross-dressers can hide if they want to ... for most of us it is impossible, so you are forced out.

Amber, a British constable, stated:

I envy the LGB community. I know they have it rough ... but when you are transitioning, it is like you have a big neon sign above your head that you are transitioning.... The gay community can come out on their own terms.

Clair, another Brit constable, stated:

The visual changes during transition is the most difficult part of being trans. Everyone can see that you are transitioning and you can't hide it.... It is a long gradual process.

Dave, an American officer, further explained how visual this 'long gradual process' is during transition:

> In a perfect world, changing genders would be like a light-switch and no one would know at work … but unfortunately medical technology isn't there. It becomes much easier to hide within society once you fully transition.… The visual signs aren't there as much, if at all.

As participants indicated, the visual cues of changing gender presentation, force most transgender individuals to involuntarily face coming out of the closet. Revisiting Chapter 1, there is a difference between the visual cues of transitioning and being a cross-dresser. Gareth disclosed that transvestites, unlike other transgender identities, possess the ability both to hide in the closet and to be forcefully 'outed'. Gareth stated he was 'outed' to some colleagues when an ex-girlfriend told them about his transvestite behaviour. Gareth stated that once his colleagues found out, he started getting bullied at work:

> On one occasion I got my locker broken into and they changed some of my kit for girls' kit, you know like my hat and stuff like that. Someone also graffitied the back of my car with 'gender bender' written on the back of it while it was parked in the police secure car park.… Another time, when I lost a pair of glasses, someone said they found my glasses and I've put them in your drawer, and when I got back to my drawer they were obviously girls' glasses … I approached HR and they told me they couldn't help me out until I filed an official report. Bearing in mind to make the official report at that time, I still wasn't prepared to go public with all of this, I just wanted it to remain under the radar, but if you go public with something like this, everyone finds out.

Gareth, who was trying to keep his transvestite status in the closet, was forcefully 'outed' to other members of his force when he eventually made a complaint; and in response his police supervisors transferred him to a different divisional area while the investigation was pending. Gareth stated that his experience was 'awful', and he eventually felt forced to come out to his family and friends after being forced out of the closet by his force. Gareth was eventually referred by his supervisors to the welfare unit and was sent to cognitive behavioural therapy due to 'his cross-dressing'.[8] His transvestite status led to a huge breakdown in Gareth's confidentiality, as he never had engaged in any form of transvestitism while at work. Gareth perceived that his transgender status would never be revealed at work, but as soon as he was forced to expose himself, he became a very visible member of the transgender community within his constabulary.

## Issues with 'coming out of the trans closet'

All transgender participants disclosed that despite their positive motivations for voluntary disclosure, 'coming out of the closet' resulted in traumatic experiences and impacted their long-term career outcomes. As Addison, a British constable, stated:

> Once I came out, the job became horrible. I was harassed and I believed it impacted my chances for promotion.

Dave, an American officer, stated:

> You think the hard part is coming out, but it isn't.... The hard part is the consequences of coming out. It hasn't impacted me career wise as much ... but I have had my fair share of putting up with bad stuff.

Like Addison, Dave and others, Liv, an American officer, stated:

> Once you come out it confirms what others think ... then you have to face the bullying and harassment.

This is similar to Davis (2009), who found that once a transgender person comes out at work, they face harsh reactions from fellow non-police colleagues. These negative and harsh reactions will be revisited in this chapter and throughout the following chapter.

Collectively, trans officers reported issues with work socialisation and exclusion to the point that some felt isolated in their work environment. Erin, a British constable, who came out as a lesbian officer first before they identified as genderqueer, described the conflict of coming out as genderqueer after a medical diagnosis of gender identity disorder:[9]

> At that point I had to disclose to the line manager at work ... which because of my previous experience and how um ... my sexuality ... I felt it would be used against me ... I thought, great, I survived being a gay woman, now I am going to come across as someone who is genderqueer, which most people don't understand.... So I am going to be very careful about this and very cautious about who I tell ... which led me probably to be a little bit isolated on my team.

Notably, most participants expressed aversion to the medical diagnosis of gender identity disorder when disclosing trans status at work. Like others, Jessie, an American officer, mirrored Ellie's statement:

> Being diagnosed with a disorder can impact your career in policing.... You have seen it and everyone knows it.... They will take your gun away

because you have a condition or you are crazy.... Being trans shouldn't be a disorder.... You feel isolated.

Ellie, a British constable, stated:

When you get diagnosed with a mental disorder it carries a stigma. Most transsexuals hate that they are diagnosed with a mental disorder in order to transition. It takes away the normality of having a trans identity.

As discussed in Chapter 1, historically to transition between genders a medical diagnosis of gender identity disorder has been required. And if someone identifies as genderqueer, a medical diagnosis is needed should they request any medical treatment. Yet, as Ellie illustrates, there is a stigmatisation of the diagnosis that signifies that there is something wrong with them – that they are outside societal gender binary norms and thus must be medically diagnosed as having a mental disorder. Shelley (2009) states: 'clinical discourses and diagnostic criteria actually reflect in a negative sense, the social injustices that trans people face' (p. 387). GID-related diagnostic criteria include 'discomfort about one's assigned sex' and the 'wish to rid one's natal sex characteristics' (Cohen-Kettenis and Pfafflin, 2009: 7) among other symptoms that pathologised all gender non-conformity behaviour as a one-dimensional disorder. Further, the use of the term 'disorder' could further stigmatise gender non-conforming individuals as abnormal because they identify outside the social gender binary.

## Not 'doing gender': genderqueer police identities

Revisiting Chapter 1, genderqueer identities do not adhere to binary categories of gender, identifying neither as 'male' nor as 'female'. As research indicates, those who outwardly challenge social constructions of binary gender within hypermasculine environments often face more social resistance than more binary identified individuals (Budge *et al.*, 2010; Law *et al.*, 2011). Theoretical approaches discussed by West and Zimmerman (1987) and Butler (1990) can be used to better understand how some transgender officers 'do gender' and 'perform gender' in their respective social environments.[10] As discussed in Chapter 3, in their theory of 'doing gender', West and Zimmerman (1987) argued that gender is a social process that is constantly negotiated versus something that is innate to men or women (Schilt and Connell, 2007).

West and Zimmerman (1987) constructed their theory to account for the reproduction of gender through social interaction. They illustrated how in Garfinkel's (1967) case study, 'Agnes', a transwoman who was assigned male at birth, learned to do femininity in the everyday social production of gender. They further stated: 'participants in interaction organize their various and manifold activities to reflect or express gender, and they are disposed to perceive the behaviour of others in similar light' (West and Zimmerman 1987: 4). Society holds everyone accountable for gendered expectations, and thus gender inequality is socially constructed and maintained in certain environments. Men continue to do dominance while women exercise deference (Schilt and Connell, 2007). Besides positioning masculinity and femininity as strict binary opposites, in hypermasculine environments, this social expectation of gender becomes super-heightened.

West and Zimmerman's (1987) concept of 'doing gender' emerged within hegemonic theoretical frameworks and is frequently used to explore gender inequality, yet feminist scholars are beginning to question whether the theory's ability can account for social change (Connell, 2010). Notably, West and Zimmerman's theory of 'doing gender' shares components of Butler's theory of 'performing gender' in *Gender Trouble* (1990), which was explored at length in Chapter 2. Butler, unlike West and Zimmerman, draws on psychoanalytic theories rather than sociological theories of symbolic interaction to frame her arguments (Schilt and Connell, 2007). Both theories state that there are expectations in terms of social norms and view gender as an overarching system that restricts gender expressions for men and women at the same time as it provides structure for a 'liveable life' (Butler, 2004: 8).

As discussed in Chapter 3, a main issue with previous gender theories is that they are too binary constrictive and do not explore those who are genderqueer. Genderqueer individuals within policing do not feel the need to adhere to socially constructed expectations of gender, in line with Harrison *et al.*'s (2012) findings. While genderqueer individuals may be perceived as 'alternative' femininities and masculinities, as Schilt and Connell (2007: 597) describe them, there are no theories as to how genderqueer individuals identify as outside gendered binaries. Genderqueer individuals devalue theoretical social perceptions of masculinity and femininity by existing as gender outliers, as individuals who identify as neither. Stone (1991) hints at this when stating that trans identities 'currently occupy a position which is nowhere, which is outside the binary oppositions of gendered discourse' (p. 295).

Holly stated that there was a trend of workplace hiring discrimination against individuals who, as she described it, do not fit into 'a linear kind of gender identification'. Holly, an American officer, additionally stated:

> People who are pre-hire candidates coming into it are generally going to meet some resistance not meeting gender stereotypes from agencies or from the background investigators regardless if they have a qualified and viable candidate will get rid of the candidate for other reasons if they are talking about not meeting a gender stereotype male or female. A lot of college graduates will identify as genderqueer, but most of them have not made it into a hiring process. It is bothersome for me, because I do not think it should matter one way or another, but I also feel that their expectations of being genderqueer and identifying that way and that it shouldn't affect them … I am not saying it should, I am saying it does.

Josie, another American officer, stated:

> No one can say for sure, but I have never heard of an agency hiring someone who identifies as genderqueer prior to employment ... I think in police culture more people are trying to be macho or assert their femininity ... there is no account for what's in-between.

Empirical research has already shown that employers have preconceptions as to which job candidate possesses the preferred characteristics to fill a specific job (Acker, 1990; Martin, 2003; Moss and Tily, 2001; Padavic and Reskin, 2002; Williams, 1995). Research has also shown that employers hire job candidates who they believe possess more 'feminine' characteristics (Hochschild, 1983) and more 'masculine' characteristics (Kanter, 1977; Acker, 1990) based on their perception of what is more desirable for certain positions. Therefore, it could be argued that those who rest outside a 'linear kind of gender identification', as Holly described it, might face employment discrimination. Further, perceptions of binary gender are strengthened by existing occupational segregation (Schilt and Wiswall, 2008). In other words, because perceptions of binary gender categories are so entrenched in American, English and Welsh police culture, those who do not adhere to strict 'male' and 'female' binaries may face overt discrimination in hiring practices. Therefore, those who identify as genderqueer and do not adhere to binaries are less likely to be hired.

For this research, I had only two genderqueer individuals who participated. Notably, all American trans participants perceived an absence of genderqueer identities within policing. The two genderqueer individuals who participated in this research were from English/Welsh police constabularies. These two constables disclosed more occupational complaints compared with participants who identified as MTF or FTM (this will be revisited in the following chapter). As previously stated, because genderqueer individuals do not associate with any realm of the binary spectrum of 'male' or 'female', cisgender individuals may have a lack of understanding of genderqueer identities, as Erin stated:

> I don't necessarily identify as a guy ... um ... I kind of ... I now understand it as being genderqueer ... I thought, great, I survived being a gay woman and now I am going to come across as someone who is genderqueer, which most people do not understand.... For me, coming out was a bit different because I identify as genderqueer.... My supervisor recently asked me if they should call me a 'he' or a 'she'. I said because I was quite a butch girl before and I don't see myself as a guy, so you can make me the butchest girl you have ever known ... whatever you want.

Yet, there are some officers who exhibit less confusion and more understanding. Erin continued:

> I remember trying to explain to a guy – I don't identify as a guy or girl, and I know it sounds weird ... and he goes, no, not really. He said, I am half black and I am half white, and I have always had an issue with one community that don't accept me, so I am sort of stuck in the middle. He said I kind of know where you are coming from ... I hadn't thought of it that way.

Notably, Erin stated that they[11] first identified as a butch gay woman before they identified as genderqueer. Erin, who disclosed they had a mastectomy and is currently undergoing hormone treatment, stated they only wanted to go so far in a gender transition:

> I always understood that if you did this on the NHS they would prescribe you with hormones. You have to be on hormones for a couple of years, then you are considered for surgery. And because I wasn't sure how far I wanted to take this or what the route or my journey was really, I thought that is not for me. So I am just going to control my body by going to the gym.... Six months after my chest surgery I decided that I wanted to explore the option of hormones.

Notably, Erin disclosed that they will never go through with any bottom surgery, as they feel more comfortable the way they are – possessing both male and female gendered characteristics.

Another genderqueer participant, Addison, faced different types of occupational issues from Erin. Notably, there were visible differences between Erin and Addison, and I believe this had an impact on how they were accepted within police culture and also impacted the amount of bias they had to face. Addison, who previously identified as a male, began to grow his hair out at work and chose to wear the classic female 'blacks' uniform with the force. Addison disclosed:

> My inspector asked if there was any reason why my hair was like it was. I replied yes. I was then told that if I arrived to her house presenting as such (my hair was clean, tidy and flicked/styled out on the sides), she would think I was a mess and could not do the job. She stated I was a mess and should get it cut as it was unprofessional, etc.

Addison disclosed that the same inspector stated: 'I have trans friends, and what you get up to in your own time is your business'. Addison reported several incidents of uniform violations and observable social exclusion because they presented themselves as genderqueer.[12] Notably, Addison visually presented a more deemed 'feminine' of centre presentation (i.e. shoulder-length hair, female attire, no facial hair, yet they possessed a very 'masculine' muscular frame) than Erin (i.e. removal of their breast, deeper voice, short hair and a muscular frame), despite the fact that neither of them identify as 'male' or 'female'. While genderqueer identities do not subscribe to binary gendered characteristics, society (due to genderism) associates gender as being 'male' or 'female'. I believe this is what led to Erin reporting more positive acceptance within police culture than Addison.[13] Notably, unlike genderqueer identities, transsexual individuals disclosed that they face a unique struggle in relation to the social acceptance of their masculine or feminine identities.

## Perceptions of masculinity/femininity and gendered talk

Participants disclosed intersectional attitudes of gender expectations when they transitioned on the job. During post-transition, officers and constables disclosed that their new cross-gender interactions changed. Transmen were no longer included in 'girl talk' (i.e. talk about appearance, romantic interests and menstruation) with female colleagues, while transwomen reported similar changes, like being excluded from 'guy talk' (i.e. conversations about sports, cars and sexual objectification of women) with male colleagues. As Jessie, an American officer, stated:

> Once I transitioned, I wasn't socially included in guy talk anymore. People assumed because I transitioned that my personality would change too.

Dave, another American officer, stated:

> Once I became Dave, women talked to me differently. Sometimes I would be included in some girl talk, but now I am treated differently.

Much like all American transsexual participants, all English and Welsh constables stated that they were treated differently after transition. Clair stated:

> I was in the army before, so I was used to the guy talk. Once I transitioned, that all changed. I felt socially rejected by men and women because I wouldn't be included in girl talk either.

Mirroring Clair, Elizabeth stated:

> I don't miss the guy talk, but I am also left out of the girl talk ... I feel that socially I am not accepted by either gender.

Tom stated:

> I still like girlie things and I miss talking about those things sometimes. I mean, just because someone transitions, it does not mean that all your

interests change.... There is an assumption that because I identify as a male I am unable to identify with female stuff ... I mean, I used to be female, but now I am treated socially much differently.

This is similar to Schilt and Connell's (2007) study of trans workplace interactions in non-police environments. Crocker and Lutsky (1986) mentioned a similar finding when they speculated that trans employees may falsely assume that because there are physical changes in the presentation of their gender identity, co-workers may think that they have changed their interests to stereotypical gender-congruent ones.

Previous research has already indicated that employers evaluate their employees' job performances and abilities in binary gendered ways (Acker, 1990; Gorman, 2005; Martin, 2003). These gendered evaluations appeared to be highlighted when participants disclosed their transition from one gender to another and how they performed masculinity during the process. This is similar to Connell's (2010) and Schilt's (2006) research on non-police trans identities and how they observed sexism in gendered organisations pre-transition. Meyer (2012) and Vries (2012) explained these observations by suggesting that trans identities are positioned as 'outsiders within', allowing them to see past 'natural' gender difference. Because a post-op trans identity experiences both social expectations of the performance and expectations of femininity and/or masculinity, they are best suited to make these critical observations. Besides observed gender assumptions of masculinity within police culture and the intersection of socialisation, the motivations for joining policing (a known hegemonic masculine environment[14]) are also explored here.

Dave, an American officer, presented himself as a masculine lesbian early in his policing career, and then transitioned when medical technologies in gender reassignment surgery had advanced. As such, Dave was able to describe his observations and perceptions of masculinity and acceptance within policing:

> Being male or masculine is more acceptable in society, and if you are a man, I don't think being feminine is as acceptable. I think that an effeminate man may have a more difficult time in law enforcement.

Liv, another American officer, stated that effeminate men and transwomen within policing are looked down on because there is a correlation between the presentation of masculinity and the performance abilities of policing. As Liv stated:

> Extremely, extremely feminine portrayals; you have a man on the job who has very feminine characteristics. Initially from the egotistical point of view, how is this person going to help or protect me?

When I explored this further with Liv, she stated:

Their egos are through the roof. They actually feel manlier saying, well, what's that bitch gonna do if this happens, you know, what's that little faggot going to do, or, he's wandering around like Peter Pan, or whatever terms they like to use.

## Subcultural divisions and biases among trans feminine identities

When conducting interviews with trans-identified police, there appeared to be a taboo topic within their subculture that is very rarely mentioned to cisgender individuals, so much so that I found no research on the topic within policing studies. Officers and constables who disclosed their controversial opinions on the topic apparently felt more comfortable disclosing this to me, I believe, because I was viewed as being relatable to the trans population because I identified as a 'butch female'.[15] As Josie explained to me, being a 'butch' lesbian often results in similar mis-gendered experiences to those in the trans community:

> You know how it feels … because of your gender presentation, and don't take this the wrong way, you know what it is like when you feel you are not passing as the gender that you are. You know what it is like to be confronted and told you are in the wrong restroom.

I believe that my role as a deemed 'insider' for being a butch lesbian aided in the open disclosure of topics that are not feely disclosed to 'outsiders'. Officers and constables who participated in this research gave very candid and, at times, controversial opinions regarding an inter-bias component of trans socialisation. This inter-bias component of trans socialisation consisted of subdivisions of acceptance between MTFs, genderqueers, cross-dressers, etc. Holly, an American officer, stated:

> I told myself that I could be a cross-dresser the rest of my life and that it wouldn't affect me, which turned out to be totally inaccurate. For most of us, it is a very secretive thing at first, and once you gain acceptance you gain different levels of acceptance, and my initial level of acceptance was … well, I can be a cross-dresser and not be transsexual, because there is a big difference between the two.

Holly, who identified as a cross-dresser prior to transition, gave a detailed insight into the social divisions between MTFs, genderqueers and cross-dressers:

> Cross-dressers are not real T. They are not real T girls. And I see it among the MTFs, not much among the FTMs … I have noticed it and I have heard it on a direct level. I have witnessed it occurring, and I have talked to other people about how they deal with other transgender people…. They feel that

they are superior to the cross-dressers.... It's ignorance for the most part. It is the same kind of bias behaviour being committed against each other in the same community.

As a member of the LGBT+ population, I have heard of inter-spectrum bias (e.g. gay attitudes towards lesbians, lesbians towards FTMs, etc.), but it was not until I conducted this research that I discovered that there is social exclusion and isolation in the form of a social hierarchy within the trans policing community itself. Notably, the trans community is diverse, and full of anomalies, and there are different subcultural expectations and perceptions. Josie, an American officer, stated:

Cross-dressers who like the feminine feel when they are dressing and there are different spectrums, but the pass-ability is really the reason why most people, why the two don't interact.... It's 'pass-ability'. You know I spent $105,000 on the medical expenses while in transition, all out of pocket. I spent that money so that when I go in public, people don't know who I am.

Holly, like other trans police, stated:

There is a culture where some trans people don't hang around with other trans people who don't pass. There is a rift between people who pass and people who don't pass. And there is a rift between cross-dressers and post-surgical women. What would they have in common? You know what I'm saying? Drag queens, you know what I am saying? I mean, we dress for different reasons. I mean, we dress as a female, you know we dress age-appropriate.... To be honest with you, I wouldn't hang around a bunch of cross-dressers if they didn't pass in the venue. If I am at a trans convention, sure, if it is a convention. But do I want them in my personal life, going out and stuff? Not really. I know it sounds awful, but it is uncomfortable for me. I wouldn't have much in common with them. You know what I am saying, some activity we do together.

Josie went on to explain why this social exclusion typically occurs:

It is not an inclusion issue that people do it, it is just a matter of trying to survive the transition.... Cross-dressers dress a little bit, they have a hard time with the age-appropriate thing, and they dress younger than they are, and they always dress not really right for the occasion. They can't walk in heels. They think they can, but they walk like men in heels.

Clair, when speaking about the social exclusion that occurs within the trans-gender community, stated:

Is there a rift? It is more like the fucking Grand Canyon.... Transsexuals like myself are nothing like those others. We don't associate with them because they dress inappropriately ... and they don't face the same issues we face.

Like Clair, Liv described a story in which she noticed the differences between herself as a transsexual and her friend who is a cross-dresser. Liv stated that her friend dresses in 'drag' every six months and it doesn't depress him. Liv stated pre-transition that she got 'really, really bad depression', and taking off her wig at home 'would kill me like I couldn't look in the mirror'. Unlike her friend, having to present herself as a man full-time disrupted her happiness. Liv goes on to say that the hostility within this *inter trans hierarchy concept* can be attributed to conflict between the part-time performance of cross-dressing and the full-time presentation of being transsexual. Liv explained why her transsexual identity is dissimilar from others who cross-dress:

In my case, you know I can literally end up hospitalised from not being able to do it.

Here, Liv is describing that being transsexual, unlike being a cross-dresser, means that one faces different medical and psychological challenges. Liv and the other transsexuals interviewed disclosed that cross-dressers have more control over how they present themselves. Thus, they could possess the ability to 'hide' their trans status from others. Arguably, possessing this perceived self-controlled power can lead to resentment from those who are forced to reveal their trans status to colleagues. This is similar to the resentment held by some within the gay community towards individuals who have not 'come out of the closet'.

All of the MTF participants interviewed for this research expressed that they had some issues with being collectively included and associated with cross-dressers or transvestites. Often this revolved around the stigma of having a medical diagnosis, and thus associating with a medical condition versus under-taking an activity that is perceived as voluntary in action. Amber, a British constable, stated:

There is definitely a hierarchy. For myself, the label that I chose is T-S woman, and the woman element comes from the fact that I am post-op and my transition process is complete and I am fully into a female life. The T-S part obviously comes from transsexual, because the medical definition of what we do is cross the sex boundaries, if you wish. Modern language calls it crossing the gender divide. This is why I uphold a transsexual definition, because secondary to what we find now is that people that regularly cross-dress that are transvestite and dual-role transvestite claim the transgender term. What I find blurs the picture, the definition between transvestite – those that have a specific term of their activities in a dictionary – and a cross-dresser will again have their own specific definition, and now the word transgender is becoming transgenderist, where a transsexual revolves around the diagnosis of having gender dysphoria, and that is why there are differences between us.... It is about the life we need to live psychologically to survive, whereas transvestites and cross-dressers do it for thrill, fun, sexual gratification, exhibition and for relaxation purposes. Their reasons are totally different.

When examining the act of gender presentation between MTFs and cross-dressers, there appeared to be a divide over how one physically presents and displays femininity. As Amber stated:

Often a cross-dresser will wear super-short inappropriate clothing. Very high heels, just doing ordinary things. Whereas us transsexuals are different.... There is a portion of us that rather would not be this way. We have to learn to accept ourselves first then move into femininity as best we can.

Gareth, a British transvestite, explained the division and differences between transsexuals and transvestites:

I sit firmly in the transvestite camp, I don't wish to take my gender issues any further, I don't feel that need to, yet I feel socially excluded from other trans identities. Transsexuals don't want to associate with me when I cross-dress.

Gareth's quote aligns with other participants' statements regarding how they choose to socialise with other trans identities. For example, if a trans feminine individual is trying to 'pass', they will not want to be seen socially with other trans feminine individuals who do not 'pass' as well, out of fear of disclosure. This is similar to how some gay individuals, who are in the closet, may not want to be seen in public with individuals who are perceived as being 'obviously' gay.

Additionally, some post-op trans constables disclosed that they no longer associate with the LGBT+ community because they have severed ties with the transgender community. This is often referred to as being 'deep stealth' because there is no disjuncture between their work identity, home identity and LGBT+ social identity. Once they have fully transitioned, they may feel disconnected from those who are transitioning or have not transitioned. As Clair, a British constable, stated:

They are nothing like me. I am a woman now, not one of those freaks who dress up part-time ... I am what you would call stealth.

Claiming a 'stealth' status and socially distancing from other trans identities can arguably lead to further reinforcement of social hierarchies that may exist in the trans feminine police community.

Participants disclosed that within the 'feminine' trans police community, a social hierarchy (i.e. the *inter trans feminine hierarchy concept*) is based on how one present's femininity and the amount of social oppression each person faces. Post-op transsexuals are often situated at the top of this hierarchy, because they have overcome specific struggles and present their 'femininity' in more structured binary ways, or, as Clair states, are 'stealth'. Genderqueer, gender fluid and other trans feminine identities are perceived as facing different forms of oppression from transsexual identities. Yet, they are perceived higher in the hierarchy than cross-dressers because they present themselves as genderqueer full-time, often facing similar oppressions as transsexuals. Situated at the bottom of the *inter trans hierarchy concept* are cross-dressers. What is intriguing about this *inter trans hierarchy concept* is that, typically, before transitioning, transsexuals have either engaged in the action of cross-dressing or have identified as a cross-dresser in the past within policing.

## Chapter summary

This chapter has explored trans officers' perceptions and experiences within policing, identifying a range of issues, such as social stigmas and the process of transgender status disclosure, genderqueer identities, perceptions of masculinity and femininity, why some transgender identities are drawn to policing, and the concept of an inter-trans feminine subcultural hierarchy, in order to answer the following research question:

> What are the occupational experiences and the perceptions of officers who identify as trans within policing?

Transgender police disclosed that they were often forced out of the closet for two reasons: (1) because transitioning involves significant visual changes; and (2) their respective departments 'outed' them without their permission. Transgender officers disclosed that if they came out voluntarily prior to transition, it was because they wanted to be authentic to others about their transgender status, to educate their policing colleagues about transgender identities in the hopes of promoting acceptance and for advocacy reasons. This finding contributes to Creed and Scully's (2000) research on LGB disclosure in workplaces.

This chapter also explored those who have very notable transgender visual cues and who identify as genderqueer. According to participants, genderqueer identities appear to be rare in policing because of entrenched gender binaries reinforced by hegemonic masculinity within police culture. As explored in the previous chapter and also this one, this adherence to strict gender binaries makes it especially difficult for those who do not identify with either. Participants claimed that genderqueer identities are overtly discriminated against within policing. Further, the reinforcement of gender binaries might further socially encourage transgender individuals to adhere more to 'male' and 'female' appearances instead of a non-binary appearance. The combination of these two factors may explain why genderqueer identities are perceived as non-existent within American, English and Welsh[16] police culture but may be more apparent in others.

This chapter also explored micro-relationships within trans feminine social cultures within policing, more specifically an *inter trans feminine hierarchy concept*. On a micro-level, there is social exclusion and isolation of some transgender individuals, who are at the bottom of a social hierarchy within the trans feminine police community. This appears to be heightened in policing, arguably because gender role ideologies are strictly enforced in a hegemonic environment (see Chapter 6). In this social hierarchy, transsexuals are perceived to be superior in gender presentation, although they appear to face more forms of oppression. Often MTF transsexual participants disclosed that they do not socially associate with other-gendered identities that would make others question their own gender presentation (i.e. 'clocking'). Notably, in this social hierarchy, genderqueer identities in policing are regarded as having a higher social status than cross-dressers, who are often disparagingly considered to be 'part-time trans'. I suspect that this hierarchy is more apparent within policing because of the enforcement of strict binaries and transsexual desires for heightened gender conformity.

Most occupational experiences of American, English and Welsh transgender officers were comparable: for example, their experiences of coming out, choosing to remain in the closet, perceptions of masculinity and femininity, choosing policing as a profession and the perception of an inter-trans feminine social hierarchy. However, there existed one major observable difference between the countries, which was the perception of fewer genderqueer identities within policing in America than in England and Wales. Arguably, because there was only one significant difference between these countries, this research illustrates that the 'working personality' within police culture is more accurately described as monolithic than fragmented, especially in the way gender and sexuality are embedded, contested and reinforced within it.

## Notes

1 While I wished to examine trans masculine occupational experiences, this research found more dominant themes in respect to trans femininity.
2 I hope future work in masculinity and femininity studies in non-police work environments will examine how relatable this concept is.
3 Refer to Chapter 3.
4 Referring to Chapter 6, cisgender perceptions of gender within police culture were found to strictly adhere to 'male' and 'female' binaries.
5 Due to ethical considerations for safe-guarding respondents, an anonymous randomisation process has been imposed throughout this book. As such, to protect participants, I opted to not reveal the respondents' specific locations.
6 Post-op refers to transsexual individuals who have medically transitioned from one gender to another. Typically, this process takes several years, and it is feasible, as I have found in this research, for some individuals to possess no stereotypical visual indications or social indications of existing as a previous gender.

7 Some members of the cross-dressing community may not identify as transgender, but all of my research participants stated that cross-dressers are members of the transgender community. As discussed in Chapter 3, academically, cross-dressers have been included within the transgender community because they present gender in non-traditional ways. Personally, I believe identification should be determined by an individual, but because my participants (even cross-dressers) identified as transgender, they were included in this research.

8 It was very apparent that Garth's medical and personal privacy was violated by his police force.

9 Gender Identity Disorder (GID) was defined as 'people who experience intense, persistent gender incongruence', in the 4th edition of the *Diagnostic and Statistical Manual* (DSM-IV) (American Psychological Association, 2013). The more recent 5th edition (DSM-V) replaced GID with gender dysphoria (GD), which 'will be used to describe emotional distress over a "marked incongruence between one's experienced/expressed gender and assigned gender"'. Rather than stigmatising gender non-conformity, the changes to the DSM aim to remove stigma from gender non-conforming individuals and place the emphasis on the symptoms of stress-related gender incongruence in society, while creating a diagnostic label to ensure transgender individuals are able to access sufficient medical care (American Psychiatric Association, 2013).

10 This was covered in Chapter 3.

11 As previously stated, the word 'they' is used since genderqueer identities typically do not associate with male or female pronouns.

12 Trans-specific uniform violations will be covered in the following chapter when administrative issues are covered.

13 This will be revisited in further detail in the following chapter.

14 See Chapter 3.

15 This is explored in Chapters 4 and 5.

16 Due to research limitations, I was unable comparatively to determine why genderqueer identities are perceived more present than within American policing cultures. Certainly this is an area that would require additional research as highlighted in Chapter 9.

## References

Acker, J. 1990. Hierarchies, jobs, bodies: A theory of gendered organizations. *Gender and Society* 4(2), pp. 139–158.

American Psychiatric Association. 2013. *Gender dysphoria* [Online]. Available at: www.dsm5.org/documents/gender%20dysphoria%20fact%20sheet.pdf [accessed: 1 October 2014].

American Psychological Association. 2013. *Answers to your questions about transgender people, gender identity disorder, and gender expression: is being transgender a mental disorder?* [Online]. Available at: www.apa.org/topics/lgbt/transgender.aspx [accessed: 7 November 2017].

Budge, S., Tebbe, E., Howard, K. 2010. The work experiences of transgender individuals: Negotiating the transition and career decision-making processes. *Journal of Counselling Psychology* 57, pp. 377–393.

Burke, M. 1993. *Coming out of the blue*. London: Continuum.

Burke, M. 1994. Homosexuality as deviance: The case of the gay police officer. *British Journal of Criminology* 34, pp. 192–203.

Butler, J. 1990. *Gender trouble: feminism and the subversion of identity.* New York: Routledge.

Butler, J. 2004. *Undoing gender.* New York: Psychology Press.

Clair, J., Beatty, J. and MacLean, T. 2005. Out of sight but not out of mind: managing invisible social identities in the workplace. *Academy of Management Review* 30(1), pp. 78–95.

Cohen-Kettenis, P. and Pfafflin, P. 2009. The DSM diagnostic criteria for gender identity disorder in adolescents and adults. *Archives of Sexual Behavior* 39(2), pp. 499–513.

Colvin, R. 2012. *Gay and lesbian cops: diversity and effective policing.* London: Lynne Rienner Publishers.

Connell, C. 2010. Doing, undoing, or redoing gender: learning from the workplace experiences of transpeople. *Gender and Society* 24(1), pp. 31–55.

Creed, W. and Scully, M. 2000. Songs of ourselves: Employees' deployment of social identity in workplace encounters. *Journal of Management Inquiry* 9, pp. 391–412.

Crocker, J. and Lutsky, N. 1986. Stigma and the dynamics of social cognition. In: Ainlay, S.C., Becker, G. and Coleman, L.M., eds. *The dilemma of difference* Boston, MA: Springer, pp. 95–121.

Davis, D. 2009. Transgender issues in the workplace: HRD's newest challenge/opportunity. *Advances in Developing Human Resources* 11, pp. 109–120.

Devor, A. 2004. Witnessing and mirroring: A fourteen stage model of transsexual identity formation. *Journal of Gay and Lesbian* 8, pp. 41–67.

Gagné, P., Tewksbury, R. and McGaughey, D. 1997. Coming out and crossing over: identity formation and proclamation in a transgender community. *Gender & Society* 11(4), pp. 478–508.

Garfinkel, H. 1967. *Studies in ethnomethodology.* Upper Saddle River, NJ: Pearson.

Gedro, J. 2009. LGBT Career Development. *Advances in Developing Human Resources* 11(2), pp. 54–66.

Gorman, E. 2005. Gender stereotypes, same-gender preference, and organizational variation in the hiring of women: Evidence from law firms. *American Sociological Review* 70, pp. 702–728.

Harrison, J., Grant, J., Herman, J. 2012. A gender not listed here: genderqueers, gender rebels, and otherwise in the National Transgender Discrimination Survey. *LGBTQ Policy Journal at the Harvard Kennedy School* 2, pp. 13–24.

Hochschild, A. 1983. *The managed heart: commercialization of human feeling.* Berkeley, CA: University of California Press.

Humphrey, J. 1999. Organizing sexualities, organized inequalities: lesbians and gay men in public service occupations. *Gender, Work & Organization* 6(3), pp. 134–151.

Kanter, R. 1977. *Men and women of the corporation.* New York: Basic Books.

Law, C., Martinez, L., Ruggs, E., Hebl, M. and Akers, E. 2011. Trans-parency in the workplace: How the experiences of transsexual employees can be improved. *Journal of Vocational Behavior* 79, pp. 710–723.

Leinen, S. 1993. *Gay cops.* New Brunswick, NJ: Rutgers University.

Levitt, H. and Ippolito, M. 2014. Being transgender: the experience of transgender identity development. *Journal of Homosexuality* 61(12), pp. 1727–1758.

Martin, P. 2003. 'Said and done' versus 'saying and doing': Gendering practices, practicing gender at work. *Gender and Society* 17(3), pp. 342–366.

Moss, P. and Tily, C. 2001. *Stories employers tell: race, skill, and hiring in America.* New York: Russell Sage.

Meyer, D. 2012. An intersectional analysis of lesbian, gay, bisexual, and transgender (LGBT) people's evaluations of anti-queer violence. *Gender & Society* 26(6), pp. 849–873.

Padavic, I. and Reskin, B. 2002. *Woman and men at work*, 2nd edn. Thousand Oaks, CA: Pine Forge Press.

Rumens, N. and Broomfield, J. 2012. Gay men in the police: identity disclosure and management issues. *Human Resource Management* 22(3), pp. 283–298.

Schilt, K. 2006. Making gender visible: Transmen as 'outsiders-within' in the workplace. *Gender and Society* 20(4), pp. 465–490.

Schilt, K. and Connell, C. 2007. Do workplace gender transitions make gender trouble? *Gender, Work & Organization* 14(6), pp. 596–618.

Schilt, K. and Wiswall, M. 2008. Before and after: gender transitions, human capital, and workplace experiences. *The B.E. Journal of Economic Analysis & Policy* 8(1), pp. 1–26.

Shelley, C. 2009. Transpeople and social justice. *Journal of Individual Psychology* 65(4), pp. 386–396.

Stone, S. 1991. The empire strikes back: A posttransexual manifesto. In: Epstein, J. and Straub, K., eds. *Body guards: the cultural politics of gender ambiguity.* Abingdon: Routledge, pp. 280–604.

Stryker, S. 1994. My words to Victor Frankenstein. *GLQ: A Journal of Lesbian and Gay Studies* 1(3), pp. 237–254.

Vries, K. 2012. Intersectional identities and conceptions of the self: the experience of transgender people. *Symbolic Interaction* 35(1), pp. 49–67.

West, C. and Zimmerman, D. 1987. Doing gender. *Gender and Society* 1, pp. 125–151.

Williams, C. 1995. *Still a man's world: men do women's work.* Berkley, CA: University of California Press.

## Chapter 8

# 'We don't hire people because they are male or female.... We are going to make this work'

## Transgender perspectives of administrative issues

This chapter centres on three major themes that emerged during this research: (1) direct forms of heterosexism and genderism within policing; (2) transition policy and leadership issues; and (3) the administrative correlates of a positive trans-supportive work environment. The first major theme, direct intersectional forms of heterosexism and genderism within policing, examines various reported forms of bias directed specifically towards the transgender community. This theme is further broken into subthemes that examine hiring discrimination, unwarranted job reassignment during MTF transitions and transgender bathroom battles where identities are policed. The second theme consists of subthemes that examine issues in workplace policy that impact MTF and FTM transgender identities.

This chapter also further examines specific administrative complaints of transgender identities within police cultures and theorises why these complaints are more targeted towards those who transition in work environments. Specific attention is paid to administrative punishments, bathroom issues while being transgender and genderist expressions within police work environments. Following upon collective research of LGBT+ identities within law enforcement (see Sears *et al.*, 2013), this research found that transgender identities in policing are subjected to both heterosexist and genderist attacks. Furthermore, referring back to Chapter 3 (i.e. Goffman, 1977), it is theorised that gendered divisions that exist in some police work environments highlight and reinforce binary acceptance. In other words, in work environments where gender differences are highlighted, transgender identities who are not perceived as adhering to gendered binaries (see Chapters 6 and 7) will face more social resistance and unacceptance. As this chapter highlights, this can then lead to more occupational complaints, like uniform violations and restroom allocations.

Endemically, all transgender participants stated that they had experienced at least one incident of transgender bias within their respective work environments. Yet, it was found that a combination of transition policies during transition and supportive leadership had an influence on overall reported positive experiences. It is theorised that effective leadership alongside transition policies which guide supervisors aid in administratively supporting those who transition. This, in turn, reduces the expression of genderist attitudes towards those who transition in workplaces. This is a profound contributory finding as not only does this chapter highlight what the issues are, it also proses solutions on what administrative changes may correct the issues.

As previously outlined in Chapter 7, the participant demographics of the transgender officers who participated in this research are given in Tables 8.1 and 8.2.[1]

## Intersectional forms of heterosexism and genderism within policing

### Heterosexist and genderist verbiage and other forms of displayed transgender bias

Sears *et al.* (2009) surveyed 400 American LGBT+ members of law enforcement.[2] They discovered that out of 60 transgender individuals in law enforcement, over 56 (90 per cent) reported negative experiences within their respective agencies (Sears *et al.*, 2009). Further, of those reported negative experiences: 15 per cent reported being terminated; 37 per cent reported being threatened with termination; 68 per cent reported being verbally harassed by their co-workers; 43 per cent reported being threatened with violence; 18 per cent reported incidents of physical attacks; and 53 per cent felt their personal safety was jeopardised due to social isolation by their peers (Sear *et al.*, 2009).

*Table 8.1* American transgender officer participants

| Pseudonym | Policing tenure | Trans ID | Region |
|-----------|-----------------|----------|--------|
| Dave | 18 years | FTM | Rural |
| Holly | 35 years | MTF | Urban |
| Jessie | 33 years | MTF | Urban |
| Liv | 19 years | MTF | Urban |
| Josie | 27 years | MTF | Urban |

*Table 8.2* English and Welsh transgender constable participants

| Pseudonym | Policing tenure | Trans ID | Region |
|-----------|-----------------|----------|--------|
| Erin | 15 years | Genderqueer | Urban |
| Tom | 30 years | FTM | Urban |
| Sarah | 2 years | MTF | Urban |
| Amber | 7 years | MTF | Urban |
| Addison | 15 years | Genderqueer | Urban |
| Elizabeth | 8 years | MTF | Urban |
| Clair | 17 years | MTF | Urban |
| Ellie | 35 years | MTF | Urban |
| Gareth | 11 years | Transvestite | Urban |

Further research carried out by the Williams Institute stated that LGBT+ discrimination and harassment within law enforcement is 'pervasive' throughout the U.S.A. (Sears *et al.*, 2013). Sears *et al.* examined 57 court cases (in 2000–2013) and administrative complaints filed by LGBT+ law enforcement members who alleged they had faced discrimination based on their sexual orientation or gender identity. They found that discrimination complaints ranged from firing and demotion to severe verbal harassment, sexual harassment, death threats, discriminatory slurs, indecent exposure and complaints of inappropriate touching.

All 14 American, English and Welsh trans participants disclosed that they had experienced various forms of heterosexism and/or genderism within policing. Liv, an American officer, disclosed after she transitioned:

> I had some very homophobic/transphobic graffiti left on a piece of paper that was our sign-in sheet at the office. It said 'Fag-hag' and 'fag-hag should die'.

Clair, a British constable, stated:

> I had notes left on my locker that said 'she-he' and 'faggot'.

Heterosexist language was disclosed to be the most commonly occurring type of behaviour used within policing when administrative incidents of heterosexism/genderism were disclosed. Previous research on transgender identities found that two-thirds of LGBT law enforcement personnel reported hearing heterosexist comments on the job, with over half reporting being treated like a social outsider (Sears *et al.*, 2013). Further, previous LGB research by Herek (1989) in the U.S.A. and Thurlow (2001) in England and Wales found that heterosexist words are the most reported type of bias behaviour within policing. Colvin's (2012) research on lesbian and gay identities within American policing found that over 70 per cent of participants stated they have had heterosexist words directed at them at work. Unlike Colvin's (2012) research, data indicated that transgender identities are also susceptible to heterosexist language alongside genderist language, despite how they presented their masculinity and/or femininity or their sexuality. American participants disclosed that the following words were directed at them:

- bull-dyke (Dave);
- fag-hag, he-she, shim (Holly);
- queer faggot, he-she (Jessie);
- faggot, tranny (Liv);
- sissy faggot (Josie).

English and Welsh constables, like their American counterparts, all disclosed that they have had heterosexist/genderist words directed at them within policing.

This finding is consistent with Colvin (2012), who found that 50 per cent of lesbian and gay British constables reported heterosexist language as being the most occurring occupational complaint. Yet, as mentioned earlier, transgender identities are also susceptible to heterosexist words alongside genderist words. Examples included:

- gender-bender (Erin);
- bull-dyke (Tom);
- faggot (Sarah);
- bent, fag (Amber);
- faggot, sissy (Addison);
- fag (Elizabeth);
- he-she, faggot, shim, tranny (Clair);
- fag (Ellie);
- tranny weirdo (Gareth).

Research on transwomen has found their sexuality to be relatively evenly split between lesbian, bisexual and asexual (Johnson and Hunt, 1990; Lawrence, 2003). Further, studies on the sexualities of transmen have found that the majority of them are sexually attracted to females (Chivers and Bailey, 2000; Devor, 1993). Further, studies on the sexualities of cross-dressers have found that the majority are heterosexual (Bullough and Bullough, 1997; Docter and Fleming, 2001; Docter and Prince, 1997). Despite most participants not identifying as lesbian or gay, all participants disclosed that they have been the victim of heterosexist verbal attacks. As Ellie stated:

> I have been called a faggot and sick. It has really bothered me, but you know I am sure you have had to put up with it too. You just keep your head high and carry on.

Clair, like others, stated that her locker and administrative paperwork had been vandalised, with words like 'queer' and 'fag' written on them. Besides name-calling, participants disclosed that they had items vandalised or stolen from them at work. Liv, an American officer, disclosed how items were taken from her at work:

> They also broke into my desk and some personal items were taken … like photographs of my children…. It was someone within the police department, it couldn't have been anyone else, as it was an officer-only area and it was a locked desk in that area.

Besides acts of vandalism and theft, all FTM participants disclosed that both verbal threats of physical violence and actual incidents of physical violence occurred frequently. Holly, an American officer, disclosed an incident where she was threatened by a male colleague in the car park of her police headquarters. She stated that a male colleague called her a 'fag, I was an abomination; I was a he-she, a shim and a bunch of other hurtful things'. There was no administrative punishment, despite the fact her employers knew of the incident. Holly stated that the same officer eventually escalated the name-calling to physical violence when 'he took a swing' at her and she promptly 'punched him out':

> I tried to explain to him that just because I changed genders doesn't mean I forgot how to fight. I boxed for a number of years.

Like Holly, Amber, a British constable, told a story about a colleague who used physical violence and name-calling:

> One guy, called Dave, about six and a half foot tall and built like a, you know, big, used to come over and thump me with his fists.... He used to call me a fucking tranny, weirdo, bastard and, you know, just make comments about gay people. And, obviously, I am not gay but trans, yet it was horrible.

Some trans police stated that instead of receiving warnings of future physical attacks, colleagues would make inappropriate 'threatening jokes', as one British constable disclosed in a work diary when the subject of her genitalia was brought up:

> Colleague approached me with a pair of bolt croppers when enroute to the found property cupboard; 'I could save you some money on surgery' and snapped them closed. I informed him that I required my penis flesh remaining intact to have it turned inside out – the colleague then commented he would try kicking me in the crotch as that may turn inside out … this incident was very inappropriate and I felt threatened.

Most participants stated that they had work experiences that escalated from name-calling to vandalism, to threats of physical harm and then eventually to physical attacks. Yet, often they were afraid to report any incidents to their supervisors because they perceived nothing would be done to combat it. Clair gave a story where workplace incidents crossed over into her personal residence:

> Every time my window got smashed, I got dog excrement through my letterbox, given a beating outside my house, you don't report it cause they are not gonna do anything about it … I was beaten up on one occasion by officers from my police force outside my house.

Clair stated that she did not report the physical incident because her force did nothing when the initial name-calling and threats started; therefore, she perceived that they didn't care and that her force was, as she claimed, 'trans-phobic'. Additionally, she stated that after the physical attack outside her personal residence by fellow on-duty officers, she was fearful of further violence had she reported it to her police administrators.

Besides biased words, threats of physical violence and physical attacks at work, all MTF participants disclosed that they were fearful of future job termination due to their trans status. This is similar to previous research on LGB identities (see Button, 2001; Colvin and Riccucci, 2002). One participant disclosed that her story of her sequential termination made the national news. Liv disclosed that her chief of police approached her while on duty during her transition to acquire some prescription painkillers, since Liv had an unused supply from a previous surgery. Her chief of police stated he had injured his back and said he would pay her for the pills. Liv refused to accept any money for the leftover pills she had and gave them to her chief, since she had known him for years. After the incident, Liv disclosed what had occurred to her immediate supervisor, whom she trusted, and he filed a complaint and accused her of being a drug dealer, despite the fact that she was potentially entrapped by her chief. Notably, Liv disclosed that the chief did not receive any type of reprimand for soliciting her for the prescribed narcotics. Liv disclosed that during the internal affairs investigation she went to the FBI out of 'fear' because she felt entrapped and potentially targeted because she was trans. At the time of writing this, she is still trying to fight her agency to get her job back.

### Perceived occupational bias in hiring practices

As previously explored in Chapter 7, participant's perceptions of hiring practices of genderqueer identities were examined. Yet, police who identified as transgender (i.e. MTF, FTM, transgender, cross-dresser, etc.) rather than genderqueer, reported similar perceptions of hiring bias within policing. Holly, like all trans participants, stated:

> We have had some transgender applications, but they have not been accepted for various reasons, mostly because they are transgender. I observed two different background investigations going on at the same time with the exact same information: one agency hired the individual and the other did not. There was no reason not to hire the trans applicants in both agencies.

Liv, another American trans officer, stated:

> There is no way any department would hire you if they thought you are trans. It is viewed as a red-flag indicator that you might have problems in the future. There is a perception that if you are trans you are mentally ill, and if you are mentally ill then you cannot be a police officer. It's sad really.

I think that is why a lot of trans people do not apply to policing, because most know they will be weeded out during the hiring process and not given a fair chance.

Mirroring Holly and Liv, Josie stated:

I have heard of trans potential applicants not even being given an application when they ask for one or any fair assistance during their application process. It has been made quite clear to the community that departments do not want trans officers.

All British constables, like their American counterparts, stated that they also perceived forms of trans bias within police hiring practices. Clair stated:

If they know you are trans, technically they can't not hire you because of it, but they can easily find another reason not to because you are.

Sarah, another British constable, disclosed that discrepancies may exist between recruitment numbers and the actual hiring numbers of trans identities:

Sure, on paper and in the public eye constabularies are saying they are hiring trans constables, but where are they at? I know several members of the community who would be great constables who applied but were not hired because they are trans. There is a difference between recruiting potential trans employees than actually hiring them.

Erin stated:

There is no way to tell what the actual hiring numbers of the trans community is.... It is unknown how many applicants are actual trans.... There are other ways they can decide to not hire you if you are trans.

While all British trans participants stated that they perceived the existence of hiring bias within policing, some participants disclosed that some constabularies were better than others. Ellie stated:

There has been improvements in some constabularies, but bias still exists in hiring practices. I know some big constabularies like Manchester are doing much better about hiring practices because they are recruiting the trans community, but there is no consistency between hiring practices in the constabularies. So, you may get hired in one constabulary, but not even considered in another.

When I inquired about how participants obtained employment, since they perceive trans bias exists in police hiring practices, all participants disclosed that they didn't transition until after employment, or, in one participant's case, they hired her without knowing she had transitioned prior to employment. This finding was anticipated because previous research has already shown that transgender identities are outwardly discriminated against during American hiring practices in other professions (see Lombardi *et al.*, 2001; Mallory *et al.*, 2011) and within law enforcement in general (see Sears *et al.*, 2013). Of particular interest is Sears *et al.*'s (2013) study, which reviewed 57 employment court cases in America between 2000 and 2013 and found several key findings that are consistent with the perceptions of participants. Sears and colleagues found that out of all the studied 57 court cases spanning all areas of employment, 40 per cent of all filed reports involving documented LGBT discrimination occurred specifically within law enforcement professions. Notably, in due course, this is an area that I intend on following up on with future research.

### 'Out of the public's eyes': transwomen's transitions

MTF participants disclosed that when going through the process of transitioning, they were often forced into another assignment or forced to take time off from work as sick leave because they are, as Josie, an American officer, stated: 'less likely to be in the presence of the general public'. Notably, I personally observed this when I worked with our department's first transgender officer, who was moved from patrol to communications when transitioning. As she disclosed to me: 'they are afraid that I will make the department look bad and they want to keep me out of the public's eyes'.

Jessie, an American officer, disclosed that she was unwillingly removed from her job assignments and transferred to a different administrative assignment:

> They pulled me off the streets so I can transition out of view of the public. I felt uncomfortable.... Many other officers had the same type of experience I had in the same time period. I personally know of some federal agents who were gonna transition and they basically put them on medical leave ... because they didn't want them in the office.

Amber, a British constable, stated:

> They moved me to a paperwork assignment and away, with less interaction with the public and others. At first I didn't like it and some would see it as some sort of punishment, but I actually enjoyed it. It allowed me to transition safely without facing dismissal for transitioning.

Amber was the only MTF constable who disclosed that she enjoyed her forced job reassignment during transitioning. Notably, she disclosed that she was just thankful that she was not terminated for transitioning. Almost all of my MTF participants disclosed that if they were reassigned during transition, they weren't reassigned willingly. As Clair, another British constable, stated:

> In a way, this can single you out, because there are some cisgender constables who actually want an administrative position, but I wanted to stay on the streets like other employees. So you can understand why some cisgender people would get upset if you get moved to a position they want.

Clair was not alone in her preference for not being reassigned to an administrative position. As Elizabeth stated:

> I love being on the street and on patrol. I did not want to be assigned to a paper-pushing position.

When looking at American, English and Welsh police comparatively, unwanted job transfers were a reported common practice within policing when transitioning from male to female, but were never reported when transitioning from female to male. I believe this can be explained in several possible ways. First, within police culture, gender ideologies exist that positively reinforce masculinity and reject femininity, as explored in Chapter 6. Therefore, within policing, it is perceived to be more socially acceptable to exhibit masculine traits than feminine traits. Second, there are socialised perceptions within policing of gendered bodies and how these bodies are perceived; this was also explored in Chapter 6. Gendered perceptions of the human body (i.e. constructs of masculinity) are often associated with strength and muscles (see Zimmer, 1987), which are desirable traits for policing (see Heidensohn, 1992; Hunt, 1990). Therefore, transmen may be viewed as being more physically able to handle aspects of their job than trans feminine identities. Third, transitioning from male to female involves more drastic physical changes in presentation (i.e. growing of hair, nails, make-up, etc.), whereas a female-to-male transition might not be as visually noticeable as it is socially acceptable for men and women to have short hair, and body armour may hide any evidence of a chest surgery. Arguably, the more perceived visual perception of non-heteronormative bodies may attract negative attention with policing (see Dwyer, 2011).

Yet, another argument could be made that MTFs could be administratively punished via job transfers because they are actively perceived as rejecting masculinity. Corsiano (2009) found that displays of masculinity are culturally the norm; therefore, any expression of femininity disrupts masculine perceptions of policing environments. In reaction to this perceived active resistance to a cultural norm (i.e. masculinity) within policing, MTFs may be more administratively punished.

Finally, one of the reported reasons given by participants for being removed from the street and put into an administrative role was uniform regulations. Unlike FTM identities, all MTF participants disclosed that they have been administratively punished, or threatened with punishment, for various occupational uniform violations while transitioning. Participants disclosed that they were administratively punished for the violations, as shown in Tables 8.3 and 8.4.[3]

Often these uniform violations were issued because of their physical presentation during transitioning. MTF officers were written up for violating 'male' uniform violations, despite the fact that they were transitioning or had previously transitioned as 'female'. As discussed in Chapter 6, this can occur because MTF police are often still perceived as 'male'.

Yet, another argument could be made that MTFs could be administratively punished via job transfers because they are actively perceived as rejecting masculinity, a perceived desirable trait of a 'working police personality'. Corsiano (2009) found that displays of masculinity are culturally the norm; therefore, any expression of femininity disrupts masculine perceptions of policing environments. In reaction to this perceived active resistance to a cultural norm (i.e. masculinity) within policing, MTFs may be more administratively punished.

*Table 8.3* American participants disclosure of formal administration punishment, or threatened administrative punishment

| American participant | Reason for uniform violation | Disclosed frequency of occurrence |
| --- | --- | --- |
| Holly | Hair-length violation | 2 |
| Jessie | Finger-nail violation | 1 |
| Liv | Hair-length violation | 1 |
|  | Wearing of earrings | 1 |
| Josie | 'Males' are not to wear make-up | 1 |

*Table 8.4* English and Welsh participants disclosure of formal administration punishment, or threatened administrative punishment

| British participant | Reasons for uniform violation | Disclosed frequency of occurrence |
| --- | --- | --- |
| Sarah | Collar-length hair violation | 2 |
| Amber | Make-up violation | 1 |
|  | Uniform violation ('wrong gendered uniform') | 2 |
| Elizabeth | Collar-length hair violation | 3 |
|  | Uniform violation ('wrong gendered uniform') | 1 |
| Clair | Collar-length hair violation | 3 |
|  | Uniform violation ('wrong gendered uniform') | 2 |
| Ellie | Collar-length hair violation | 1 |
| Addison | Collar-length violation | 1 |

Comparatively, when examining participant disclosure of uniform violations,[4] gendered uniforms were an observable difference between American participants and British participants.[5] American participants, who wear unisexed uniforms, reported fewer incidents of uniform violations, while British participants reported more frequent incidents.[6] Arguably, gendered uniforms could be perceived as reinforcing polarity between what is desirable (i.e. masculinity) and what is not desirable (i.e. femininity), since male masculinity is more frequent and accepted within policing (see Appier, 1998; Crank, 1998; Heidensohn, 1992; Hunt, 1990).

Further, a gendered divide in uniforms may further heighten observable gendered differences within police culture. Goffman (1977)[7] explained that observed gendered differences could lead to more social divisions with cultures. These social divisions could be a plausible explanation for why more British MTFs than American MTF officers are punished for uniform violations. By adopting a unisex uniform, American officers are slightly reducing this observable social division.

### Trans bathroom battles

Public bathrooms are an area of contention for trans officers, and even more antagonistic for officers who identify as MTF. Whittle *et al.* (2007) conducted research on trans identities within the U.K. and found that 47 per cent of transgender individuals do not use bathrooms assigned to their acquired gender, with 7 per cent of the transgender population reporting that they have been asked to use different toilets in public spaces. Minter and Daley (2003) found that 62 per cent of 75 transgender people in San Francisco experienced denial of access and/ or harassment while using public toilets.

Transgender individuals, when using the toilet, face being assaulted, mocked, attacked and even arrested.[8] Often transgender individuals will seek a public toilet that they perceive as being stigma free and physically safe, like unisex or disabled toilets. If a gender non-conforming person chooses the wrong toilet, they face violent resistance if someone in the room disagrees with their choice within police institutions. This disagreement is often called 'the policing of gender' or 'misgendering' and serves to devalue or delegitimise expressions that deviate from normative conceptions of gender. According to Judith Butler (1990), rejection of individuals who are perceived as non-normatively gendered is a component of creating one's own gender identity. People who are uncomfortable with the gender presentation of someone else can use gender segregation as an excuse to assert that the person is somehow a deviant or, worse, violently express their disagreement with that gender presentation.[9]

All trans participants disclosed issues of being allowed to use public toilets in police institutions. Holly, an American officer, gave a commonly disclosed MTF example of her fight to use the bathroom at work:

In my case, I had people who did not want me to use the women's restroom. They put up a fight with the command staff about it.... There was a decision made that I would use a unisex restroom, which was located on the opposite side of the complex and down three floors from my workstation. Not convenient by any means of the imagination ... I felt it was my space.... It was my private space ... and I would use it and I was good with that. So, then some other women on the floor started using that same restroom, which basically caused me to have an inability to use a restroom. So there was no access and that created some issues, and when I voiced it they set up a back-up bathroom, which was basically down three floors from my workstation in the basement next to the range ... and they put a lock on the door and they wanted a sign placed on the door basically saying 'restroom in use'. They might as well have stuck a flag that said that 'Holly is in here, don't come in'.

Here, Holly is describing how she feels socially excluded from other females and targeted because of her trans status due to the gender-segregated bathroom at work. By not allowing Holly to use public toilets, police administrators are reinforcing societal perceptions of gender, which leads to displays of genderist behaviour within police culture. Arguably, allowing a work environment to police genders, as Butler (1990) states, in bathrooms, can encourage further genderist types of biased behaviours. Notably, Holly had fully transitioned when her bathroom battle began, and by all accords, she is a woman. Her agency 'policed her gender' because she is perceived as a 'stigma outlier' in respect to traditional police female identities. This perception of being a stigma outlier can lead to social isolation and exclusion within police communities, as covered in Chapter 4.

Unfortunately, Holly's bathroom battle did not end when she was forced to change to an isolated private bathroom. Holly continued:

Very soon after they installed locks on this one bathroom ... instead of putting a key lock they put a latch on the inside. I used that lock and that restroom because that was what I was asked to do. When I was in there one time someone was banging on the door. The banging became a little bit more aggressive and I asked them to wait because I was almost done. It was a small restroom with four unoccupied stalls. The banging kept getting louder and more violent. I put myself back together and went to the door, and as I am opening the door a female sergeant kicked in the stall door.... This particular sergeant knew full well the reasoning behind it, because she was one of those people who baulked about it and complained to the chief, the command staff, city manager and a bunch of other people about why it was there and I should not be allowed to use the women's restroom. So, she kicked in the door and proceeds to dress me down.... She said I had no right locking the door and I shouldn't be here anyway – you should use the restroom on the other side of the building.... You shouldn't even be in the building, sort of things.

Josie, like Holly, disclosed another bathroom story in which she started using a disabled toilet to change in and to use the bathroom 'while people adjusted' and 'out of consideration for everybody'. Josie did this after a fellow cisgender female police officer said she should not be allowed to use the women's toilet and complained to her supervisors. Eventually Josie thought this was unfair, and after continued 'squawking' from other female officers, she went to the human rights and disability commission to petition to use the female toilet. Josie notably won her legal battle, and as she puts it:

> I am proud that I am now permitted to use the restroom like all the other women, but I am sad because I had to fight for a basic right at my workplace.

As with the American officers, British trans constables stated that when an officer discloses that they are transgender at work, police administration officials and colleagues are consumed by which bathroom they are going to use in police facilities. As Clair stated:

> When you first come out, people are so concerned about which bathroom you are going to use. Most trans people will go out of their way to use a disabled or unisex bathroom just to avoid confrontations.

Tom, like other British constables interviewed, stated that he uses the unisex toilets to avoid any confrontations, but often he has to use the men's toilets. When I asked Tom why he goes out of the way to try to use the unisex toilets most of the time, he stated:

> I didn't want to like embarrass the blokes more than anything, you know? I didn't want to upset anybody, so I was just very mindful about what toilets I would use.

Unlike other constables, some British constables stated that there are no unisex toilets at their police institution. As Sarah stated:

> I did anything possible to not use any public bathrooms. I have had women in the past confront me and tell me to leave the loo. It is embarrassing, it is like people are saying I am not a woman despite the fact I am one now.

Much like Sarah, Clair stated:

> Often, I would have to hold it as long as possible to avoid any confrontations.

I believe these bathroom confrontations could be similar to what Munt (1998) and Skeggs (1999) contended. Munt (1998) stated that gender-segregated toilets serve as sites where gender is tested and proved. Therefore, if one is not perceived as 'passing' this gender test, then they may be confronted. Skeggs (1999) stated that within toilet spaces, those 'who appear feminine are authorized and granted the power (in this small space) to evaluate others' (p. 302). Thus, some women who use this power may be more likely to confront and police the gender of other women (Skeggs, 1999). Those who are confident in their feminine presentation (con)test others' gender because they perceive that they visually display femininity in a socially acceptable manner.

Further bolstering this argument, Greed (2003) contended that the site of the toilet is not 'biologically' or socially designed for women and that public toilets are segregated dichotomously by sex and looks. In incidents where boundaries of gender difference are overtly enforced, it is socially illustrated how sites and bodies are mutually constituted within sexed power regimes. This once again can be connected to Goffman's (1977) arrangement theory between the sexes.

Butler (1990) explained that by understanding sexed reactions, it is possible to examine how sexed spaces come to exist through the continual maintenance and enforcement of gendered norms. Therefore, trans constables can experience embarrassing and potentially abusive confrontations, along with the taken-for-granted presence of 'normal' women's bodies, makes these spaces female. By being sex-segregated spaces, toilets exist as sites that (re)constitute cultural conceptions of dichotomised binary sex. Concurrently, as toilets take on the markers of femininity, these markers feminise or de-feminise bodies. Through marking the 'abnormal', the 'normal' is reinstated and (re)produces bodies within the category 'woman'. This is how genderism can become heightened in spaces within police culture. As Cooper and Oldenziel (1999) stated:

> The very creation of bathroom spaces, which are routinely separated by sex, reflect cultural beliefs about privacy and sexuality. Separating women's and men's toilet facilities prevents either sex from viewing, accidentally or otherwise, genitals of another.... So, women's and men's bathrooms assume heterosexuality and the existence of only two sexes ... which rejects overt sexual expression.
>
> (p. 26)

Further, some transwomen disclosed that because they are trans, they are perceived as sexual deviants by some cisgender individuals. Amber, a British constable, stated:

> For a woman to think that a transsexual woman would sexually assault you in the bathroom is absurd. I think that is why some women object or confront you. I am a woman and I have a right to use the bathroom too.

Because transgender individuals do not conform to societal expectations of binary gender, their presence in a sex-segregated area raises anxieties about gender and sexuality. These anxieties can magnify into perceptions that MTFs, because they once possessed a penis, could sexually assault other women in public toilets.

## Police transition policies and leadership issues

### Police transition policies

Previous research on the non-police trans population has revealed that employers lack knowledge of appropriate workplace accommodations and support which is needed for individuals who are transitioning (Budge et al., 2010). Part of this workplace accommodation involves the implementation of a transition policy. In police forces where certain expressions of feminine identity were not permitted, transwomen disclosed that there were continuity failures due to a lack of a transition policy. For research purposes, a transition policy typically outlines uniform violations and how they apply to transgender employees while also enabling administrative guidance on how to manage the needs of trans employees during transition. Trans-specific administrative policy issues may be as simple as changes in uniform policy for constables who are transitioning. Issues, for example the growing of long hair, wearing of earrings, growing and painting of fingernails and the wearing of deemed gender-specific clothing for transwomen, are not properly addressed if a policy does not exist to guide acceptable uniform standards.

Most participants disclosed that their forces did not look to incorporate a transition policy until they had personally notified their personnel unit of their desire to transition. And in those cases, other police agency's transgender policies were always referenced. The disclosed reasons why a transition policy was not previously used by their respective police forces were:

1   There is a perception that a transition policy is not needed due to the small size of trans populations within policing.
2   There is a general lack of knowledge of gender identity issues, legal requirements and appropriate administrative action within forces.
3   There is perceived hostility and fear towards transgender people generally, from both management and staff.

In forces where there was no transition policy guidance, transwomen stated that they typically had to face more administrative complaints than cisgender females because no policy existed to protect them during their transition. Additionally, because there was no transition policy at their respective forces, participants disclosed that their supervisors had no guidance on managing their specific administrative issues. Arguably, based on what my participants disclosed, a transition policy helps protect trans employees alongside administrators by providing guidance on supervisory concerns like uniforms, bathroom usages, etc.

Sarah disclosed that trans identities can feel isolated and targeted when there is no transition policy in place, because some supervisors are perceived as lacking understanding of trans identities. Sarah provided an excellent example of this by disclosing her story of being on patrol and being asked by several schoolchildren if she was a male or a female. Sarah answered the question honestly and told the schoolchildren that she used to be a man but is now a woman. One boy told his parents of the discussion, and they filed a formal administrative complaint with her department. In response to the complaint, her immediate supervisor recommended that a leaflet be written about her to hand to people in case they had questions since there existed no transition policy within her constabulary. Before Sarah's constabulary published the proposed leaflet, her Inspector asked her if it would be 'detrimental if the media got a copy of it'. Sarah responded to her supervisor by stating:

> I sent an e-mail back and said if it was about trans issues on a wider scale, ya, that's fine, but if it's just about me then that's a bit discriminatory ... which could single me out.

As Sarah's story illustrated, by not having a transition policy in place which would offer guidance on how to deal with specific issues like Sarah's story described, she felt 'singled out'.

Liv, an American officer, believed that the lack of a transition policy in her department hindered her and placed unwanted attention on her transitioning process. Liv, who eventually lost her job during her legal battles against her agency during the course of this research, stated that her discriminatory treatment for being trans started when she was administratively punished for uniform violations during her transition. She started wearing earrings at work after giving her department six months' notification that she was transitioning. Liv states:

> They started with the uniform policy and then they pulled a memo from 1994. There was no policy; there was just a memo from a former chief ... I got ordered to take them out, and they were like, okay, if you are not violating any policies, we will leave you alone.... So earrings came out, and then of course what did they do? You know the other girls were ordered to take them out because they had to cover themselves, and now all the girls hate you because everything is changing because of you.

Liv tried to argue to her chief that if other women are allowed to wear earrings, then she should be able to also. In response, the chief banned all earrings and this began to create tension between her and the other female officers. Liv continued:

> We then had a meeting about hairstyles, because all of the girls wore their hair in a long ponytail.... So I wore the ponytail for about a month, they approved a hairstyle, and I started to wear it. There were no issues for 5 months, and then out of nowhere the bomb dropped and there was: your hair is touching your collar. And I'm like, what are you talking about, every girl's hair touches the collar ... and they're like, we're changing everything, we are rewriting policies, and don't take this the wrong way, it is because of you ... I said you are going to make the whole building hate me.

As Liv's story illustrates, having a transition policy in place can assist a trans officer during transition while not administratively singling out an officer during transition. Holly, another American officer, stated that having a transition policy in place can occupationally help trans-identified officers to transition:

> Having a policy in place that allows the employee to make their own decisions and have their own destiny. They are able to have a hand on the policy that addresses their sense of gender, their sense of self and how they choose to identify.

Notably, all transgender police who participated in this research believed a transition policy was imperative within administration. As Josie, an American officer, stated:

> People in this job don't have that guidance without policy. How can they work without a policy?

Erin, a British constable, describes the lack of transition policy as:

> I always use the fire-drill analogy when I try to encourage forces to develop a trans policy ... I say, you don't actually wait for there to be a fire before you actually do your fire drill – why are you waiting for someone to join your force or stick their heads out of the barrel a bit and say 'by the way I want to transition' for you to say, god, we need some sort of policy around this?

Often constables are faced with direct supervisors who use policy to guide them on supervisory actions when dealing with administrative issues within policing. Just like American forces, most English and Welsh agencies have little or no guidance on a transition policy, as they vary between different constabularies, with no standardised adaptability or support from ACPO. Sarah described the importance of an approved universal policy across England and Wales:

> But we have ACPO ... which is chief constables ... sort of coming together ... and a lot of things ... if they have a unified transition policy or something

like that, which you then should disseminate so all police forces would get the message. In a way, they are failing us by not doing so.

During the course of this research, I discovered that out of 43 constabularies, nine[10] had independent occupational transition policies that were deemed 'not-privately' marked and posted online for the public to view. Besides assisting trans constables during transition, publicly acknowledging that a constabulary has a transition policy in place lets the non-police community know they are attempting to promote trans equality. As Erin, a British constable, stated:

> Imagine how that would benefit a force with a transition policy posted online. It shows to the community you are supporting LGBT+ rights.

Tom, a British constable, additionally disclosed that transwomen have a more difficult time hiding behind the uniform and that uniform policies are commonly used as a tactic by management to 'bully' some transwomen who are transitioning. Erin described how one agency without a transition policy treated a transwoman during her transition:

> One woman wanted to grow her hair and then the inspector wanted a report and a picture of what it was going to look like and how long it was going to take … and I was thinking … there is no way you would ask any other female that … but he was what you would call an old-style inspector who had a military background, and he was obviously way out of his comfort zone in managing someone who is undergoing gender reassignment.

Having a transition policy in place can provide guidance to supervisors, offer support for trans constables who are negotiating a gender change and demonstrate to the non-police population that their force is acknowledging trans identities. Arguably, this in turn can facilitate a supportive work environment and provides positive continuity guidance across forces.

## Administrative impacts on a positive trans-supportive work environment

Because participants revealed that a transition policy is linked to what they define as a supportive work environment, participants disclosed that they also believed that both a transition policy and *positive proactive leadership* were related to the severity of heterosexism/genderism they experienced within policing. *Positive proactive leadership* comprises of a mixture of components of the *leader-member exchange theory* (see Truckenbrodt, 2000) and the following supervisorial features: role modelling of perceived equality, strictness in combating observed bias, and being perceived as less judgemental and more approachable.

### Leader-member exchange theory

If we examine concepts of the leader-member exchange theory, relationships between those who lead and those who follow are viewed as more vital than the qualities of leaders (Truckenbrodt, 2000). Leader-member exchange theory[11] suggests that those in authoritative roles are likely to form different relationships and connections with their subordinates. According to the leader-member exchange theory, leaders should be friendlier, more communicative, more supportive and more personable with those they are supervising. By leaders using this approach they are more likely to establish trust and respect-based relationships within work environments (Bauer and Erdogan, 2015). Dave perceived his leadership as not being limited to contractual-type obligations, as described by Colvin (2014). Instead, he perceived his leadership as also having trust, open communication and information disclosure. Dave disclosed that his occupational relationship with his chief has aided in his perceived social acceptance within policing.

Yet, Dave disclosed a story in which another immediate supervisor had spoken to him:

> He told me that I was going to be subjected to a hostile if not violent work environment and wanted to know if it was that big of a deal. I said it was and if it came down to that, I would defend myself.

Notably, Dave stated that he only had a few bias incidents at work and that he believed that his overall positive experiences within his department were directly connected to positive proactive leadership, mainly his chief and other command staff. What was interesting about Dave was that he came from a very small police department in the south-eastern U.S.A., an area known for holding morally conservative views. Despite this, out of all the participants, he reported the most positive occupational experiences during his transition.

Jessie, an American officer, also stressed how important the relationship she had with her supervisor had been to her acceptance within policing, which could also be explained by the leader-member exchange theory. Jessie disclosed how she was torn between wanting to transition and still wanting to be a police officer. Therefore, she went to her chief looking for guidance:

> I just spilled it all out. My approach was to say, 'Look, I can understand if you say I can't be an officer here, but, you know, I will do anything. I will work in dispatch…. Just let me stay employed'.

Jessie disclosed that she believed that going directly to the chief paved the way for the organisation to assist and support her during her transition. Jessie went on to say:

> The chief listened and he said, 'Look, we hired you because we thought you could do the job as a police officer. For almost 20 years you have

demonstrated you can do that at a high level. This isn't gonna change that. We don't hire people because they are male or female.... We are going to make this work'.

Jessie went on to disclose that her agency sat down with her and her supervisors to discuss what she needed from them during her transition and how she thought they should inform the organisation, and to reaffirm that they were going to work with her at all times during her transition. Jessie, working alongside her supervisors, planned to announce to her agency that she was transitioning, and collectively they devised a transition policy and distributed an information pack to other officers within her medium-sized department. The information pack had terms, described what being trans was, and gave additional trans-awareness information. Jessie stated that once she went back to work after her surgeries, everyone was professional to her, creating a trans-supportive work environment. As Jessie states:

> I think a good part of my treatment was of course due to leadership. There was no division, nobody wanted to object, or think that this was not right.... There were no cracks in the leadership.... The response was amazing and I was proud of my police department.

Jessie's and Dave's stories are perfect examples of how positive proactive leadership using the leader-member exchange approach[12] can impact social acceptance, leading to fewer reported complaints of trans bias within work environments. Often the upper administrators' responses and reactions to these officers' transition disclosures set the course for their acceptance within their respective units. In incidents where officers did not directly disclose their transition status to upper management, they typically reported more incidents of peer social exclusion, isolation and lack of support from immediate supervisors.

### Positive proactive leadership support

Additionally, when I examined the reported negative experiences of all 14 participants, I discovered that trans identities that had both positive proactive leadership and a transition policy occupationally in place reported fewer incidents of heterosexism and/or genderism. Notably, these participants reported more positive perceptions and experiences, such as feeling more supported and having more positive group socialisations. As Dave best summarised what participants stated:

> My supervisor told me that he would constantly have my back during my transition, by doing so, he set an example for my colleagues about his support and that he wouldn't tolerate any negative attitudes about ... my

transition or transgender people in general. By having this support I feel more loyal to my department, and I am happier ... I plan on staying here till my retirement.

Role modelling was disclosed by participants as being a component of positive proactive leadership, because supervisors are responsible for safeguarding the equality of the organisation as a whole. Supervisor behaviour is perceived as reflecting the norms of a police organisation (see Huberts *et al.*, 2007). Therefore, if an employee observes that a supervisor engages in heterosexist and/or genderist behaviour, then they will perceive the organisation as a whole as potentially possessing the same views and deeming such actions to be acceptable. Here is where the old adage 'leading by example' can be applicable. As Holly, an American officer, stated:

> Officers look up to their supervisors, whether they admit it or not. If they see them making fun of someone or whatever, then those under them will think it is okay behaviour.

Like Holly, Josie stated:

> You have to lead by example. People expect that those in charge represent how others act.

Strictness of supervisors in applying clear norms and sanctioning misbehaviour of employees when heterosexist and/or genderist behaviour is observed was disclosed as being a quality of positive proactive leadership. If we examine prior research, it has been well documented that employees are less likely to engage in negative non-rewarding behaviour to avoid administrative punishments (see Butterfield *et al.*, 1996; Huberts *et al.*, 2007; Trevino, 1992; Trevino and Nelson, 1999). Additionally, enforcing administrative punishments when heterosexism and/or genderism are observed establishes guidelines of what is acceptable and unacceptable behaviour. Therefore, by establishing what is deemed to be acceptable and unacceptable behaviour, mechanisms of group socialisation are altered to facilitate rather than hinder the emergence of a trans-supportive work environment. As Tom, a British constable, stated:

> You have to punish those to change people's behaviour. Once others see that it isn't allowed, then others will modify their behaviour.

Trans participants disclosed that once they come forward for administrative support (i.e. if a complaint is filed or if they need administrative assistance during transition), it is very important that their supervisor supports them continuously throughout the process. Additionally, it was disclosed that trans participants perceived that the more personable their supervisors were towards their concerns and needs, then the more supportive they viewed their supervisors' leadership.

Dave, an American supervisor and member of SWAT, disclosed his story of how he came out to his chief and his force and how positive proactive leadership led to a supportive work environment for him:

> I sat down with the chief and it was like a two-minute conversation. And I said, 'Chief, I am transgender and I am starting my transition, do you have any questions?' And he goes, 'I thought that and wondered', and we talked about it for a few minutes. I then came out to my SWAT team and I would say for the most part they have been supportive. I have a very supportive group of people that I am here with ... you know? I appreciate that ... so it definitely makes it easier.

Dave attributed his acceptance within policing to his supervisor being 'very open, he's non-judgemental, he's supportive, so I think a lot of it is due to him and his attitude ... that is definitely something that has an impact, is the leadership'.

### Police transition policies plus positive proactive leadership

Previous research has shown that having formal policies in place that include trans employees may lead to a better work environment (Huffman *et al.*, 2008), yet appropriate support and leadership is also required according to this research. Further, Schilt and Westbrook's (2009) found that when open work-place transitions do not receive top-down support, cisgender men and women are more likely to express resistance towards their trans colleagues. Erin, a self-identified genderqueer British constable with 15 years' experience, describes how important a transition policy is alongside positive proactive leadership support:

> My division is very friendly and I have a cautious advisor.... She knows about my background and she is cool with it.... My team know about it and they are cool about it. So I have a very supportive, accepting team around me.... They are not perfect, now don't get me wrong. You can have the best policies in the world ... um ... as I have learned, you have some very good policies, but it comes down to personnel, and they can decide to ignore those policies and take it into their own hands, and that is when problems generally start.

Out of all the 14 participants, those who reported the most negative occupational experiences had neither positive proactive leadership *nor* a transition policy in place. The experience of one British constable, recorded in her notebook/work diary, illustrates this perfectly:

Meeting with head of HR, SGT and INSP. It was confirmed no change in policy would occur without an expert being consulted. I voiced that I was getting headaches during foot patrol, as my hat was applying pressure onto the hairclips in my hair and ponytail – was advised to get a new hat from stores to elevate the problem. Also told that while it was acceptable to have hair to a female standard my fingernails were however not and I was advised to trim them to a male length as two civilian members of staff had commented on them. When I defended that female officers routinely ignored the appearance standard (number of earrings in ears, non-natural coloured make-up, painted fingernails) I was told that wasn't an issue for the current meeting.

Clearly, this constable's request to be treated equally as a fellow female colleague went unanswered. The fact that her force did not have a transition policy in place to support her uniform presentation, coupled with the fact that there was no policy guidance for her supervisors, left her feeling, as she described it, 'targeted'.

When participants disclosed working in supportive environments, there was always a transition policy combined with positive proactive leadership in place (i.e. disallowed bias behaviour towards the employee, emotionally supported the employee transitioning, etc.). Conversely, when my participants experienced unsupportive work environments, missing was either a transition policy or a lack of positive proactive leadership, or both. Figure 8.1 illustrates the relationship between having a policy versus not having one and positive proactive leadership versus unsupportive leadership in relation to trans occupational experiences.

## Chapter summary

This chapter has explored the occupational issues that trans officers face within police culture in America, England and Wales. The following themes emerged from the interview data: hiring bias, discrimination via unwanted job reassignment, lack of transition policies and the impact of leadership in combating

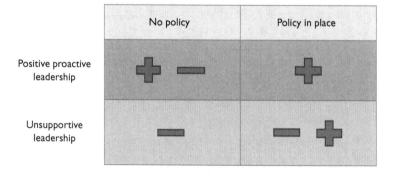

*Figure 8.1* Transition policies and leadership.

heterosexist and/or genderist behaviour. In combination, these have provided much needed information to answer the following research question:

What are the reported positive and negative administrative issues that transgender individuals face within policing?

Based on the many positive and negative experiences that were disclosed, the severity of heterosexism and genderism seemed to vary according to whether two administrative factors were present: the existence of a transition policy, and the existence of positive proactive leadership. Transgender police who reported positive work environments disclosed that both are needed to create a trans-supportive work environment. In respect to leadership, trans police reported fewer negative incidents when they were able to rely upon positive proactive leadership.

The data indicated that positive proactive leadership includes several elements. First, supervisors must be positive role-models by setting a good example for their employees to follow. By not engaging in heterosexist and/or genderist attitudes or behaviours, this is discouraged amongst subordinates. Second, supervisors of transgender employees must be strict in applying clear norms and sanctioning misbehaviour of employees when heterosexist and/or genderist behaviour is observed. Third, supervisors should at all times during pre/post-transition provide continual supervisory support of trans employees who ask for assistance or are observed to need help. Finally, supervisors of transgender police who possessed humanitarian values, who had some form of personal connection to their employees and showed that they cared, made a particularly positive impact.

According to participants, a negative work environment for transgender officers equates to heterosexist and genderist verbal attacks, vandalism of personal items/areas, theft of personal items, threats of physical violence and actual physical violence. Further, participants perceived that job discrimination towards transgender individuals is rampant within police culture. As highlighted, uniform violations along with the denial of bathroom usages or the 'policing of gender' also contribute to a negative work environment for transgender individuals. I theorised that this occurs because gender differences are highlighted within uniforms and the segregation of bathrooms. As previously discussed in Chapter 3 (i.e. Goffman, 1977), it is theorised that this observed social division between 'male' and 'female' leads to the heightened displays in respect to the policing of gender.

MTF police specifically disclosed that they have been the victim of misgendering and verbal attacks for using the bathroom assigned to their new gender at police institutions. It was suggested that because masculinity and the reinforcement of gender binaries is predominant in police culture, bathroom confrontations between police may occur more frequently. Therefore, my findings suggest that those who visually challenge the gender binary will face more social resistance in gendered spaces. Further, there appeared to be more occupational complaints against MTF British constables than against MTF American officers. This unexpected finding might be attributed to the traditional binary gendered uniforms used within British policing. Compared with the unisexed uniforms used in America, the gendered uniforms used in England and Wales provide an extra visual cue, enabling the enforcement of gender role ideologies and creating heightened stigma for infractions. This situation increases the probability of British officers receiving more uniform violations. Notably, all of MTF participants reported some type of gendered uniform violation, but it was a far less frequent occurrence for the American officers.

Through capturing the in-depth accounts of trans police working in America, England and Wales, this chapter has clearly illustrated the importance of two key factors for promoting a positive work environment for trans officers: (1) positive proactive leadership and (2) a transition policy which provides guidance for supervisors and trans officers alike. The evidence presented here indicates that having both in place can lead to positive trans occupational experiences, whereas having neither in place is likely to result in more complaints and grievances.

## Notes

1 Due to ethical considerations for safe-guarding respondents, an anonymous randomisation process was imposed throughout this book. As such, to protect participants I opted not to reveal the respondents' specific locations.
2 Law enforcement can comprise local, state and federal members within policing, sheriff offices, corrections, etc. These findings were explored in Chapter 3.
3 Formal administration punishment is included with threats of administrative punishment because as threats of formal administration punishment also imply administrative unacceptance, I was unable to confirm formal reports versus threats of formal reports due to organisational employee confidentiality concerns, and participants disclosed that threats were just as upsetting as the formal filing of a report.
4 Refer to Tables 8.3 and 8.4.
5 Caution should be taken when examining this data due to the small sample size and as I have stressed throughout this research, the data should not serve as a generalisation or as a representative sample. I was only allowed to examine empirical evidence of those who participated in this research.
6 As stressed throughout this work, due to the small sample size, caution should be taken when examining these figures. This only represents voluntarily disclosed incidents from participants and should not serve generalisations or as a representative sample. Further, a collective comparison will be revisited in Chapter 9.
7 Goffman's (1977) arrangement theory between the sexes will be revisited again in the following section. Also, Goffman's (1977) arrangement theory is discussed in detail in Chapter 3.
8 Currently in America, there are several bills that have been proposed which would allow for those whose gender identities are questionable to be arrested for using public restrooms. One bill in Texas is proposing that a $5,000 finder's fee could be collected for outing someone who is transgender in public restrooms.
9 Refer to Chapter 3.
10 These included South Yorkshire, Nottingham, Metropolitan Police, Cambridgeshire, Kent, Gwent, Thames Valley, Derbyshire and City of London Constabularies.

11 This theory focuses on the behavioral functions of leadership and how behavioral actions impact the relationship between those who lead and those who are being led.

12 This approach includes: clear communication, nurturing internal and external relationships, an appreciation of individual differences and diversity, etc.

## References

Appier, J. 1998. *Policing women: the sexual politics of law enforcement and the LAPD.* Philadelphia, PA: Temple University Press.

Bauer, T. and Erdogan, B. 2015. Leader-member exchange (LMX) theory: An introduction and overview. *The Oxford Handbook of Leader-Member Exchange.* Oxford: Oxford University Press, pp. 1–9.

Budge, S., Tebbe, E., Howard, K. 2010. The work experiences of transgender individuals: Negotiating the transition and career decision-making processes. *Journal of Counselling Psychology* 57, pp. 377–393.

Bullough, B. and Bullough, V. 1997. Are transvestites necessarily heterosexual? *Archives of Sexual Behavior* 26, pp. 1–12.

Butler, J. 1990. *Gender trouble: feminism and the subversion of identity.* New York: Routledge.

Butterfield, K., Trevino, L. and Ball, G. 1996. Punishment from the managers' perspective: a grounded investigation and inductive model. *Academy of Management Journal* 39, pp. 1479–1451.

Button, S. 2001. Organizational efforts to affirm sexual diversity: a cross-level examination. *Journal of Applied Psychology* 86(1), pp. 17–28.

Chivers, M. and Bailey, J. 2000. Sexual orientation of female-to-male transsexuals: A comparison of homosexual and nonhomosexual types. *Archives of Sexual Behavior* 29, pp. 259–278.

Colvin, R. 2012. *Gay and lesbian cops: diversity and effective policing.* London: Lynne Rienner Publishers.

Colvin, R. 2014. Transformational leadership for IT implementations and internal control. *SAIS 2014 Proceedings.* Paper 4. [Online]. Available at: http://aisel.aisnet.org/sais2014/4 [accessed: 8 November 2017].

Colvin, R. and Riccucci, N. 2002. Employment nondiscrimination policies: assessing implementation and measuring effectiveness. *International Journal of Public Administration* 25(1), pp. 95–108.

Cooper, P. and Oldenziel, R. 1999. Cherished classifications: Bathrooms and the construction of gender/race on the Pennsylvania railroad during World War II. *Feminist Studies* 25(1), pp. 7–41.

Corsiano, M. 2009. *Policing and gendered justice: examining the possibilities.* Toronto: University of Toronto Press.

Crank, J. 1998. *Understanding police culture.* Cincinnati, OH: Anderson Publishing.

Devor, H. 1993. Sexual orientation identities, attractions, and practices of female-to-male transsexuals. *Journal of Sex Research* 30, pp. 303–315.

Docter, R. and Fleming, J. 2001. Measures of transgender behavior. *Archives of Sexual Behavior* 30, pp. 255–271.

Docter, R. and Prince, V. 1997. Transvestism: a survey of 1032 cross-dressers. *Archives of Sexual Behavior* 26, pp. 589–605.

Dwyer, A. 2011. 'It's not like we're going to jump them': how transgressing heteronormativity shapes police interactions with LGBT young people. *Youth Justice* 11(3), pp. 203–220.

Goffman, E. 1977. The arrangement between the sexes. *Theory and Society* 4(3), pp. 301–331.

Greed, C. 2003. *Inclusive urban design: public toilets.* Woburn: Architectural Press.

Heidensohn, F. 1992. *Women in control? The role of women in law enforcement.* Oxford: Clarendon Press.

Herek, G. 1989. Hate crimes against lesbians and gay men: issues for research and policy. *American Psychologist* 44, pp. 948–955.

Huberts, L., Kaptein, M. and Lasthuizen, K. 2007. A study of the impact of three leadership styles on integrity violations committed by police officers. *Policing: An International Journal of Police Strategies and Management* 30(4), pp. 587–607.

Huffman, A., Watrous-Rodriguez, K. and King, E. (2008). Supporting a diverse workforce: What type of support is most meaningful for lesbian and gay employees? *Human Resource Management* 47(2), 237–253.

Hunt, J. 1990. The logic of sexism among police. *Women and Criminal Justice* 1(2), pp. 3–30.

Johnson, S. and Hunt, D. 1990. The relationship of male transsexual typology to psychosocial adjustment. *Archives of Sexual Behavior* 19, pp. 349–360.

Lawrence, A. 2003. Factors associated with satisfaction or regret following male-to-female sex reassignment surgery. *Achieves of Sexual Behavior* 32, pp. 299–315.

Lombardi, E., Wilchins, R., Priesing, D. and Malouf, D. 2001. Gender violence: Transgender experiences with violence and discrimination. *Journal of Homosexuality* 42, pp. 89–101.

Mallory, C., Herman, J. and Badgett, M. 2011. *Employment discrimination against lesbian, gay, bisexual, and transgender people in Oklahoma.* The Williams Institute. [Online]. Available at: http://escholarship.org/uc/item/79w0b14t [accessed: 8 November 2017].

Minter, S. and Daley, C. 2003. *Trans realities: a legal needs assessment of San Francisco's transgender communities.* San Francisco, CA: National Center for Lesbian Rights and Transgender Law Center.

Munt, S. 1998. *Butch and femme.* London: Cassell.

Sears, B., Hasenbush, A. and Mallory, C. 2013. *Discrimination against law enforcement officers on the basis of sexual orientation and gender identity: 2000 to 2013.* The Williams Institute. [Online]. Available at: http://escholarship.org/uc/item/3h220044 [accessed: 8 November 2017].

Sears, B., Hunter, N. and Mallory, C. 2009. *Documenting discrimination on the basic of sexual orientation and gender identity in state employment.* The Williams Institute. [Online]. Available at: http://williamsinstitute.law.ucla.edu/research/workplace/documenting-discrimination-on-the-basis-of-sexual-orientation-and-gender-identity-in-state-employment/ [accessed 8 November 2017].

Schilt, K. and Westbrook, L. 2009. Doing gender, doing heteronormativity: 'gender normals', transgender people, and the social maintenance of heterosexuality. *Gender and Society* 23, pp. 440–464.

Skeggs, B. 1999. Matter out of place: visibility and sexualities in leisure spaces. *Leisure Studies* 18, pp. 213–232.

Thurlow, C. 2001. Naming the 'outsider within': Homophobic pejoratives and the verbal abuse of lesbian, gay and bi-sexual high-school pupils. *Journal of Adolescence* 24, pp. 25–38.

Trevino, L. 1992. The social effects of punishment in organizations: a justice perspective. *Academy of Management Review* 17, pp. 647–676.

Trevino, L. and Nelson, K. 1999. *Managing business ethics: straight talk about how to do it right.* New York: John Wiley and Sons.

Truckenbrodt, Y. 2000. The relationship between leader-member exchange and commitment and organizational citizenship behavior. *Acquisition Review Quarterly* 7(3), p. 233.

Whittle, S., Turner, L. and Al-Alami, M. 2007. *Engendered penalties: transgender and transsexual people's experiences of inequality and discrimination.* [Online]. Available at: www.pfc.org.uk/pdf/EngenderedPenalties.pdf [accessed: 8 November 2017].

Zimmer, L. 1987. How women reshape the prison guard role. *Gender & Society* 1, pp. 415–431.

## Chapter 9

# Research contributions and future police policy recommendations

## Main themes and contributions

During the course of this research, several dominant themes emerged. Revisiting Chapter 6, cisgender police categorisations of heteronormativity and gender ideologies were explored together with the consequences of these (mainly negative) perceptions of LGBT+ colleagues. Cisgender participants disclosed that LGB officers, in conjunction with transgender officers, were collectively perceived as violating heteronormative perceptions of gender ideologies. Thus, I interpreted that the data suggested that transgender identities are observed more negatively within police culture than LGB identities. Cisgender participants disclosed that heteronormative perceptions of masculinity influenced their opinions of gender role ideology and their views of job and gender performance. Those who are not apparent as conforming to heteronormative aspects of 'masculinity' were observed as more likely to experience negative forms of social rejection. Further, participants disclosed that officers who were interpreted as challenging social expectations of 'maleness' (i.e. transwomen) were more likely to be socially rejected within policing compared with officers who were interpreted as challenging 'femaleness' (i.e. masculine and/or lesbian women).

In Chapter 6, I argued that this potentially occurs because trans feminine identities are perceived as a threat to the 'working personality' hegemonic masculinity component within policing, which in turn can be interpreted as a disruption to a fundamental aspect of police culture itself. In other words, trans feminine identities challenge police culture because they 'offend' or complicate perceptions of masculinity. Further, data suggested that masculinity performance is culturally, socially and biologically associated with genital constructs. Those who are MTF were perceived by cisgender participants as defiantly challenging these constructs, because psychologically, socially and biologically they distance themselves from elements of masculinity and aspects of the male body. Therefore, MTFs are perceived as gender betrayers and police cultural rebels for not embracing their 'maleness'. FTM police identities, on the other hand, did not appear to be as socially rejected as other transgender identities according to participants.

To further explain why certain transgender identities are perceived as not accepted within police culture, participants suggested that cisgender hetero-normative sex/gender/sexuality ideologies rest upon the perception that there are two, and only two, opposite sexes who are attracted to each other, and these are determined first and foremost by a person's physical body, primarily their genitals. Therefore, transwomen are not perceived as 'female' because they lack a vagina, and transmen are not perceived as 'male' because they do not possess a penis. This binary heteronormative perception that gender is biological reinforces and generates genderist ideologies within police culture.

When exploring the occupational experiences of transgender police in Chapter 7, social stigmas towards heteronormativity and gender role ideology were disclosed as being influential in transgender occupational experiences. Transgender officers stated that they were often forcefully 'outed' because tran-sitioning involves significant visual changes, or their respective departments 'outed' them without their permission. Further, transgender officers disclosed that if they came out voluntarily prior to transition, they had various motivations for doing so. These motivations included a need to be authentic to others about their transgender status; for educative reasons, because they wanted to let those in policing better understand transgender identities for socialised acceptance; and/or for advocacy reasons, because they wanted to represent something positive for the transgender community.

Chapter 8 explored the specific occupational complaints of heterosexism and genderism and the administrative issues associated with employing LGBT+ offi-cers. Analysis of the interview data indicated that the severity of heterosexism and genderism faced by officers varied according to two factors: the existence of a transition policy, and the existence of positive proactive leadership. First, parti-cipants revealed the importance of supervisors setting a good example and not encouraging subordinates' heterosexist and/or genderist behaviours. Second, supervisors must be strict in applying clear norms and sanctioning misbehaviour of employees when heterosexist and/or genderist behaviour is observed. Third, supervisors should at all times during pre/post-transition provide continual reasonable supervisory support for trans employees who ask for assistance or are observed to need help. Finally, supervisors of transgender police must possess personal empathy and an emotional connection to the employees they supervise (in other words, demonstrate that they care).

One particularly interesting finding from Chapter 8 was the discrepancy between the frequency of occurrence of uniform violations by transgender indi-viduals within American, English and Welsh policing. English and Welsh con-stables, who wear gendered uniforms, reported more occurrences of uniform violations than their American counterparts, who wear unisex uniforms. Notably, American MTF officers reported fewer complaints about hair-length violations, make-up violations, fingernail violations, etc. than their English and Welsh counterparts. It was suggested that the use of gendered rather than unisex uni-forms creates an extra visual perception of conventional gender norms, which heightens the stigma associated with those who contradict gender role ideologies (see Goffman, 1977). This was an unexpected differential finding between American and English/Welsh policing and points to clear recommendation for policy, as discussed later in this chapter.

Chapter 8 also pointed out that comparatively, despite geographical location or respective force size, positive occupational experiences are once again related to the presentation of masculinity within policing. So, the more masculine someone identifies along the trans spectrum, the more likely they will be to report less negative experiences than their more feminine counterparts. Second, regardless of geographical location or respective force size, the more positive (i.e. supportive) a trans officer's supervision is, the more likely they are to report a positive occupational existence. Third, there is an association between having a transition policy in place combined with positive (i.e. supportive) leadership and positive trans occupational experiences. Fourth, there is an association between not having a transition policy in place combined with negative (i.e. unsupportive) leadership and an increase in negative occupational experiences. Participants who belonged to forces that have did not have a transition policy, nor positive proactive leadership, reported more negative occupational complaints. Finally, trans officers and constables who come out directly to their highest supervisor – that is, their chief or superintendent – reported more positive top-down leadership support from their respective forces than those who came out first to their immediate supervisor.

This research also found that components of genderism exist within the trans feminine police culture on a micro-level. This is evident in the social exclusion and isolation that is present in the form of a hierarchy within the trans community itself examined in Chapter 7. I refer to this theory as the *inter trans feminine hierarchy concept*. Within the *inter trans feminine subcultural hierarchy concept*, those who are not post-op transsexuals are viewed as less of an oppressed identity and lack inadequacies in presenting 'femaleness'. Often post-op MTF police refuse to associate with others who may be perceived as 'not being female', like those who part-time cross-dress. For example, if a post-op MTF presents her gender as female and her gender is not questioned by observers in society, then her identity as a female might be challenged if she is seen in the presence of a noticeable transgender individual. In essence, they may be 'clocked' or identified as being trans by being seen with those who are more distinguishable as trans. This theoretical idea highlights that transgender identities (much like cisgender identities), can possess bias towards other members of the transgender community. So, transgender bias and the reinforcement of adherence to strict binaries can occur within all members of police culture, cisgender and transgender. From a sociological perspective, this is an intriguing finding, because most post-op transsexuals have engaged in the action of cross-dressing or have identified as a cross-dresser in the past. Therefore, genderqueer individuals and cross-dressers are socially rejected by some cisgender individuals and transsexual individuals alike.

## Intersectionality in transgender policing studies

As highlighted in Chapters 6, 7 and 8, this empirical research raised several points that should be considered regarding intersectionality.

1   This research answered the empirical call that sexuality and (trans)gender identities should be attended to separately (see Hancock, 2007). For example, previous research has analysed LGBT+ identities within policing collectively with the assumption that gender presentation, gender identity and sexuality are mutually dependent variables. Notably, this has occurred because of the research notion that shared identities for political reasons identify LGBT+ individuals as a social category (see Fish, 2008). By comprehensively analysing gender presentation, masculinity, femininity, gender identity and sexuality independently, this research found that the intersection of these categories are more than the sum of their parts (see Hancock, 2007).

2   This research found that the intersectionality of gender presentation, masculinity, femininity, gender identity, and sexuality of plays a role for both transgender police and non-transgender police heterosocial expectations of gender performance.

3   This research found that a hypermasculine police culture not only impacts dynamic constructions of sexuality, but that it also creates dynamic institutional constructions of gender expectations.

4   Within LGBT+ police social categories, this research found that there exists not only intergroup differences within policing but also intra group differences between the transgender communities specifically.

Notably, further feminist intersectional research is warranted on transgender police experiences to further refine and sharpen the role intersectionality plays broadly upon current 'queer criminology' research of LGBT+ identities.

## Policy implications

Previous research has indicated that transgender employees, like other minority groups, experience substantial stigmatisation in workplaces (see Barclay and Scott, 2006; Berry *et al.*, 2003; Dietert and Dentice, 2009; Gagné *et al.*, 1997). Transgender police disclosed that they were socially excluded and marginalised like other minority populations, but that they experienced another layer of problems due to the stigma related to their gender identity. Similar to other minority groups, workplace discrimination was experienced as interpersonal in nature, and sometimes subtle (e.g. perceived biases in hiring, unwarranted job reassignment during transitioning and being unable to use police bathroom areas), although its effects were nonetheless injurious (Hebl *et al.*, 2002; King *et al.*, 2006). Compared with previous police research (Burke, 1993, 1994a, 1994b;

Colvin, 2012; Jones, 2014; Jones and Williams, 2013; Loftus, 2008), this research presented a specific comprehensive account of the occupational experiences of transgender officers and identified factors that facilitate a trans-supportive work environment.

Based on this research, and in particular the findings presented in Chapter 8, strategies at integration, especially a better understanding of trans identities, depends directly on administrative factors like positive leadership and the implementation of a transition policy. Further, participants stressed how important it is to have social support from the upper ranks, i.e. 'positive leadership', which was directly related to their job satisfaction. Conversely, when positive leadership was absent, transgender police faced less social acceptance, more complaints of heterosexist/genderist workplace incidents and lower job satisfaction. Being administratively supported through positive top-down leadership from middle and upper management seemed to produce positive feelings and a sense of loyalty towards their organisation, similar to research conducted in non-police organisations by Law *et al.* (2011). Based on this research, the following recommendations are offered with the aim of improving the occupational experiences of transgender identities within American, English and Welsh policing:

1    There must be non-discrimination and zero-tolerance harassment policies within all police organisations.
2    There must be equal opportunities in recruitment, during hiring practices and during all stages and aspects of police employment.
3    There must be a transition policy to protect both the employer and the employee who wish to transition at work.
4    Police institutions should consult with transgender members of staff on policies and incorporate their input on the formation of transgender policies if there is not a policy in place.
5    Police agencies should make it known publicly that they support transgender rights and encourage the hiring of transgender police by providing their transition policy transparently online.
6    Transgender employees should have the same access to bathroom and changing areas as cisgender police and/or there should be unsexed bathrooms within police institutions for those who prefer to use them.
7    Any workplace disclosure during transitioning must be handled sensitively and professionally at all times – medical privacy and decency must be maintained throughout all stages of an employee's medical transition.
8    Transgender employees who identify as genderqueer should not face administrative punishment for not adhering to binary gendered work rules (e.g. hair length and fingernail length), since they do not identify with conventional gender role ideologies.

For English and Welsh forces specifically, two additional policy recommendations are suggested:

1  Dress-code policies must accommodate transgender employees; therefore, it is recommended that British agencies move away from gendered uniforms and/or allow constables the freedom to choose their preferred gendered uniforms.
2  Constabularies in England and Wales should acknowledge and educate all employees on ACPO's *Transgender People in Employment Guidelines* (2009), as most unwarranted complaints could be avoided if these policies were known and followed.

While I applaud forces that have already implemented positive leadership and transition policies, it is obvious that there needs to be more overall consistent improvements within administrative practices to successfully accommodate trans identities within policing. This is particularly apparent in forces where trans officers reported extreme levels of heterosexism and genderism which involved administrative complaints. I suggest that by implementing these policy recommendations, transgender police will face fewer occupational complaints, an area worthy of future research attention. This could be explored in two different ways: by examining agencies before and after policy change recommendations, or by comparing agencies that do not have these recommendations with those that do.

## Comparing American, English and Welsh police cultures

Reviewing results from this research, in respect to perceptions of gender, there appeared to be stark similarities in how transgender identities are perceived and treated within police cultures. As highlighted in Chapters 6, 7 and 8, all participants identified important barriers that may affect transgender integration and acceptance into police culture. These barriers often centred on the reinforcement of masculinity, often hyper masculinity, which is institutionally instilled into all facets of police culture regardless of region. Further, due to this infusement of hypermasculity into police cultures, there exists strict gendered divisions as to what is acceptable 'female' presentation and 'male' presentation. These deemed acceptable gender presentations in turn lead to social unacceptance of identities who challenge perceived 'femaleness' and 'maleness'. These rigid expectations of what gender is, and how it is preformed, lead to group unacceptance of transgender identities in police culture.

That said, there did exist small identifiable differences between American, English and Welsh police cultures: police uniforms and genderqueer identities. Transgender participants reported more incidents of administrative punishment and administrative complaints in respect to uniform violations in English and Welsh police cultures than their American counterparts. As theorised in Chapters Three and Seven, I believe this can be explained through heightened visual differences of the uniform itself. Referring back to Goffman (1977), social interactions and spaces are constructed in ways that highlight gender differences. Since there exists a highlighted gendered difference between the uniforms between men and women in English and Welsh police cultures, transgender identities who either change gender or exist in-between genders report more complaints. Their American counterparts, on the other hand, reported less administrative complaints because there does not exist a gendered division of uniforms. This theoretical contribution illustrates how gendered uniforms can impact gendered acceptance within work environments.

Another small identifiable difference between American, English and Welsh police cultures was the more perceived presence of genderqueer identities. Referring to Chapter 7, it was revealed that genderqueer identities were more likely perceived to exist in English and Welsh police cultures than American police cultures by transgender police. Yet, it is unclear why genderqueer identities are more apparent in English and Welsh police cultures than American ones. Yet, English and Welsh genderqueer identities, as other transgender identities, face similar work and social barriers, which include the social reinforcement of strict gendered binaries and overt discrimination by colleagues.

## Limitations of this research

While this research has made several contributions to the literature, limitations should be noted. The first limitation would be the usage of qualitative research as a research method. As discussed within Chapter 5, when conducting qualitative research (much like quantitative research) there exists outside influences which might impact the data, such as researcher bias and other idiosyncrasies.[1] Further, unlike quantitative research, validity issues may arise from these outside influences leading to criticism that qualitative research is not scientific in nature because it does not deductively support or refute any possible theories. Instead, qualitative research can only better understand the meaning that individuals give to a phenomenon inductively. Qualitative research attempts to overcome these issues by encouraging researchers to identify personal stances and biases, yet one of its major weaknesses is that the researcher is often unable to remain in the background. Thus, a researcher's presence alone in the analysis of data arguably can impact the meaning that is derived from any recorded data.

While some qualitative researchers argue that real objectivity is inherently difficult within itself (see Patton, 1990; Shenton, 2004), my objectivity could easily be questioned. I was at times connected to several portions of this research, thus I was unable to remove who I am as a researcher from what I was researching. As a member of the LGBT+ community and a former police officer, I openly acknowledged that during the course of this research, I possessed researcher bias.[2] Notably, throughout this research, I adhered to being as transparent as possible, yet I acknowledged that my connection to this research could have influenced how I interpreted that data or even how I even constructed my methodology.[3]

As a practitioner turned researcher, a limitation of this research also exists in who I am as a researcher. As pointed out in Chapters Four and Five, as a police officer I was trained to present 'facts' with little room for exploration or interpretation. For example, when writing a police report, I had become accustomed to presenting evidence as factually as possible, without any analysis. This is very different to academic research, where the very notions of 'facts' and 'objectivity' are contested. Another researcher with the same data may have chosen to analyse the data differently, or to explore a different theoretical angle. Notably, a large bulk of this research relied upon me as a researcher and how I interpreted the data.

Another limitation to this research was the small sample size. Notably, there are very few individuals who identify as transgender, especially within policing, and even fewer who were willing to participate in my research. As such, this research can only represent the perspectives of its participants and should not be interpreted as representative of all police officers serving in America, England or Wales (whether they be trans or cisgender). Therefore, it is suggested that further research is necessary in order to provide a prevalence estimate of the types of workplace experiences and issues revealed by this research.

A further research limitation was that my sample lacked any BME participants. All of my participants were white; there were no BME transgender participants. Therefore, future research on this topic should aim to address this limitation by focusing on the experiences of BME officers in order to enable an intersectional analysis of race, ethnicity, gender and sexuality within policing. If given the opportunity to do this research over again, with more time in which to do it, I would have attempted to explore this issue by reaching out to different police networks and specifically sampling from agencies that comprise a larger BME policing population.

## Chapter summary

As long as police culture perpetuates and upholds binary gendered ideologies, those who challenge our societal perceptions of gender and sexuality may be victims to forms of heterosexism and genderism. Yet, collectively as a society, we must acknowledge and encourage the integration of those who challenge gender roles within policing. The reality is that police should reflect the communities they serve (see Adlam, 1982; Attwater *et al.*, 1980; Bent, 1974; McNamara, 1967), and it is of vital importance that officers are aware of transgender issues, and encourage transgender employment within policing.

In this book, I empirically examined how cisgender ideologies impacted transgender experiences within policing. During this process, I followed the theoretical traditions of symbolic interactionism while examining how social products shape and are further shaped by institutional perceptions of masculinity (see Goffman, 1977, Kessler and McKenna, 1978; Schilt, 2010; West and Zimmerman, 1987). Masculinity within policing still constructed and reinforced within American, English and Welsh policing. Femininity, the antithesis of masculinity, is viewed as undesirable at times within policing cultures. So much so, perceptions of masculinity and how to perform it are a result of a combination of social products that are the foundation of institutional practice (see Schilt, 2010). West and Zimmerman (1987) stated that people are accountable to expectations of masculinity and femininity, depending if they are perceived as 'male' or 'female'. As highlighted throughout this book transgender identities because of their perceived lack of heteronormative conformity, will continue to face occupational barriers until ideologies within policing change. As Clair, an MTF constable, stated: 'It takes balls to be trans within policing'.

## Notes

1  See Chapter 5.
2  While I did not see this as a research shortcoming, others may view it as such.
3  Please refer to Chapters 4 and 5.

## References

Adlam, K. 1982. The police personality: psychological consequences of being a police officer. *Journal of Police Science and Administration* 10, pp. 344–349.
Association of Chief Police Officers. 2009. *Transgender people in employment guidelines.* London: ACPO.
Attwater, E., Bernhart, B. and Thompson, S. 1980. The authoritarian cop: an outdated stereotype? *Police Chief* 47, pp. 58–59.
Barclay, J. and Scott, L. 2006. Transsexuals and workplace diversity: A case of change management. *Personal Review* 4, pp. 1–30.
Bent, A. 1974. *The politics of law enforcement.* Toronto: Lexington.
Berry, P., McGuffee, K., Rush, J. and Columbus, K. 2003. Discrimination in the workplace: The firing of a transsexual. *Journal of Human Behavior in the Social Environment* 8, pp. 225–239.
Burke, M. 1993. *Coming out of the blue.* London: Continuum.
Burke, M. 1994a. Cop culture and homosexuality. *Police Journal* 65, pp. 30–39.
Burke, M. 1994b. Homosexuality as deviance: The case of the gay police officer. *British Journal of Criminology* 34, pp. 192–203.
Colvin, R. 2012. *Gay and lesbian cops: diversity and effective policing.* London: Lynne Rienner Publishers.
Dietert, M. and Dentice, D. 2009. Gender identity issues and workplace discrimination: The transgender experience. *Journal of Workplace Rights* 14, pp. 121–140.
Fish, J. 2008. Navigating queer street: Researching the intersections of lesbian, gay, bisexual and trans (LGBT) identities in health research. *Sociological Research Online* 13(1), p. 12.
Gagné, P., Tewksbury, R. and McGaughey, D. 1997. Coming out and crossing over: identity formation and proclamation in a transgender community. *Gender & Society* 11(4), pp. 478–508.
Goffman, E. 1977. The arrangement between the sexes. *Theory and Society* 4(3), pp. 301–331.

Hancock, A. 2007. Intersectionality as a normative and empirical paradigm. *Politics & Gender* 3(2), pp. 248–254.

Hebl, M., Foster, J., Mannix, L. and Dovidio, J. 2002. Formal and interpersonal discrimination: A field study of bias towards homosexual applicants. *Personality and Social Psychology Bulletin* 28, pp. 237–253.

Jones, M. 2014. Cultures of difference: examining the career experiences and contributions of lesbian, gay and bisexual police officers post-Macpherson. PhD thesis, Cardiff University.

Jones, M. and Williams, M. 2013. Twenty years on: Lesbian, gay and bisexual police officers' experiences of workplace discrimination in England and Wales. *Policing and Society: An International Journal of Research and Policy* 25(2), pp. 1–24.

Kessler, S. and McKenna, W. 1978. *Gender: an ethnomethodological approach.* Chicago, IL: University of Chicago Press.

King, E., Shapiro, J., Hebl, M., Singletary, S. and Turner, S. 2006. The stigma of obesity in customer service: A mechanism for remediation and bottom-line consequences of interpersonal discrimination. *Journal of Applied Psychology* 91, pp. 579–592.

Law, C., Martinez, L., Ruggs, E., Hebl, M. and Akers, E. 2011. Trans-parency in the workplace: how the experiences of transsexual employees can be improved. *Journal of Vocational Behavior* 79, pp. 710–723.

Loftus, B. 2008. Dominant culture interrupted: recognition, resentment and the politics of change in an English police force. *British Journal of Criminology* 48(6), pp. 756–777.

McNamara, J. 1967. Uncertainties in police work. In: Bordua, D., ed. *The police.* New York: Wiley, pp. 163–252.

Patton, M. 1990. *Qualitative evaluation and research methods.* Newbury Park, CA: Sage.

Schilt, K. 2010. *Just one of the guys? Transgender men and the persistence of gender inequality.* Chicago, IL: University of Chicago Press

Shenton, A.K. 2004. Strategies for ensuring trustworthiness in qualitative research projects. *Education for Information* 22(2), pp. 63–75.

West, C. and Zimmerman, D. 1987. Doing gender. *Gender and Society* 1, pp. 125–151.

# Appendix A

## Sample interview schedule

**Sample interview schedule: cisgender participants – first interview**

1 Description of what my research entailed. I advised participants that I was examining LGBT+ bias within policing, more specifically attitudes towards transgender identities.
2 Rapport building.
3 What type of person is needed to perform policing effectively? What is an important quality to possess to be a good officer?
4 What is your opinion of LGBT+ identities?
5 What have your experiences been with LGBT+ identities while on patrol? For example, have you had a bad or positive experience patrolling the LGBT+ community?
6 Tell me how you feel about transgender identities in general.
7 Do you have any issues patrolling the transgender community? If so, can you explain these issues and why you believe they exist?
8 I am interested in any interaction you have had with LGBT+ members within policing. Do you believe you work in a supportive LGBT+ environment?
9 Do you view your department supportive of lesbian/gay/bisexual identities within policing, specifically?
10 Do you view your department supportive of transgender identities within policing?
11 I am interested also in the interaction you have observed other officers to have had or your interactions with LGBT+ identities. Can you describe your most positive experience with members of the LGBT+ community? More specifically, interactions with the transgender community?
12 Could you describe your observed or personally experienced negative interaction with members of the LGBT+ community? More specifically, interactions with the transgender community?
13 By now a good sense of participant's perceptions towards LGBT+ identities should be known. You have described your opinions about the transgender

community while on patrol and within policing. Can you tell me if you have always felt this way or has your perception changed since entering policing?

14   Is there anything that I have not asked or we have talked about that you feel is important? Is this something that you would like to discuss?

## Sample interview schedule: cisgender participants – subsequent interviews

1   Follow-up upon what was discussed in the previous interview.

2   Pick up from last interview. Has anything changed or is there anything you would like to add to what was discussed previously?

3   I wanted to clarify some statements about what you have observed and your perceptions towards LGBT+ identities with policing. How do you believe policing can improve relationships with the LGBT+ community, if this is something that you believe can be improved upon?

4   How can your administration aid you in addressing or overcoming these relationships?

5   Can these recommendations work within policing, if warranted? Further, how can policing aid in the integration of transgender identities within policing, if warranted?

6   Issues specific to the participant were followed up in further detail, if relevant.

## Sample interview schedule: transgender participants

1   Description of the purpose of research. I stressed to transgender participants that I am exploring transgender bias within policing and my desire to improve work environments for transgender police. I stress that my research is not just limited to their experiences of being transgender, but it is also focused on perceptions towards LGB identities.

2   What type of person is needed to perform policing effectively? What is an important quality to possess to be a good officer?

3   Do you believe lesbian, gay and bisexual identities are viewed differently within policing than transgender identities? How do you believe that they are viewed as similar?

4   What has been your most positive observed experience with police inter-actions with the LGBT+ community? If a participant disclosed a particular interaction with a specific LGBT+ identity, I would ask further questions relevant to the experience and how they interpreted the interaction.

5   What has been your most negative observed experience with police inter-actions with the LGBT+ community? If a participant disclosed a particular interaction with a specific LGBT+ identity, I would ask further questions relevant to the experience and how they interpreted the interaction.

6    What are some issues within your department that you have had to overcome?

7    If you chose to transition on the job, how did you find your 'coming out' experience?

8    Was the department open to your needs during your 'coming out' process?

9    Was you department supportive during your transition? If a participant disclosed that they were genderqueer, I did not ask transition questions unless they brought it up. I did so because I was aware that some genderqueer identities do not take any steps to medically transition.

10   What administrative police improvements would you recommend that should be implemented to improve transgender integration into police culture?

11   What specific occupational issues should be changed to accommodate the needs of those who are transgender?

## Sample interview schedule: transgender participants – subsequent interviews

1    Brief synopsis of what the results are showing. I disclosed what my cisgender participants disclosed in respect to their perceptions of transgender identities. I used this as an opportunity to confirm with participants if they are surprised with the results. I would then explain that in this interview, I want to shift the focus more towards how things can be improved within policing for them.

2    I explained to participants that during my first interview with transgender officers that there appeared to be a hierarchy of social acceptance within the transgender police community itself. I asked participants if they agreed or disagreed with this.

3    I discussed with participants that preliminary results are indicating that leadership and having a transition policy in place have been observed as creating more positive transgender experiences within police culture. I then asked the participant how important both of these are to them administratively within policing.

4    Issues specific to the participant were followed up in further detail, if relevant.

# Appendix B
## Common trans terms

**AG or Aggressive**  A masculine identified woman; primarily used by LGBT+ community of colour.

**Ally**  An individual who confronts heterosexism, sexism, homophobia, heteronormativity, etc. for a concern for the well-being of lesbian, gay, bisexual, transgender and other individuals in the LGBT+ spectrum. Allies consider heterosexism as a social injustice.

**Androgyne**  An individual who has traits stereotypically ascribed to males and females.

**Asexuality**  An individual generally characterised by not having a sexual attraction or desire for partnered sexuality. Some asexual individuals have sex and there are different ways of being asexual. Being asexual is different from being celibate, which is a deliberate withdrawal from any type of sexual activity.

**Bigendered**  A person who identifies as having two genders, exhibiting cultural and stereotypical characteristics of both male and female roles.

**Bisexual**  An individual whose primary sexual and affectional attraction is drawn towards people of the same sex and other genders.

**Butch**  A term used to describe some types of masculine lesbian women who do not conform to stereotypical feminine presentations. The term can also be used as a descriptive adjective towards any person who has a masculine presentation, despite their sexual orientation or gender.

**Cisgender**  A gender identity that society considers similar to the biological sex assigned at birth. The term is frequently used by transgender individuals to distinguish themselves from others on the sexual spectrum.

**Clitoroplasty**  Medically-created clitoris.

**Cross-dresser**  Most commonly used as the most neutral word to describe how a person dresses in clothing stereotypically associated with another gender within society. This term has been used to replace 'transvestite', which is viewed as outdated and offensive, since it was historically used to diagnose medical/mental health illnesses.

**Drag King**  A woman who dresses up as a stereotypical male but may not have a masculine expression in their usual life. Typically, this is performed in reference to a stage act or performance.

**Drag Queen**  A man who dresses up as a stereotypical female but may not have feminine expression in their usual life. Typically, this is performed in reference to a stage act or performance. It is sometimes used incorrectly in a derogatory manner, to refer to all transgender women.

**FFS**  Facial feminisation surgery.

**FTM (F2M)**  Female-to-male transgender person.

**Gay**  An individual whose primary sexual and affectional attraction is towards people of the same gender.

**Gender**  A social construct to classify an individual as a man, woman or other identity. This is different than the sex one is assigned at birth.

**Gender dysphoria**  A medical diagnosis that concerns the constant and over-whelming desire to live in the opposite gender that a person was not born into. Often this medical diagnosis is needed for individuals to begin their gender transformation. Many transgender individuals request that the diagnosis be classified as physical rather than psychological, but they feel that there needs to be a medical diagnosis to ensure continued availability of treatment.

**Gender expression/presentation**  This is how an individual expresses oneself in terms of dress and/or behaviours that society characterises as masculine and feminine. Since gender identity is internal, one's gender identity is not necessarily perceived by or visible to others.

**Genderfluid**  An individual who is viewed as having a fluid nature representative of two or more genders, which shifts naturally in gender identity and/or gender expression and presentation.

**Genderfuck**  A form of gender identity in which an individual exhibits an intentional attempt to present a confusing gender identity that contributes to the collapse of stereotypical perceptions of gender.

**Gender identity**  An individual's self-conceptualisation of their own gender. In other words, a person's internal sense of where they exist in relationship to identifying as male or female.

**Gender non-conforming**  An individual who does not conform to gender expressions or gender roles expected by society.

**Gender outlaw**  An individual who refuses to be defined by the stereotypical conventional definitions of gender roles. This term was popularised in *Gender Outlaw* by Kate Bornstein.

**Genderqueer**  An individual who identifies as neither male nor female, identify as a combination of both, or who present themselves in a non-gendered way.

**GRS**  Gender reassignment surgery.

**Hormone therapy**  The medical administration of hormones to aid and facilitate the development of secondary sex characteristics as part of the transition process. FTM may take testosterone while MTF may take oestrogen and androgen blockers.

**Intersex**  An individual who is born with external genitalia, chromosomes or internal reproductive systems that are not associated with typical medical definitions of male or female.

**Lesbian**  A woman whose primary sexual and affectional attraction is towards people of the same gender.

**Metoidioplasty**  A surgical procedure to create a small penis by extending and using the clitoris. Typically, after this surgery a second one is preformed to allow urination through the penis.

**MTF (M2F)**  Male-to-female transgender person.

**Non-monosexual**  Individuals who have a romantic, sexual or affectional desire for more than one gender. Individuals who identify as bisexual would fit into this category.

**Omnigendered**  An individual who possesses all genders and exhibits stereotypically perceptions of males and females. This term is typically used to challenge the notion that there are only two genders.

**Oophorectomy**  The surgical removal of the ovaries.

**Orchidectomy**  The surgical removal of testicles.

**Pansexual, omnisexual**  An individual who has romantic, sexual or affectional desire for people of all genders and sexes. This term is typically used instead of 'bisexual' due to the challenge that there are only two genders.

**Penectomy**  Removal of the penis.

**Passing** or **Legible**  An individual who's gender identity and presentation matches in casual situations. A person who successfully 'passes' appears in all aspects as the gender they are assuming.

**Phalloplasty**  The surgical creation of a penis.

**Queer**  A term used by individuals who want to be identified as such. It could include anyone who chooses to be labelled as such along the entire LGBT+ spectrum.

**Same gendered loving**  A term commonly used by some African-American individuals who love, date and/or have an attraction to someone of the same sex. This term is used by individuals who want to distance themselves from terms that are associated with the perceived 'white-dominated' communities.

**Sex**  A category based on the biological characteristics (i.e. genitalia) assigned at birth.

**Trachael shave**  Medical procedure that reshapes the Adams apple.

**Trans**  An umbrella term encompassing those that identify with a gender or gender expression that is different in some way from the sex they were assigned at birth. This includes those that identify as transgender, non-binary gender people and cross-dressing people.

**Transfag**  A trans male identified individual who is attracted to other male identified individuals.

**Transition**  The period during which a person begins to live as their new gender. Transitioning can include legally changing one's name and gender on paperwork, taking hormones, having surgeries, etc. to reflect their new gender.

**Transman**  see also FTM.

**Transwoman**  see also MTF.

**Tryke**   A trans female identified individual who is attracted to other female identified individuals.

**Two-spirit**   This term encompasses indigenous individuals who fulfil one of many mixed gender roles found typically in Native American and Canadian First Nations indigenous groups. Dual-gendered, or 'two-spirited', are viewed differently in indigenous communities and are typically seen without stigma and are considered emissaries from the creator. It should be noted that they can be treated with deference or respect, but this may not always be the case.

**Vaginoplasty**   A surgically created vagina.

**Womyn**   Some individuals spell the word with a 'y' as a form of empowerment to remove the 'men' component from the traditional spelling of 'women'.

## Note

The above definitions should be used as a contextual reference and do not represent the myriad of sexual and/or gender identities that are possible in each category as there exists numerous individualised ways in which one can identify or express themselves. Terminology was derived from this research and informative websites (see GLAAD, Stonewall, etc.).

# Index

Page numbers in *italics* denote tables, those in **bold** denote figures.